SELLING YOUR CRAFTS

REVISED EDITION

SELLING YOUR CRAFTS

REVISED EDITION

SUSAN JOY SAGER

ALLWORTH PRESS
NEW YORK

08 07 06 05 04 03   5 4 3 2 1

Published by Allworth Press
An imprint of Allworth Communications, Inc.
10 East 23rd Street, New York, NY 10010

Cover design by Mary Ann Smith, New York, NY

Page composition/typography by Integra Software Services, Pvt. Ltd.,
Pondicherry, India

ISBN: 1-58115-266-3

Library of Congress Cataloging-in-Publication Data:
Sager, Susan Joy.
Selling your crafts/Susan Joy Sager.—Rev. ed.
p. cm.
Includes bibliographical references and index.
ISBN 1-58115-266-3 (pbk.)
1. Selling—Handicraft. 2. Handicraft industries—Management. I. Title

HF5439.H27S23 2003
745.5'068'8—dc21
2003041783
Printed in Canada

CONTENTS

INTRODUCTION

Look no further—you have in your hands a complete source of information to help you sell your crafts and run a crafts business successfully.

This book will give you profiles of production craftspeople, craft teachers, craftspeople who earn their living in other fields, and famous craftspeople, as well as the suggestions and opinions of craft administrators. All the basic information necessary to market and sell your work, step-by-step, is presented in this book using easy-to-understand examples, forms, and recommended reading. Although I suggest you read the book cover-to-cover, you can also use it as a reference book.

The people who have attended my ArtBiz seminars fit different profiles ranging from craftspeople who have been thinking of starting a business selling their crafts, to those interested in supplementing their present income with sales of their work, to hobbyists who want to sell only enough of their work to cover the costs of their supplies. Do you know which profile you fit? Your profile affects how you will go about marketing your work in important ways.

Just as you needed to study and learn your craft, you now need to learn how to run a successful craft business in order to sell your crafts. This book will give you the basic tools you need to set up and manage your craft business, market and sell your crafts, and the resources available to keep you informed as your business grows. The best way to learn how to run a craft business and sell your work is by getting started, practicing, asking questions, evaluating what did and did not work, and doing it all over again.

After reading this book, I hope that you will realize that although there are many ways to sell your crafts, your success as a craftsperson can only be defined and evaluated by you. Read the profiles of craftspeople in chapter 2 and see which ones most closely fit your lifestyle choices, dreams, and goals. Take the self-assessment questionnaire in chapter 5. Then read the rest of the book to move forward in your goal to sell your crafts.

Running a business and selling a handmade product is a constant source of joy and frustration as well as of learning and growth. You will never know it all or have everything ready before you start. There is no time like the present to get started selling your crafts.

I am writing this book in the hope that after reading it you will have the knowledge required to make informed decisions about selling your work, starting a business, running your current business more professionally, or even whether selling your crafts is the appropriate career choice for you at this time.

I would like to thank Tad Crawford of Allworth Press for the opportunity to write this book, Daniel Grant for suggesting it, the people I profiled who freely gave their stories, all the places that offered my seminars, gave me publicity, and believed in me, my students who asked thought-provoking questions and provided inspiration, my friends and family, and especially my husband, Scott Moody, who offered encouragement, read the first draft, added expertise to the chapters on computers and the Internet, and did the dishes.

SUSAN JOY SAGER

Summer 2002

Once again, I would like to thank Tad Crawford of Allworth Press for the opportunity to revise this book and Daniel Grant for suggesting it. I'd also like to thank my husband, Scott, for the many extra hours of parenting, as well as my son, Miles, for sleeping through the night and enjoying his outings with Daddy.

THE PROFESSIONAL CRAFT WORLD: AN OVERVIEW

CHAPTER 1

TRENDS AND TRAINING

Unless you have taken a craft history course, you may not realize that the craft field as we know it today—with degree programs, workshops, craft fairs, galleries and shops, organizations, conferences, and magazines—is a fairly recent development in the professional craft field.

Crafts were originally created out of necessity to serve a purpose such as providing a place to sit, a bowl to eat from, or a blanket to keep warm. As our culture later grew into an industrialized society, factories began to mass-produce items that had formerly been made by hand.

Reemerging interest and appreciation of things made by hand wasn't really evident until the late-nineteenth century when the Arts and Crafts movement was founded by social reformer, John Ruskin, and artist, William Morris, in England. It soon began to gain momentum in the United States. As a result, art and crafts societies started to form all over this country and exhibitions were organized that brought recognition to the objects made by individual craftspeople or small factories. New influences continued to increase with each new wave of immigrants.

In the early 1900s, several professional training programs for crafts were started such as the College of Ceramics at Alfred University in Alfred, NY, and the Oregon School of Arts and Crafts (later renamed Oregon College of Art & Craft) in Portland. By the 1930s, membership organizations had begun to form such as the Southern Highland Craft Guild in North Carolina and the League of New Hampshire Craftsmen, both still active today. Most importantly, the Cranbrook Academy of Art in

Michigan, one of the foremost educational programs for crafts in this country, began during this period, utilizing faculty trained in Europe.

An important *Index of American Design* was created during the depression in the 1930s by the federal government's Work Project Administration (WPA) program. Using watercolors to document crafts and folk art from the colonial era to the end of the nineteenth century, this index of approximately 1,600 images is still housed in the National Gallery of Art in Washington, D.C. In addition, two books written by craft researcher Allan Eaton, *The Crafts of the Southern Highlands* and *Crafts of New England,* helped bring national attention to our craft heritage.

The 1940s was a period for increased educational opportunities for craftspeople. Veterans could go to college and study through the GI Bill. Many colleges and universities expanded their programs at this time, especially in the arts and crafts. Instead of being trained as apprentices by master craftsmen to learn their craft, craftspeople now studied in art schools and university art departments to earn bachelor's and master's degrees in their area of specialization.

Starting in the 1950s, the American Craft Council (ACC) gave a common voice to craftspeople who had previously worked in isolation. ACC helped begin an exchange of ideas and techniques through a national conference, publishing *American Craft* magazine, and the American Craft Museum in New York City. Up until this time, most of the craftwork being made was primarily functional rather than aesthetic in orientation.

The craft field experienced another change in the 1960s when young people began the back to the land movement. Making crafts to use and sell, and experimenting with new materials and techniques, the craftspeople of this period brought many changes. For example, in 1962, Harvey Littleton led a glass workshop that is attributed with starting numerous glass programs across the country. He showed craftspeople how to make glass in the studio rather than solely working in a glass factory.

At the same time, fairs organized by the American Craft Council moved the field forward by connecting buyers with craftspeople. Craft fairs not only gave craftspeople a way to sell their work but served to educate the public about crafts. According to Mary Nyburg, owner of Blue Heron Gallery in Deer Isle, Maine, and president emeritus of the American Craft Council, the first wholesale craft show organized by the Northeast Region of the American Craft Council wasn't until 1966. Held in Stowe, Vermont, the entire show grossed $18,000—an amount celebrated by the organizers. Although it seems hard to believe, says Priscilla Merritt, wife of the Haystack Mountain School of Craft's founding director, Fran Merritt, when she first started her craft gallery Centennial House, in Deer Isle in 1962, it was difficult to find enough craftspeople who could produce work to fill the shop. In the last two decades, the number of craft fairs and craftspeople trying to market their work has increased dramatically.

In the 1970s, numerous organizations and publications started. The Society of North American Goldsmiths (SNAG), the Glass Art Society (GAS), the National Council on Education of Ceramics Arts (NCECA), and the Artists Blacksmith Association of North America (ABANA), were formed to actively promote and educate their members by holding workshops, conferences, and publishing newsletters and magazines. Magazines such as *Fiberarts, Fine Woodworking, Metalsmith,* and the *Crafts Report,* a business journal for craftspeople and retailers, were also launched at this time. New galleries opened and people began actively collecting crafts.

By the 1980s, craftspeople began to realize that increasing competition was making it more difficult to have their work accepted into fairs, shops, and galleries and that they needed to learn how to market their work and run a business. A craftsperson could no longer just show up or show actual work to get into a show as they had done in the past. Instead, craftspeople were asked to represent their work through slides and photographs and go through a formal application procedure to be accepted into a juried fair or show. In addition, craftspeople had to adjust their production schedules to meet the increased demands placed on them by buyers.

Crafts continued to be created for public spaces to bring beauty, enjoyment, and a sense of pride to our environment, while providing an excellent way to support and encourage craftspeople. While the WPA program in the 1930s funded many art and craft pieces for public places, the state-administered Percent for Art programs as well as architects and interior designers now carry on this legacy. The Percent for Art programs allocate 1 percent of a public building's budget to build either a new structure or addition and provide up to $40,000 to commission art or craft pieces for that building.

The craftspeople of today tend to be older than their counterparts of the 1960s and 1970s. Many craftspeople are just starting their businesses at midlife, changing careers to realize their dream of making a living from their crafts. Maryon Atwood, director of the Worcester Center for Crafts in Massachusetts, says: "I see the trends of each person having multiple careers reflected in our professional crafts program. Most of our students have attended college, even earned degrees, and have a lot of experience. These students are very serious, motivated, aware of the preciousness of time, and are interested in what I call a 'heart's desire' career."

Workshop programs are a viable alternative to traditional degree programs, offering a short-term way to learn a new skill or to find out quickly if a career in a craft is the right choice. Students of all ages can study with a master craftsperson for a session ranging from a weekend to several weeks. Michael Munroe, former director of the American Craft Council, explains: "Although craftspeople used to be primarily taught in formal degree programs using a progression of courses, students now have the freedom to study with who they want when they want because of the incredible growth in nondegree programs." Craft schools offering workshops include the Haystack Mountain School of Crafts in Maine, the Penland School in North Carolina, the Arrowmont School of Arts and Crafts in Tennessee, the Southwest Craft Center in Texas, Anderson Ranch in Colorado, and the Oregon College of Art & Craft, to name a few.

For students still interested in enrolling in a traditional program, there are more than 180 institutions including independent art schools, colleges, and universities, that offer degree programs in forty-seven states. Majors areas of craft study include blacksmithing, book arts, ceramics, furniture design, glass, jewelry/metals, papermaking, textiles, and wood.

In an article titled "You've Got a College Degree in Your Craft, What Now?" from the March 1996 issue of the *Crafts Report,* writer Daniel Grant says that according to the National Association of Schools of Art and Design, more than 2,300 bachelor of fine arts (B.F.A.) and 620 master of fine arts (M.F.A.) degrees were awarded in the academic year 1993–94. It is unlikely that the art market has expanded to accommodate and support this throng of artists. It is even less likely that many, if any, of these graduates found teaching positions, since according to the College Art Association, schools in the market for experienced artist-teachers received, on the average, 110 applications for every job opening.

While these statistics are sobering, going to school to get a certificate or degree in your craft is still the best way to receive overall training. While most of the craft administrators profiled in chapter 3 suggest taking workshops as a way to start, most suggested a formal program of study in the crafts as the preferred method of training. Following the degree, working as an apprentice and taking a business course (if not offered in the degree program) were also strongly suggested. For information on undergraduate degree programs, contact the National Association of Schools of Art and Design at 11250 Roger

Bacon Drive, Suite 21, Reston, VA 20190, (703) 437-0700; *www.arts-accredit.org.* For information and a directory on graduate degree programs contact the College Art Association at 275 Seventh Avenue, New York, NY 10001, (212) 691-1051; *www.collegeart.org.*

In her book *Crafting as a Business,* Wendy Rosen shares the following statistics to help put the craft market of the 1990s into perspective:

- The U.S. economy gets an annual boost of $2 billion from craft sales
- Craft booth space has gone from 1,600 to 6,000 booths in trade shows since 1980
- 40,000 U.S. retailers buy American crafts
- 3,000 American craft retailers polled in *NICHE* magazine indicated that they made a combined $644 million annually in sales
- Approximately 10,000 craft artists nationwide sell contemporary crafts to galleries in the United States
- On average, buyers attending the Boston Buyers Market spent $10,000 at the 1992 show

The Service Corps of Retired Executives Association (SCORE), published the following statistics in 1996 about small businesses and entrepreneurship in its brochure, *No One Knows More About Small Business Ownership:*

- Small businesses account for 99.7 percent of all employers
- Small businesses account for 54 percent of employment
- Small businesses generate 52 percent of sales
- There are 22 million small businesses in the United States

The craft market has grown tremendously in the last several decades and is a very different field today than it was even thirty years ago. Not only are there more opportunities and a greater audience for crafts in general, there is also more competition for craftspeople. The need to develop a recognizable style, have good business skills, as well as the ability to articulate your passion for your work to the customer, are all necessary skills that must be learned and practiced in order to stay competitive.

Although we have been experiencing a period of prosperity, today's work tends to be so perfectly made that it is hard for consumers to tell the difference between a handmade product and manufactured or imported work. While this is an alarming trend to some, it shows the precision of current methods and materials. The biggest challenge facing craftspeople may be how to differentiate their work from manufactured goods, thus justifying higher prices.

Is the cost of buying a handmade piece worth the pleasure someone will get from owning it? Why would a consumer buy something from a craftsperson instead of a less expensive alternative from a manufacturer? This question raises the important issue of educating the public about the value of crafts in our lives.

CHAPTER 2

PROFILES OF CRAFTSPEOPLE

The crafts field provides a variety of avenues through which to pursue selling your crafts. I have assembled a number of profiles of craftspeople in this chapter in order to demonstrate what it's like to be a production craftsperson, a craft teacher, a craftsperson who makes her living in another field, as well as a famous craftsperson. It is my intention that these profiles will be inspiring and provide role models to help you make informed choices about the business of selling your work.

In the next chapter, I offer the views of craft administrators from craft organizations, schools, craft magazines, gallery owners, and fair promoters. These experts give their thoughts on the ideal type of education you need to become a professional craftsperson, current trends, suggestions for selling your work, as well as ways to help keep you motivated.

Full-Time Production Craftsperson

A career as a full-time production craftsperson requires running a small business and selling your work through markets such as shops, galleries, and fairs. Earning your living is the result of making sales and receiving payments rather than receiving a paycheck from someone else. A production craftsperson also needs to provide benefits such as health insurance or retirement pensions for herself and her employees.

Following are two profiles of working production craftspeople. Missy Greene, a potter, lives and works in Deer Isle, Maine. Eric Swanson has a wood-

Ray Michoud

Figure 1. *Brook Trout #1.* By Melissa Greene; Clay

working studio in Boston, and learned his trade by working rather than by studying in a professional degree program. Eric employs a small staff and sells directly to architects, contractors, and other clients.

Missy Greene

Missy works alone and makes her living selling her pots through juried craft shows, her own showroom, and through shows in other galleries around the country. Her pots are very high quality, selling for anywhere from a few hundred to a few thousand dollars each.

Missy first decided to be a potter when she was a teenager. "I didn't really have instruction in clay until I was a senior in high school," Missy remembers. "I worked in a pottery shop, made pots through college, and learned about glazes and working with clay through a series of independent studies."

While Missy was still learning and developing her style, she began teaching ceramics and started selling her work. "I was teaching in Connecticut at the Guilford Handcraft Center when I set up a studio in a garage and had my first pottery sale," she recounts. "That was the beginning. The sale was really successful. Then I became the studio manager at Weselyn Potters and began teaching at the Creative Arts Center. At this time, I was making very labor-intensive pieces using clay and quills, which helped me get into my first juried craft show but didn't allow for much profit. I was making part of my living from selling my pots and the rest from teaching. At this point, I decided to go to graduate school and see if I could figure out how to make my living from just selling my work."

Currently, Missy makes large wheel-thrown vessels with animal and figurative imagery inspired by a variety of cultures and natural surroundings. "During graduate school, I took some great classes in African art, world music, and archeology that really inspired my work," says Missy. "I started developing a style which I still use today where I paint[ed] images like loons on white earthenware and used smoke firing techniques to create marks."

After graduation, Missy had two gallery shows, one in Maine and another in Connecticut. "I stopped in at the Plains Gallery in Portland, Maine, with slides of my work. I didn't know anything about selling wholesale but the gallery was interested in my work and gave me my first show," remembers Missy. "The pots sold like crazy. I couldn't believe it. It was an amazing time. Then I had another show at the Green Gallery in Connecticut which was also successful."

With the teaching experience, her own studio sale, and the gallery shows behind her, Missy felt ready to enter her first big juried craft fair. "I applied and got into the American Craft Council (ACC) juried craft fair in Springfield, Massachusetts. I didn't have anybody to ask how to do the fair, I had pedestals from hell, and I was a complete wreck. But by the end of the fair, in addition to making retail sales, I took home $20,000 in wholesale orders. I immediately went up to my parents' summer home in Maine, set up my studio in the driveway, and began to work long hours to fill those orders. Getting all those wholesale orders was more than I could have imagined at that time from just one fair."

Following her success at the ACC Springfield fair, Missy applied and was accepted on her first try to the ACC fair in Baltimore, as well as the Smithsonian Craft Fair in Washington, D.C., one of the most prestigious fairs in the country. She was on a roll. "I now know that doing juried craft fairs is fickle," says Missy. "One year I got the Best in Clay Award at the Philadelphia fair and then the next year I didn't even get into the fair! The promoters try to keep the fairs fresh and the jurors are always different, which makes it hard to plan and keeps you on the edge, never knowing if you will get into the

Figure 2. *Eric Swanson and Cleo*. Swanson Woodwork; Boston, Massachusetts

fairs or not. However, one year I came home with just one pot after doing the Philadelphia fair!"

Missy presently does about four juried craft fairs a year and sells work out of her gallery showroom in Deer Isle and several other galleries. "I'm more established now and I don't have to work so hard," says Missy. "I used to work in the studio all the time unless I went away to a fair. Now, with a family, I only work half days in the studio because I don't want to use day care. I feel so grateful to be able to do what I do and make a good living. I never imagined this would happen to me."

Eric Swanson

Eric worked his way up the ladder in unionized shops around the country as an apprentice, journeyman, fitter, foreman, installer, shaper, and molder for fifteen years before starting his own business specializing in "unique mill-work, cabinetry, and furniture made to order" in 1995.

"I was a fitter or a wood machinist and cabinetmaker by trade," says Eric. "I specialized in cutting, joining, and shaping wood. In large shops, the fitter is the one first given the plans made by architects and designers to figure out the quickest and most practical way to turn a two-dimensional design into three dimensions. To be a good fitter, you need to be able to read plans, visualize in three dimensions, and work under pressure because the fitter provides the assembly line with work."

Although Eric studied the bass at the Manhattan School of Music in New York City for a year, he left school to work in custom woodshops as an apprentice. "I was living a weird double life," remembers Eric. "I worked all day at the shop, practiced music for a couple hours, played music somewhere, finally slept maybe five hours a night, and got up to do it all over again."

Although playing music is still important to Eric, he continued working with wood in commercial shops. "Something changed when I started working at a shop in New York City. It was a well-run shop, the owner had a lot of integrity, and it was a place with both deep traditions and a lot of expertise," remembers Eric. "I worked there for a couple years, made a lot of mistakes, and got some great experience. It was an honor working with people from all over the world who had been in the trade since they were little kids and did things perfectly every time. To me, they were real craftspeople who were not interested in self-promotion but in just doing their job well."

Eric went to work in another large shop as a journeyman, then became a fitter, and eventually a foreman. "Every time I changed jobs, I learned a new bag of tricks," says Eric. "And I got more responsibility. It was great training."

After he rented a bench space in a cooperative shop and did machine maintenance to offset the costs, Eric chose to open his own shop. "I was tired of the union scene and the economy had just crashed," says Eric. "I had a taste of being on my own and was finding it hard to think about working for someone else again. I decided to start my own business."

Eric wrote a simple business plan and projected his expenses for six months. The original $13,000 that Eric saved and borrowed disappeared quickly. Even though he was sharing space with a couple of other woodworkers and bartering his technical skills, the going in the beginning was tough. "One woodworker owned all of the equipment in the shop and the other was just getting by after ten years of working on his own," explains Eric. "One started teaching and the other decided to give up his business, so I bought the equipment and took over the entire shop. It was a good opportunity for me, but came much sooner than I had planned. I bought more used machinery to supplement what was there and reorganized the shop."

Eric got work from other shops as a subcontractor, but the margin of profit wasn't high enough to be very profitable. "In the beginning, I worked all my connections with other shops and traded my expertise as a machinist. I was doing the same type of work I had always done except instead of working for just one employer, now all the local shops were my employer," explains Eric. "Then I also started getting work directly from clients, architects, and contractors." Although Eric has primarily gotten work through word of mouth, he has also had a good response from direct mail and telephone solicitation. "Whenever it gets slow, I call people and let them know I'm looking for work," says Eric, "and I can usually get the business I need."

Learning how to estimate the time involved in a project to meet deadlines and make a profit has not been easy but is necessary to stay in business. "I started tracking my hours, what my costs were, and analyzing where the money was going," notes Eric. "Discovering a computer program to keep track of my finances, like Quicken, changed my life. For example, I just finished a $90,000 job that should have been $100,000 because the customer made changes which resulted in a loss of efficiency, so I lost money. After looking over the numbers, I can now see where I should make changes next time. I now know that I should have asked the customer for a per diem charge for every day that the job was delayed due to the customer's changes. Instead, I had an employee who I was paying sitting around waiting for the okay from the customer to go ahead with the project."

Another thing Eric learned by tracking his finances is how much it costs just to turn on the lights in his shop and pay worker's compensation. "It costs me $100 a day just to be here. And I've learned that I can't do all the jobs by myself," he says. "Even with employees, things don't always go according to plan. I had three employees until three weeks ago when two gave notice and left. I had to hire a subcontractor to get a job done on time that I had to pay twice as much as I would have paid my employee. I've also learned I can't control everything. I've decided to get smaller again and start to rent out some of the shop space to other craftspeople to cut my overhead and expenses. If you want to run your own business successfully, you have to learn how to stay flexible.

"The ironic part for me is, if I still worked in a union shop, I would be making three times the salary I have been able to earn these last few years and I wouldn't have nearly the same level of responsibility. Although I'm still not making a livable wage, I am hopeful that this year will be different," says Eric. "I'm still here trying to make it work because it is very interesting and compelling to run this business and I have almost got it right. In five years, I hope I have creativity, variety, and security in my life, that I'm still self-employed or in a partnership, and that the business is still growing. I also hope I'm making a decent wage and able to take a vacation. I keep reminding myself that this is a business, not a religion."

Working as a production craftsperson can be very rewarding because you control everything and get to do the thing you enjoy the most—make your crafts. As you can see in the profiles of Missy and Eric, making a living as a production craftsperson takes time to build up the business, while learning how to run it efficiently. While Missy is finally at a stage where she can step back a little and reduce her hours, Eric is still in the startup phase of his business and needs to keep putting in more effort until he is more established and his business has stabilized.

As Eric has learned, being able to estimate work, hire new employees if necessary, and negotiate changes with clients are vital to the financial success of his business. Although Missy works with deadlines to produce work for retail sales and fill wholesale orders, she only has to worry about her own capabilities and can plan accordingly.

Craft Teacher

Craftspeople who work as full-time teachers, whether at the high school or college level, seem to have the best of both worlds: a steady income with benefits, plus a period of time off to work uninterrupted in the studio. Many other craftspeople supplement their incomes by teaching on a part-time basis through adult education programs and short-term workshops that, although they may provide a welcome paycheck, usually does not provide benefits.

Here are two profiles of craft teachers: Chris Gustin, a potter and Iver Lofving, a ceramic artist. Following are some of their insights about teaching and making their own work.

Chris Gustin

A ceramics teacher for twenty years at the college level, Chris learned to make pots during high school at a local community center before he started working in a ceramics factory. "My father ran a business manufacturing and distributing giftware made of clay around the country," says Chris. "After school, I worked in the factory. My older brother was also married to a potter so I had another connection to making pots through them. I've been around clay all of my life."

Nancy T. Smith

Figure 3. *Chris Gustin.* Potter and former professor

After attending college for a year, Chris came home to apprentice with the manager of the factory who passed away two months later. For the next two years before returning to school, Chris helped manage the factory. "My brother convinced me to return to school. After running the factory, I studied with Ken Ferguson at the Kansas City Art Institute. I was really ready to learn after running the factory and decided to turn myself completely over to Ken and learn all he could teach me about ceramics. At that time, I geared myself primarily to make studio pots and it was well worth it." Chris continued his studies at Alfred University earning an M.F.A. degree in ceramics. "The education I received at Alfred totally changed how I saw pots," remembers Chris. "It was a major influence and brought me back into the process."

After graduation, Chris did a three-month residency at the Archie Bray Foundation for Ceramic Arts in Montana and then moved to Connecticut to start his own studio. "I rented an old building with my sister-in-law and started to work on my dream of being a studio potter," says Chris. "The reality was I was basically working alone, getting a lot of rejections, nobody wanted my pots, and my work wasn't right for the craft fair market. So I kept making my work, got some publicity and exposure, and began teaching at the 92nd Street Y in New York City. One of the best things that happened during this time was that I got two pieces into a show at the American Craft Museum called Clay Glass Young Americans. A lot of opportunities came out of that show for me, including a teaching job at Parsons in New York. A typical schedule back then was working one or two days a week teaching, with the balance spent working in my studio."

In 1980, Chris was hired to teach ceramics at the Program in Artisanry (PIA) at Boston University. "One of the students had seen my work and called me to see if I would apply for the job," recounts Chris. "I drove up to Boston, spent time talking with the students, and they hired me."

In 1982, Chris renovated a former chicken barn for his studio and home in South Dartmouth, Massachusetts. "If I had known then what a big project it was," admits Chris. "I wouldn't have done it. But the risk was important for me at that time." Chris commuted to Boston three days a week to teach at PIA and spent the rest of his time in the studio.

In 1985, PIA left Boston University and merged with the Swain School of Design in New Bedford, a much closer commute for Chris. Two years later, PIA/Swain merged with UMass Dartmouth. Ten years later, Chris submitted his resignation to leave his teaching job and return to working in his studio full-time to expand a part-time tile business he had started a few years earlier.

"I have found that teaching is a separate career from making," says Chris. "Even though teaching informs making, it requires getting people to listen and learn, not just giving information. It takes a lot of energy. The students and my teaching career have been great. And although I know I'm good at teaching, I've decided that life is just too short. I'm at a point now after twenty years of teaching where I want to do something else with my time. I have also been trying to figure out how to balance work with my family. In the past, I could work in the studio during the summer months or my days off, but lately my studio stuff always seems to take priority over family matters. I'm married, have a daughter, and need to work in my studio just five days a week and spend the other two days with my family.

"I started the tile business, Chris Gustin Ceramics, to make functional tiles for floors using beautiful colors that are not easily found in the commercial market," says Chris. "I worked with a few architects and got the company started. I've realized I can't expand it if I teach, and I really want to develop it. The interesting thing to me is that my running the tile business really makes sense to my students. There is a sadness about leaving the teaching job, but I'm excited to be able to be a role model for my students of someone who is trying something new instead of becoming complacent. I'm giving up something I love for something I love. And at this point, I'm willing to take some risks to feel alive."

Maili Bailey

Figure 4. *Iver Lofving*. Ceramic artist and high school teacher

Iver Lofving

A ceramic artist, printmaker, and painter, Iver is also a high school art and Spanish teacher. "I'm beginning my sixth year of teaching," says Iver. "The school year is usually very hectic, but during the summer I get a lot of work done in my studio. We spend the summer in Swan's Island, Maine, where I try to keep a schedule of at least five hours a day working in my studio. With the security of the paycheck from teaching, I can take the time to do my work in the summer instead of looking for work. However, during the winter, it's harder to find the time to work in the studio."

Iver received a B.F.A. degree from Alfred University and a master's degree in education from the University of Maine. After going to New York City to see if he could make it as an artist, Iver decided to join the Peace Corps. "I was assigned to Guatemala and Costa Rica for two and a half years to help people build small water tanks to provide a clean water supply," remembers Iver. "In the United States, we live in a different world, but not one that is necessarily better. I found that being in a different culture really gave me perspective on how the world works."

Although Iver was inspired by Guatemala and did paint a few watercolors, it seemed like a luxury to make art. When he returned to the United States, he started teaching Spanish and art at a private school in Vermont. Then he moved to Maine, began his master's degree program, and became a Peace Corps representative. "I always took art classes even when I was getting my masters at the University of Maine," says Iver. "I also coordinated a show featuring art from Guatemala, as well as photographs and textiles, that were displayed in the student union and very well received."

After becoming certified to teach Spanish and art in the public schools,

Iver got a job at Skowhegan High School in Skowhegan, Maine, where he is still teaching. "I go to workshops whenever I can to keep inspired," says Iver. "I did a summer residency at the Watershed Center for Ceramic Arts in Edgecomb, Maine, which was wonderful. I also go to weekend workshops for art teachers at Haystack in Deer Isle, Maine, whenever I can. It's a chance for the teachers to make art and is a very magical time for us. I like teaching and feel it is a socially redeeming profession. And I hope that I am having an impact on some of the students by helping them get into something worthwhile."

Both Chris and Iver acknowledge that although teaching allows them time in the studio, it requires a strong commitment to helping other people learn. Iver noted the importance of finding ways to rejuvenate and keep inspired as a teacher and a maker such as attending workshops. For Chris, after twenty years of teaching, starting his own business while spending enough time with his family is what's important to him at this stage in his career.

Craftspeople Who Make Their Living in Another Field

There are many craftspeople who have chosen to make their living using other skills while maintaining a craft studio, selling and showing their work on a part-time basis. While many people start this way, some craftspeople choose this option as either a way to keep their work separate from the demands of the marketplace or to simultaneously pursue another interest.

Profiled here are Marcia Macdonald, a metalsmith in Wilmington, NC, with an undergraduate degree in design and an M.F.A. degree in metals who earns her living as a designer, and Joli Greene, an artist in Portland, Maine, who has made peace work a priority.

Marcia Macdonald

Although Marcia has been accepted by some of the best craft fairs in the country, she likes the security of getting a paycheck and keeping her work separate from making a living. "I like to ask myself questions about what I'm doing in my work and keep from getting trendy or stale. I don't want to keep making the same thing over and over," says Marcia. "I have a lot of ideas and although I admire people who do production work, I personally would find it too stifling. It is also a lot of work and very costly to do these high-end fairs."

Before a recent move to North Carolina from Oregon, Marcia split her

Figure 5. *Marcia Macdonald.* Metalsmith and designer

time between working in her studio and working part-time for a wholesale
gift company designing products. "I liked problem solving for the company
and although I thought about my projects when I wasn't at work, they didn't
take energy away from thinking about my own pieces," says Marcia. "Having
the outside job also allowed me the freedom to make pieces that didn't necessarily have to be salable. With the outside job, I knew I could pay the rent. It
was my security blanket."

After receiving a B.F.A. degree in design, Marcia went to the Penland
School in North Carolina to study jewelry as a scholarship student. The experience convinced her to pursue her love of metals in graduate school. "While
I was at Penland, I heard about a metalsmith named Fred Woell," remembers
Marcia, "who taught at the Program in Artisanry in Massachusetts. I enrolled
in the M.F.A. program and studied with Fred for a couple years. He was the
first teacher to tell me to put my own imagery in my pieces. During my time
in graduate school, I also learned how to structure my time, discipline myself
in my craft, and work with professional craftspeople who, in addition to teaching, also showed their work."

During graduate school, Marcia had the opportunity to teach a two-
dimensional design course for undergraduate students. "A design background

is so important because it gives craftspeople a vocabulary," says Marcia. "So many people take up a craft that have never studied design and the lack of a design background really shows in their pieces." After receiving her M.F.A. degree, Marcia went to the Oregon College of Art & Craft in Portland to work for a year as the metals resident. "I was paid to be there, teach classes, and do my own work," explains Marcia. "It was a wonderful experience."

Marcia likes to work with a variety of materials, ranging from metals and stones to wood, and found objects. "I'm currently making brooches and neck pieces that are mixed-media, narrative, assemblage pieces," says Marcia. "I use whatever materials I need to get my ideas across. Currently, my work is becoming more personal because I'm starting to see my life as one big picture. I also feel there is something else I'm here to do besides just making art objects. My needs are shifting. I'm becoming more spiritual and I want to nurture that. I want to help people and feel it is more important to me than either money or making objects. Even though I know I will always make objects, I won't be satisfied unless I'm making a difference in other people's lives."

Figure 6. *Joli Greene.* Artist and peace activist

Joli Greene

Although she has spent much of her career working in service to others through teaching and peace work, if asked what she does, Joli will answer without hesitation, "I'm an artist." Joli, aware of her ability to work in a variety of mediums, says all of her work, whether making a basket or teaching, is simply shifting mediums and selling her creativity in different ways. For over twenty-five years, Joli has worked as an artist, arts administrator, social worker, and peace activist. "I find my other work just as meaningful as my creative work," says Joli. "If I can pass along the joy I feel about life to another person, then I will feel I have been successful."

Joli started out in the early 1970s studying fine art at Syracuse University in New York while doing illustration work for the zoology department. She has also worked as an arts administrator, teacher, employment counselor, touring artist in both prisons and schools, and as a peace activist. Her work in the federal Comprehensive Employment and Training Act (CETA) program coordinating after-school art programs for underprivileged children provided a chance to acquire valuable administrative skills. More importantly, the experience paved the way for a later chapter in her life, combining her love of working with children with her humanitarian efforts to help promote peace. After injuring her back to the point that production weaving was no longer an option in the late 1980s, Joli started keeping a journal to look at what she was doing, see if any themes emerged, and decide how to spend her time.

"I wanted to look at what I was doing with my time here on earth and affect consciousness to create a better world," says Joli. "I wanted to achieve more than selling scarves to tourists to get by. What I found out about myself is that part of me feels alive when I work with kids and when I teach, and that anything I do to stimulate other people's creative process just feels right. As a result, I have tried to gear my life to do just that."

Joli began working at World Peace Camp and later toured Russia with two groups, Peace Fleece and the Wednesday Spinners, from Maine. The trip involved working and teaching with Russian spinners, weavers, and shepherds. The following year, Joli was asked by the Soviet Peace Committee to live and work in Russia as its first sponsored artist to work with Russian children. While in Russia, Joli taught the children to put on plays, design sets and costumes, and perform music. Even though supplies were scarce, the group toured Russia with professional theaters donating space. The following summer, the group attended the World Peace Camp in the United States, going on tour with American children performing at places like the United Nations and Paul Newman's Hole in the Wall camp for children with cancer and AIDS. "When I first arrived at the Hole in the Wall camp," Joli remembers, "I thought it would be really hard; but I found the place was so full of joy, it had almost a festival atmosphere!"

At the present time, Joli is again shifting gears. "It's time to go back to the studio," asserts Joli. "Time to clear out a space for myself and start teaching some workshops again. Right now, I'm working on illustrating a children's book with a Tibetan monk based on stories from the Tibetan culture." Joli hopes to not only learn compassion from studying the Tibetan culture, but also to help the Tibetans preserve their culture through her illustration work with the book.

"I'm still selling baskets and stepping up the process to make things out of love instead of as a machine," says Joli. "I would not be the artist I am today without having had the accessibility of a place like Haystack to work without interruption, in different mediums, as both a student and a teacher, and to see what my peers are doing in a noncompetitive environment. I think people need encouragement to maintain their vision, and Haystack has been a place that has helped to nurture mine."

Although earning a living using other skills takes Marcia and Joli away from their studios, it also frees them to make less marketable work. The challenge for them is to find the time and motivation to keep working in the studio after the demands of another job. For Marcia, working as a product designer didn't take all of her creative energy and allowed her to still feel excited and have the energy to work in her studio. For Joli, whether she is currently teaching, doing peace work, or working in her studio, she feels creative and happy.

Famous Craftspeople

Even the famous craftspeople whose names and work we recognize are constantly promoting themselves, selling their work, and planning for their future. Although name recognition is important, it is something that doesn't usually happen by chance. Many craftspeople may be famous or well known in their fields, usually after years of hard work, and yet still have to concern themselves with earning a living.

Profiled here are two craftspeople, Thomas Moser, a cabinetmaker who didn't start his business until his late thirties, and Dale Chihuly, a glass artist who has been making glass since the 1960s and is considered a pioneer in his field.

Thomas Moser

Thos. Moser, Cabinetmakers employs one hundred people in its Auburn, Maine shop producing the finest handcrafted hardwood furniture for residential and contract furniture makers. Thos. Moser furniture is not only signed and dated as a work of art, it is guaranteed for the lifetime of the original owner.

"Even as a kid," recounts Thomas, "I was a maker. I didn't acknowledge that part of me again until after I had earned a Ph.D. and had been a college professor for several years. Wood was always my avocation, and in my late thirties, I decided to turn my hobby into my livelihood." Twenty-five years later, Thos. Moser, Cabinetmakers has four showrooms: Portland (Maine), New York City, San Francisco, and Philadelphia.

"In the beginning, we had a hard time getting the business going— everybody does," remembers Thomas. "Most people fail because they don't realize or accept the fact that, in addition to making your work, you have to spend about 40 percent of your time marketing and doing administrative work. The notion that somehow people will magically buy your work without having to sell it isn't realistic. When I started, I was married with four kids and was the sole provider for my family. I had decided to leave teaching but had no intention of living anything but a middle-class lifestyle."

In the beginning, Thomas worked hard taking whatever woodworking jobs he could get to make payroll. "I had students who worked for me in the beginning," says Thomas. "And I didn't always get to do the kind of work I wanted. We even sold our house and put that money into the business. I surrounded myself with skillful woodworkers, and after losing money the first several years, we turned the corner and started to make a profit. After five years, we were fully supported by the business."

There have been several significant phases to building the business. "In 1973, when we started the business, or what I call our craft period," says Thomas, "I was interested in reacquainting and rekindling the craft of fine woodworking that had been lost to mass production with the industrial revolution. I did not make art." During this early period, Thomas wrote three books and ran courses in the summer in a program he called the Maine School of Cabinetry. "The emphasis was on discovery," explains Thomas. "That profit was a means to an end. The people who worked with us then were very serious about woodworking, very well educated, and interested in running their own business someday. Fifteen of them run small woodworking companies today. I call them the alumni association."

The next phase of the business began in the early 1980s and lasted for the next ten years. "We moved the business and gained efficiency through a division of labor," says Thomas. "Someone glued, the next person cut joints and assembled, and then the pieces went to the finishing room. We began to hire local people who in another place and time might have worked in a mill.

We provided a good working environment and the business grew 31 percent per year for the next ten years."

The current period has been one of professional management. "I realized that I am not an administrator, but a wood-worker," admits Thomas. "So I hired an M.B.A. from Harvard who ran the business for five years. And I learned a great deal from him."

At present, there are primarily two markets for the furniture. "The commercial market involves architects and selling to aca-demic libraries, conference rooms, private institutions and foundations, museums and galleries," says Thomas. "The residential mar-

Figure 7. *Thomas Moser*

ket is sold through our showrooms, our catalog which we market nationally, and by word of mouth. With very few exceptions we do not sell our furni-ture wholesale. Our customers tend to be forty-five years or older, in manage-ment or professional jobs, and are very highly educated with at least a master's degree. Very few products sell to such a highly educated market. And 40 per-cent of them are repeat buyers."

Although Thomas has a shop at home where he is currently rebuilding a boat, he works in a prototype shop at the business where he does experi-mental work. "We do applied research," says Thomas. "We usually work out our designs and test our products thoroughly before production begins. We even break chairs to see how they break. I do very little of this. We also do a lot of basic design, which is the part I enjoy. Right now, for example, I am working on fourteen new designs. I know what I want them to look like, but I am trying to figure out if they can be made efficiently. One piece took only three days to figure out, while another one I have been working on for three years!" In addition to working in the prototype shop, Thomas lectures, does public relations work, and teaches a few courses.

Thomas suggests that people who are starting out ("if they are still young enough," he says) should "work for someone else first to learn the business, such as in a millworking shop instead of for a single craftsperson. The art part will come in the late hours at night when they are working alone. They need to know how things are made, be good at estimating jobs, and learn the business part. The ability to be organized and work well with people is not something you learn in school. If they don't, they will be like me and it will take them twenty-five years to get it right."

Dale Chihuly

Note: When I called to set up an interview with Dale Chihuly, one of his staff told me that he was so busy I would probably not be able to interview him for several months. Instead, I was sent a large media kit including numerous articles written about Dale Chihuly, an artist's statement about one of his current projects, and a page of slides. Here is Dale Chihuly's story gleaned from this extensive media kit.

It was 1965 when Dale Chihuly blew his first glass bubble in his basement studio using colored flat glass and metal tubing. By the late 1990s, he had created some of the largest pieces of glass ever blown by hand. Named "America's First National Living Treasure" by the nation's fifty governors, Dale Chihuly is the founder of the Pilchuck Glass School, in Seattle, established the glass department at the Rhode Island School of Design (RISD) in Providence, and is one of four Americans to have had a one-person show at the Louvre in Paris. His list of accomplishments, awards, and collections are too many to note here.

According to Jeff Davis in an article titled "Glass Master," published by the *St. Louis Dispatch* on July 16, 1996, Chihuly's glass work is sculptural, incorporating bright colors and unusual shapes. "Call it art, call it craft, I don't care what they call it," Chihuly has said of the public response to his work. "Somewhere down the line, long after I'm dead, someone will figure out what it was and how important it was. In the meantime, I get my kicks out of people seeing the work." Chihuly spends his time teaching, collaborating with other artists, traveling, developing new techniques, and showing his work. "I guess that I've essentially been a director for about twenty years now," Chihuly explains. "There's really nothing new about that. What is new is the vast number of shows and installations we now do." With a crew that includes a dozen workers on the glassblowing team and another dozen assigned to installation, Chihuly rejects the twentieth-century notion of artists working alone in their studios.

In another article, entitled "Chihuly's Glass Menagerie" in the March 1997 edition of *Arts* magazine, writer Jennifer Komar notes that many of Chihuly's projects are public installations and experimental projects. "Public installations are my favorite form of art because so many people get to see them," says the artist. "I'm lucky that my work appeals to so many people of all ages. It's more accessible than most public work. A lot of that has to do with the material."

Even with all the recognition he has received, Chihuly's life has not been without personal tragedy, losing both his brother to an accident and his father to a fatal heart attack while a teenager in the 1950s; as well as losing the sight in his left eye in a car accident in 1976. As a result of this accident, Chihuly no longer blows glass himself, instead supervising a team of glass artists using drawings and verbal instructions to communicate his designs.

Russell Johnson

Figure 8. *Chihuly Over Venice.* By Dale Chihuly; Ireland

In an article titled "Brooklyn's Hot Show Steams, Sizzles During 'His Glassness' Visit" in the *Christian Science Monitor* on October 13, 1994, writer Carol Strickland reports that Chihuly, called "the Tiffany of Contemporary Glass" and "His Glassness," received his M.F.A. degree from the University of Wisconsin in Madison. There, Chihuly studied with Harvey Littleton, who is considered to be the father of the contemporary glass movement. He continued his studies in Venice on a Fulbright after graduation with some of Italy's finest artisans at the renowned Venini factory where he learned the notion of teamwork in the hot shop. "I was the first American glassblower who didn't do the work myself," Chihuly explains. "Now it's more common, but originally there was a lot of resentment towards that. I went on the road so people could see the process and understand. I wanted to make sure they know how the work is made."

A recent body of work executed in 1995–1996 called *Chihuly Over Venice,* was a public installation on a grand scale and involved glass artists from four different countries: Finland, Ireland, Mexico, and Italy. In an artist's statement on the project, Chihuly explains, "I was thinking about grand chandeliers hanging over the canals of Venice, and I said why not go to four countries with great glass traditions and blow chandeliers with both American and glassmasters from each of the countries—a collaboration of cultural techniques and talent that would be unique for each country." Chihuly elaborates, "I would go with no preconceived ideas and take it day-by-day. The results would be impossible to predict, and each chandelier would be unlike any other. We would break down the cultural barriers and dispel the secrets that have so long restricted and insulated the great glass houses. In the end, the chandeliers, made from thousands of individual parts and representing the work of hundreds of glassblowers, would be sent to Venice—the 'Wizard of the Sea'—the most mysterious and secretive city of all."

Famous craftspeople such as Thomas Moser and Dale Chihuly have worked hard and long to get to where they are now. Instead of making the craftwork themselves, each craftsperson has hired other people to work for them, whether under their direct supervision, such as Chihuly with a team of glassblowers, or in Thomas Moser's factory carrying out his tested designs. This production capability has allowed them to produce numerous pieces and helped to make them well known in their respective fields.

Each career choice profiled has positive and negative aspects. A full-time production craftsperson must be willing to produce work in multiples and may require the services of employees. Craft teachers must wait until school is out to concentrate on their craftwork. Craftspeople who earn their living in another field think of their work as only part of their identity. Famous craftspeople are always promoting their work and moving on to a new level of challenge and achievement.

You may find that you have several stages to your career as a craftsperson. For example, you may start out making your craft as a hobby, sell some work on a parttime basis, and then begin earning a living as a production craftsperson. Or you may change from doing production work to becoming a craft teacher, or vice versa. It's up to you. No choice is inherently better. There are many craftspeople who are currently doing a combination of making their own work, selling their work, and teaching to earn a living.

CHAPTER 3

CRAFT ADMINISTRATORS

Craft administrators come from a variety of backgrounds and interests with many beginning their careers as artists and craftspeople. They might have become craft administrators because they got involved in organizing an exhibit, writing a grant, or starting a cooperative gallery. Other craft administrators study arts administration at the graduate level and are truly professional administrators. While still interested in their own work, these administrators spend the majority of their time working for organizations that promote education or services for other craftspeople, rather than working in their own studios.

The following excerpts from interviews with craft professionals have been collected in order to give you a personalized overview of the craft world. These people work for craft organizations, schools, magazines, or run galleries. I asked them to share their thoughts on how the craft world has changed, to recommend fields of study, and offer suggestions for selling craftwork. Some of their comments and suggestions may surprise you.

Michael Munroe
Former Director, American Craft Council, New York, NY

"After studying at the University of Wisconsin as an undergraduate, I earned an M.F.A. in Design in 1971 from the Cranbrook Academy of Art. After graduation, I worked as a professor of design and gallery director at [the State University of New York] SUNY [in] Oneonta where I curated a crafts

Figure 9. *Michael Munroe*

exhibition. The Director of the Renwick Museum in Washington [D.C.] saw an article about the exhibit and called me to come to Washington in 1974 to become the curator there. For over twenty years, I worked there curating many exhibits including recently picking out the pieces for the White House Collection of American Crafts that has been traveling around the country. Then I became the director of the American Craft Council.

"Throughout the 1940s to early 1970s, art departments in universities and art schools flourished. During that time, if someone earned a degree, they could usually get a teaching job. The system finally produced too many graduates. I think that it was the lack of teaching jobs that led to the emergence of craft artists who became entrepreneurs to survive. This has contributed to the enormous growth of craft fairs we have seen in the last twenty years. Now, instead of aesthetic risk, students are taught more about marketing and how to make money selling their crafts.

"There is no one correct formula for what you need to do to become a craftsperson. Although I was taught in a certain progression of courses, there are a diversity of approaches available now. I suggest people interested in becoming a craftsperson do an apprenticeship or they could pick someone they want to study with or techniques they want to learn and take several workshops at any of the craft programs around the country. After a quick sampling of workshops, they could quickly find out if being a craftsperson is what they want to do.

"To craftspeople interested in selling their work, nothing is more critical than to develop a style that is recognizable and get this image in front of as many people as possible. Enter competitions where the work is juried and get your work in shops. Spend as much time as possible making and promoting your work."

Maryon Atwood
Director, Worcester Center for Crafts, Worcester, Massachusetts

"I was a fine arts major and studied painting at Monmouth College [Illinois] and the Art Institute of Chicago. My arts administration career started when I got involved in a local arts council doing fund-raising. After that, I worked as the associate director of the museum at the University of Connecticut and eventually became the development director. Then I came to the Worcester Craft Center as the director.

"In addition to our certificate program, we offer classes in eight studio mediums as well as a gallery and gift shop. To craftspeople just starting out, I recommend a two-year studio-based certificate program. It is not only a less expensive alternative to a four-year B.F.A. program, but a way to work with real artisans who are practicing and selling their work.

"A disturbing trend I'm seeing is that selling work has started to replace the focus of educating people about the value of crafts in our everyday lives. Teaching and passing on traditions about the importance of crafts are important goals to us here.

"It is very important for craftspeople not to become isolated. They need to make time to keep current by seeing shows, visiting galleries, and reading periodicals. They also need to look for influences for their work in all mediums, not just their own area of interest. It is also important to write on a regular basis by keeping a journal or notebook. Craftspeople need to make time to regenerate and participate in a lifelong learning process."

Priscilla Merritt
Owner of Centennial House Gallery and wife of Fran Merritt, founding director of Haystack Mountain School of Crafts

"The craft world has changed tremendously since we started Haystack with Mrs. Bishop in 1951. At that time, I started the weaving program at Haystack. Later, after we had moved the school to Deer Isle, I ran my shop, Centennial House, for twelve years selling crafts. There were very few craftspeople then. In the 1950s and 1960s, they had a much simpler life than they do today because they could work in the winter and sell to shops in the summer. Nothing is that simple anymore. In 1962, there was very little choice of merchandise to put in the shop because there were so few craftspeople then. Now there are a lot of shops and galleries as well as a large craft community with individual showrooms scattered throughout Deer Isle.

"I recommend that a craftsperson just starting out get a college degree in the arts and then apprentice for one or two years. Workshops are good, but too short. A degree in art from a college or trade school not only gives a craftsperson a broad background, but the credentials to teach as well. Craftspeople also need to take advantage of libraries, such as the one at Haystack, to keep informed and inspired.

"For someone trying to sell their crafts, depending on how they may want to present themselves, I suggest a basic business background. Although it doesn't have to be involved, they need to learn organizational skills."

Mary Nyburg
President Emeritus of the American Craft Council; Potter and Owner of Blue Heron Gallery, Deer Isle, Maine

"One of the biggest changes in the field I see is that there are so many shows today. I can still remember the first wholesale fair organized by the northeast region of the American Craft Council in 1966.

"Trends I see in the work itself are that collectibles seem to go in fads. Glass is very popular right now. Clay seems to be moving to be more colorful and sculptural, while at the same time, there is a return to wood-fired pieces. Baskets are emerging as well as furniture.

"I recommend craftspeople take a simple course in business and get a formal education in crafts. After they graduate, they should get an apprenticeship with a working craftsperson to really learn the business.

"Their work not only needs to be of the highest quality, but they need to develop a good working relationship with the galleries that promote and sell their work. They need to be very careful of the quality of their work, not take too many orders before they can handle them, and pay close attention to delivery times. For example, if a gallery wants work delivered in June, don't send it to them in August."

Marilyn Stevens
Former Editor of the *Crafts Report*, Wilmington, Delaware

"The biggest change I see in the field is less of a distinction between craft and gift markets. For example, more craftspeople are exhibiting at gift shows. As a result, craftspeople need to find ways to distinguish their work from imports or manufactured pieces. They also need to educate the public and articulate their passion for their work by telling the story behind what they do. They need to give the public a reason to buy their pieces by sharing the romance behind what they do. Using hangtags that add value to the piece by telling the history, or family inspiration or what I call a "hook," might be one way to do this.

"Craftspeople must perfect their techniques to produce the best product possible whether they study for a degree, take a studio course, or enroll in a workshop. More people are also coming to the craft field in their forties, seeking fulfillment after having worked in the mainstream business world, as opposed to the 1970s when most craftspeople began working right after school.

"In addition, they also need to develop a complete understanding of what they are giving the end user who purchases their pieces. And, finally, they need to think of themselves as running a small business and find specific business courses designed for craftspeople."

Stuart Kestenbaum
Director, Haystack Mountain School of Crafts, Deer Isle, Maine

"I sort of backed into being a crafts administrator. I have a degree in comparative religion from Hamilton College [New York]. After college, I apprenticed to a potter in the early 1970s and then worked in administration through the CETA program at the Children's Museum in Portland. I got involved in grant writing and was hired at the Maine Arts Commission, first only part-time as a field coordinator, then to run the Artists in Residence program, and finally became the assistant director. I came to Haystack as the director in 1989. I also write poetry, mostly in the off-season.

"To jump-start a career in the crafts, I suggest aspiring craftspeople immerse themselves in order to find out if they really like doing their craft full-time. By taking a two- or three-week workshop at places such as Haystack, Penland, or Arrowmont, students are exposed to a number of role models in one short session.

"For practical training on how to manage a career in crafts, I recommend craftspeople take a business or professional development workshop offered by local guilds and organizations. Also, I think people should look at a lot of work, notice what they like and where it is sold, read publications, and basically stay informed about the craft world. I always say writers should be readers and the same goes for craftspeople. Remember what other people have done, that being a professional craftsperson is possible, and figure out what you need to do it.

"A trend I have noticed is an increase in the technical proficiency of craftspeople. With the use of new techniques and materials, the range of acceptable expression in the craft world has also opened up. For example, Haystack used to offer several sessions in weaving each summer. The current fiber offerings have expanded to include surface design, quilts, mixed media, and embellishment. Another example is in glass where I see craftspeople making more sophisticated work. Glass artists used to learn a technique from a book or magazine and then try to replicate it on their own. Now they can take workshops at any number of places to learn how to do these techniques from another craftsperson."

Carolyn Hecker
Founding Director, Maine Crafts Association, Deer Isle, Maine

"As an undergraduate, I minored in printmaking. In 1976, I received a masters in arts administration from American University [Washington, D.C.]. I worked for the Smithsonian as the associate education coordinator in a program that offered classes for 10,000 students each year, age two to ninety-two years old. I also did a project called "Craft Art 1977," which included five juried exhibitions and an opening at the Renwick Museum. Then I left to start Greenwood Gallery with workshop programs at local universities before coming to Maine. I helped found the Maine Crafts Association in the early 1980s and was the first director. Recently, I retired to run my husband, Ron Pearson's, jewelry business. I am currently organizing a traveling exhibition of his work.

"Craftspeople are more aware of the need for marketing now. The crafts population is an older one, although the schools are still strong. One change I have noticed is that weaving used to be more popular. There is always experimentation and using new materials.

"Craftspeople need to know what they are doing, be passionate about their work, assess what is out there, and talk with people in both the business and academic worlds to keep informed. They also need good design skills.

"There is still a lot of validity in studying in an academic program. If you are interested, I suggest you visit the schools and talk with students. Although many programs still do not offer business training, they offer technical training and give you exposure to art. Although there just isn't enough time to develop skills in a workshop, they are necessary—no matter what your level—to learn new techniques or brush up on one.

"Apprenticeships, although they are not easy to come by, and working with a mentor are great ways to learn the field. My husband, metalsmith Ron Pearson, had many apprentices over the years, sometimes as many as twelve people at one time. The CETA program approved their training for one year and the majority of them went on to work in the field of metals.

"Craftspeople should also subscribe to publications geared to their medium such as *Metalsmith* or *Fiberarts,* and join local craft organizations to get in touch with their peers. They should also join national organizations, such as American Craft, to see what is being shown in galleries around the country and to find out about events no matter where they choose to live."

Wendy Rosen
Founder of the Rosen Group, Inc., Baltimore, Md.

Wendy began her career in advertising sales and started her own company, the Rosen Group, in 1980. The Buyer's Market of American Crafts, sponsored by the Rosen Group, hosts two large craft fairs a year in Philadelphia and Boston, has grown to include a publishing division including *NICHE* and *American Style* magazines. She is also the author of *Crafting as a Business* and *Cash for Your Crafts.*

"Today, some of the best artwork in America is found in television commercials, comic books, music videos, movies, T-shirts, and other embellished everyday products. In America's mainstream, people seem to prefer to wear their art rather than put it on a wall. Some of today's best art is also found in painted furniture, contemporary ceramic teapots, and fashion jewelry. The art of the next generation is not the art of our parents.

"Tomorrow's craft consumer may take many forms, but one thing is clear: most of these new consumers will buy for very personal reasons, not for investment, not for social status. Tomorrow's craft collector will seek to make connections with other cultures, their values, and their nostalgic past.

"Just a few years ago, most craftspeople were selling their work out

Figure 10. *Wendy Rosen*

of the backs of their vans. Through retail fairs and festivals, they were seeking a way to make a living through their work. In the late 1970s and early 1980s, the number of craft shops and galleries grew at an incredible rate. The marketplace demand for crafts exceeded supply so heavily that many craftspeople could not keep up with the overwhelming demand. Yet, until the early 1980s, thousands of craftspeople had no organized or reliable way to sell to shops and galleries. In the early 1980s, things began to change. Today there is a clear path to success.

"With internships, mentor programs, the Art Business Institute, and wholesale markets like the Buyer's Market of American Crafts, trade publications for galleries, such as *NICHE* magazine, and *AmericanStyle* (a glossy, full color newsstand magazine for collectors), craftspeople have all the tools to find collectors and to cultivate new customers for all types of craftwork. With these new tools, craftspeople have taken their place in society as highly respected, creative, hardworking entrepreneurs—neighbors who make a valuable contribution to the community at large. Career craftspeople are living the American dream!"

Conclusions

The comments of these craft administrators offer an overview of the craft field as they see it today as well as a glimpse into what it was like years ago. According to these administrators, not only are the methods and materials changing, but so are the ways in which craftspeople are educated and work is sold. The emergence of workshop programs, for example, offers an alternative to traditional certificate and degree programs and facilitates spreading new techniques and knowledge to people who may previously have had limited access to learn new techniques.

A topic of concern that came up repeatedly in these interviews was the value of keeping traditions alive, educating the public about the value of crafts, and learning how to communicate the story and passion behind an artist's work. As the crafts market is forced to compete with both mass-produced and imported items, it is important to ask, Why are crafts important in our lives? How can a craftsperson differentiate his or her work from imports? What if the work looks so slick that buyers think it isn't handmade? Craftspeople need to learn how to communicate with the users of their products and let them know the value of their work when their pieces may be priced higher than something that can be bought in a regular store.

A time-honored tradition in the crafts field, being an apprentice is still the best way to learn how to run a crafts business, as is suggested by the numerous recommendations for finding these type of opportunities. Workshops and books can offer some guidance, but learning how to run a business from a crafts professional is a great way to get started. Apprenticeships will be discussed in more detail in the next chapter.

While taking a business course is a rather new concept in the craft world, it was advised by most of the craft administrators I spoke with because everyone realizes how competitive the field is today. Business training can save you both time and money, as well as the aggravation of running a poorly organized business.

CHAPTER 4

MENTORING

Who would you turn to for advice about selling your crafts and running your business? There are many people and places in our lives that guide us in our careers through their example or by offering much-needed advice. Mentoring, whether in the form of an apprenticeship, a mentor relationship, or a residency, can give you the support you need to move from being an aspiring craftsperson to a professional one.

Apprenticeships

Traditionally, before there were workshops and degree programs, craftspeople worked as an apprentice to a master craftsperson to learn the trade. Although apprenticeships are not easy to come by, they offer an aspiring craftsperson an invaluable experience to learn about running a business from a professional.

The resurgence of handcrafts has led to a rebirth of apprenticeships. Although some basic techniques and principles can be learned in school, most craftspeople find that success depends, to a great extent, on working with another experienced craftsperson. An apprenticeship can help them refine their skills, understand production methods, business procedures, and how to handle all aspects of earning a living in crafts. The relationship between the craftsperson and apprentice is a special one, and careful thought should be given to whether the craftsperson and the apprentice will get along well, if the craftsperson is a good teacher, and what the specific arrangements and working conditions will be. Will the apprentice have the opportunity to work on their own work? Who will pay for the materials? Who is responsible for what? The relationship between the craftsperson and the apprentice is a two-way street because the apprentice benefits from the learning experience and the craftsperson benefits from the apprentice's contribution to the production process.

Many arrangements exist between apprentice and craft artist. Sometimes the apprentice works for free or pays the craftsperson for the opportunity to work with them and learn their business. In other cases, the craftsperson pays the apprentice, usually minimum wage. If you are considering becoming an apprentice or hiring one, consult the state and federal labor laws in your area to find out what the current legal requirements are regarding apprenticeships. Put your arrangement in writing, to avoid any misunderstanding, and keep a copy for your records.

Thomas Mann, of Thomas Mann Design Inc. in New Orleans, worked for two silversmiths when he was in high school learning firsthand how to run a craft business. He now employs apprentices, in addition to his regular employees, in his own business to help him produce his line of jewelry.

The book *Apprenticeship in Craft,* edited by Gerry Williams, was written for those specifically interested in apprenticeships. When asked what he would recommend to potters interested in obtaining an apprenticeship, Williams said, "Call ahead and visit as many potters locally as possible to just get acquainted and let them know you are looking for work. If you really like one or two of them, be persistent, but not obnoxious, and keep in touch until something works out. You may find that soon you will either have an unstructured relationship or a formal apprenticeship." Contact Gerry Williams at Studio Potter, P.O. Box 70, Goffstown, NH 03045; (603) 774-3582; *www.studiopotter.org* for more information on ordering *Apprenticeship in Craft.*

To find an apprenticeship opportunity, you should start by asking other craftspeople for suggestions. Try advertising in the newsletter of your local crafts organization, and check *American Craft Magazine,* which can be found in bookstores or by calling (800) 724-0859. Reference books like *Who's Who in American Art* (available in most libraries) and *The Guild,* published by Kraus-Sikes Inc. (available in bookstores or by calling 800-969-1556), are valuable resources.

Mentors

In their book *Making It On Your Own,* Sarah and Paul Edwards say that if you were an Olympic athlete, enthusiastic audiences would cheer you on to great feats. Your coaches would encourage, prod, and guide you to success. If you were part of a top sales team for one of the nation's leading corporations, you would attend regular seminars and training programs with experts to charge you up and build your skills and confidence. But if you are one of today's growing number of self-employed individuals, who cheers you on? Who picks you up? Who gives you the boost you need? Chances are you have to do most of that yourself.

A mentor, or trusted advisor, can also teach you how to run your business, introduce you to important people, and provide support and encouragement. Many people become mentors after they are established in their careers because they want to give back to the crafts community, pass on techniques, and teach someone the business skills they worked so hard to master.

In addition to ongoing mentor relationships, consider short-term arrangements such as assisting craftspeople at a craft fair to learn how to make sales and interact with customers. To meet the needs of their new exhibitors, the Rosen Group, sponsors of the Buyer's Market of American Craft, offers short-term mentor opportunities at their fairs where new exhibitors can be matched up with a seasoned craftsperson exhibiting at the fair. For information on its mentor program, contact the Rosen Group at 3000 Chestnut Avenue, Suite 300, Baltimore, MD 21211; (410) 889-2933; *www.americanstyle.com.* You can also call your local crafts organizations or show promoters for referrals if you are interested in being matched up with a current exhibitor as a short-term mentor.

Don't forget noncraft business organizations such as the following:

- *The Small Business Administration* (SBA) can be reached at (800) 8-ASK-SBA. Check out the SBA's Web page at *www.sba.gov* for more information on mentor programs.
- *The Service Corps of Retired Executives Association* (SCORE) is available in ten regions across the United States and can be contacted at (800) 634-0245 or through the organization's Web site at *www.score.org.* Dedicated to helping small businesses through no-fee mentoring, business counseling, and low-cost workshops, SCORE offers confidential one-to-one or team business management counseling. According to its brochure, *No One Knows More about Small Business Ownership* (1996), SCORE coun-

seled 157,849 cases, held 4,016 workshops with 98,837 clients, and do-
nated 1,024,748 volunteer hours.
- *The Women's Business Development Corporation* (WBDC) in Maine offers
  a mentoring program targeted to women business owners. The program features three components: an experienced businesswoman to
  serve as the mentor, an entrepreneur ready for business, and technical assistance from the WBDC staff. The program provides training,
  skills development, support, and networking over a sixmonth period.
  Contact WBDC at P.O. Box 658, Bangor, ME 04402; (207) 947-5990 for
  more information.

Residencies

Residencies at places such as a craft school or art center offer the aspiring
craftsperson an alternative to a traditional apprenticeship by providing studio and equipment access, a chance to gain some teaching experience, a network of role models, plus exhibition and sales opportunities. By removing
craftspeople from their everyday obligations to family and work, a residency
can provide uninterrupted time to work in a supportive atmosphere to try
new techniques, create a body of work, and learn how to sell your work.

In the book *Artists' Communities,* Tricia Snell, executive director of the
Alliance of Artists' Communities, maintains that there is a growing grassroots
movement to create new residencies that directly serve artists' most important needs. This is a response to the falloff of public programs that support
artists. Collectively, artists' communities represent a century-old, national support system for artists and thinkers. A survey done in 1995 showed that there
were over seventy communities in this country providing 3,600 residencies to
artists, craftspeople, and writers.

Residencies can last from a couple weeks or months to a year depending on needs and availability. Although many communities must charge a
nominal fee to cover some of their operating costs, others require volunteer
work in exchange for the opportunity. Some pay the residents a stipend. If
you have to pay for the opportunity to be a resident, it may be worth it for
the contacts you will make, the time you will have available to develop your
work and business skills, and the access you will have to facilities.

Here is a sampling of some of the residency programs available for
craftspeople around the country. For current information, fees, and application details, please contact the programs directly.

Contact Information/Medium

- *Anderson Ranch Arts Center* P.O. Box 5598, Snowmass Village, CO 81615; (970) 923-3181; *www.andersonranch.org* [All crafts]
- *Archie Bray Foundation for the Ceramic Arts* 2915 Country Club Avenue, Helena, MT 59602; (406) 443-3502; *www.archiebray.org* [Ceramics]
- *Arrowmont School of Arts and Crafts* P.O. Box 567, Gatlinburg, TN 37738; (865) 436-8887; *www.arrowmont.org* [All crafts]
- *Fabric Workshop and Museum* 13151 Cherry Street, 5th floor, Philadelphia, PA 19107; (215) 568-1111; *www.fabricworkshopandmuseum.org* [Textiles +]
- *Oregon College of Art & Craft* 8245 SW Barnes Road, Portland, OR 97225; (503) 297-5544; *www.ocac.edu* [All crafts]
- *Penland School of Crafts* Conley Ridge Road, Penland, NC 28765; (828) 765-2359; *www.penland.org* [All crafts]
- *Peters Valley Craft Center* 19 Kuhn Road, Layton, NJ 07851; (973) 948-5200; *www.pvcrafts.org* [All crafts]
- *Pilchuck Glass School* 430 Yale Avenue North, Seattle, WA 98109; (206) 621-8422; *www.pilchuck.com* [Glass]
- *Watershed Center for Ceramic Arts* 19 Brick Hill Road, Newcastle, ME 04553; (207) 882-6075; *www.watershedcenterceramicarts.org* [Ceramics +]

If you decide to pursue a residency at one of these programs, call for information and then plan a visit. Stay for a couple days to meet the current residents and see the studio facilities. If a long-term residency doesn't fit your current circumstances, ask about scholarship opportunities for a workshop.

For more listings, refer to *Artists Communities* by the Alliance of Artists' Communities. The book provides information on facilities and housing, admissions background, scholarships, fellowships and stipend opportunities, as well as statements by former residents and the community's director. *Artists Communities* is available in bookstores or by contacting the Alliance of Artists' Communities at 210 SE 50th Avenue, Portland, OR 97215; (503) 239-7049.

If you are thinking about selling your crafts, either an apprenticeship or residency would be an ideal way to start your career. An apprenticeship offers you a chance to learn how to run a craft business from a professional craftsperson. You might also be given access to the studio and have the opportunity to create your own work during your time off. A residency gives you an opportunity to continue working in the studio on your own work, access to professional craftspeople, and might include opportunities to teach or exhibit your work. Both an apprenticeship and a residency also provide the chance to develop a network of professionals that you can store away until you have a need to contact someone for advice or a referral. You may be able to find one of these opportunities locally, or you may need to relocate.

If you are ready to start your business but would like someone to talk to for support and guidance as the business develops, finding a mentor or mentor program might be the solution. A mentor is someone you can call for advice or arrange to have regular meetings with—someone who can answer your questions, offer support, and give you suggestions or referrals, when necessary. They have been where you are now and have decided to devote their time and energy to helping someone else get started. While you might move to do an apprenticeship or residency, depending on where you live, you probably won't have to move to find a mentor. Remember, a mentor does not necessarily have to be a craftsperson.

Whether you try a traditional apprenticeship, find a mentor, or apply for a residency, the experience will offer the support and skills you need to move forward in your career. Use the opportunity to make contacts, learn how to run a crafts business, and develop your work. You may be at a stage in your life where you can move anywhere to take advantage of one of these opportunities, while at another time you will need to find an opportunity closer to home. Even a chance to assist and learn from another craftsperson on a short-term basis can be valuable.

CHAPTER 5

SELF-ASSESSMENT

Are you thinking of turning a craft hobby into a business? Have you just graduated from school and are wondering if you are ready to make your living selling your work? Or have you been running a professional studio for some time but need to rethink your direction because of a recent change in the market? A self-assessment can be a very useful part of your planning process because it helps you to review your goals, discover your lifestyle choices, and match these with your current situation.

In her book *Supporting Yourself as an Artist,* Deborah Hoover warns that if her book ensured that you would get rich, buy a fabulous studio at rockbottom prices, or become famous, everyone would be an artist. If you expect or feel entitled to make money immediately from your work, then being an artist is probably not the right career choice for you. Most likely, the reason you are an artist is your compulsion or inspiration to create. If you also have the talent, then you have the opportunity to build a successful career as an artist. But talent is not enough to ensure that you will be financially successful as an artist. You will probably have to work very hard to support yourself. Those of you who have these qualifications should, after having read this book, be better informed about the opportunities and the problems you will confront during your career. Unlike many artists before you, you will have the benefit of knowing how to deal with some of the decisions that lie ahead—decisions that are critical to your personal and professional well being. You will also be able to acquire the skills and knowledge you need to survive as an artist. In a very real sense, you will know how to help yourself.

Which of the following is your perception of success? Is it (1) making your craft on a regular basis and selling it to earn your living; (2) working in your studio and selling something once in a while; or (3) just enjoying working in your studio and not worrying about sales? Your choice about what you would really like to do with your work is all that matters, not any external definition of success. Once you know what you are aiming for, you can then take the steps necessary to accomplish it.

Take a few minutes and complete the self-assessment questionnaire on the following pages. This is not a test—be honest with yourself.

If you chose mostly answer *a,* you are probably already earning a living from the sales of your work. You have a good background in the crafts and business, the studio and portfolio you need, you know who your customers are, are promoting your work through several venues, and you know the importance of networking and lifelong learning.

If you chose mostly answer *b,* then you enjoy the security of a paycheck and yet you have a strong interest in supplementing your income with selling your work. If you should decide to make the transition to earning all of your income from selling your work, you are learning valuable skills through your part-time selling experiences. Consult an art advisor if you decide you want help to plan a transition.

If you chose mostly answer *c,* then you probably enjoy making your work but are either not interested in selling it or are unsure of how to go about running a craft business. Consult an art advisor if you decide to start earning all or part of your income from selling your work at some point in the future.

Reviewing the results of your self-assessment illustrates the role you are comfortable filling at this time. If you are not already selling your work regularly, you are either poised to start selling your work full-time, or recognize that you need to take additional steps to learn more about how to sell your work. Some of you may decide that selling your work to earn your living is not for you. If you are interested in selling your work, take a few minutes to see what strengths and weaknesses you noticed in your self-assessment and pay close attention to those chapters in this book that relate to those weaknesses.

Self-Assessment Questionnaire

Circle the answer that best describes your current situation.

1. What is your level of education and experience?

   A. I have a degree in my craft or I have done an apprenticeship to learn my craft and the business. I continue to attend as many workshops as I can on both my craft and business.

   B. I have a degree in another feld but have taken numerous workshops to learn both my craft and how to run a business.

   C. I have taken a few workshops in my craft.

2. I want to make my living by:

   A. Selling my work full-time.

   B. Selling my work part-time and maintaining another source of income.

   C. Working at a noncraft job.

3. I prefer my income to be the following:

   A. It doesn't matter, as long as I earn enough money annually.

   B. A regular paycheck supplemented with sporadic sales of my work.

   C. A regular paycheck.

4. My studio is described as the following:

   A. It has all the equipment I need, a large workspace with adjacent offce, a show room to meet customers, and space to store my inventory and ship my work.

   B. A decent workspace with the basic equipment I need.

   C. A space in a spare room or part of my garage or basement.

5. My portfolio includes:

   A. Color slides taken by a professional photographer, black-and-white photographs, a publicity photograph of me working in my studio, and a shot of my booth.

   B. Color slides of some of my work and a few photographs.

   C. I don't have a portfolio.

6. The following sentence describes my craftwork:

   A. A line of several different pieces created in multiples with a distinctive style as well as a series of one-of-a-kind pieces.

   B. Some pieces made in multiples and some one-of-a-kind pieces.

   C. Many different styles—I like to experiment and never make the same thing twice.

7. Which description sounds like customers who would buy your work:

   A. They like to collect unique things for the home as well as purchase handmade gifts.

   B. I guess they like to buy unique gifts for others or for themselves, but I'm not sure.

   C. I don't know who my customers are.

8. Where do your customers see your work?

   A. At numerous fairs, juried shows, shops, advertisements, or my annual studio sale.

   B. At a fair or studio sale a few times a year or in a group show once in a while.

   C. I don't show my work often.

9. I belong to the following organizations:

   A. My local, state, and national craft organizations.

   B. My local craft organization.

   C. I'm not a joiner of groups.

10. What are your goals for the next five years?

   A. I want to support myself with sales of my work earning a livable wage.

   B. I want to keep the security of my other job, but if the sales from my work continue to increase, I will consider pursuing my craft business full-time.

   C. I want to make pieces I enjoy without being concerned about sales.

SETTING UP YOUR CRAFTS BUSINESS

CHAPTER 6

BUSINESS PLANNING

What is all this fuss about planning a business? After all, you may have already started selling your work and haven't needed to do any business planning yet. But if you don't have a plan, how are you going to know if your business is doing well? Business planning can include projecting what you want to accomplish with your business, a timeline for achieving those objectives, and methods to measure your success. The most common format used is called a business plan.

There are several good reasons for you to write a business plan right *now*. The planning process required to write a business plan will help you clarify your goals for your business so you can make informed decisions. A business plan will give you something against which to measure the success of your business as it develops. And, finally, if you need to finance your business or expand it, applications for bank loans or proposals for potential investors usually require a well-thought-out business plan.

If you are thinking that there is no way you can write a business plan, keep reading and use the simple form included in this chapter to help you get started. Would you go on a trip to a new place without a map? Would you start a business without taking the time to write a business plan? To help keep you from feeling lost, plan to set aside a couple hours each week to work on a section of your business plan, and before you know it, you will be looking at a finished plan.

A business plan should not be done once and filed away, but reviewed and updated on a regular basis to help you measure your success and figure out what to do next to advance your goals. A business plan should be seen as a tool to help you manage your business more efficiently so you can spend more time in your studio.

Getting Started

There is a lot of preliminary work to be done before starting a business, such as naming your business, setting up your studio, producing inventory, obtaining insurance, learning how to handle finances, as well as marketing and selling your work, as outlined in this book.

During the first year you are in business, you will probably be in a trial-and-error phase. Searching for the right markets for your work, learning how to price and sell, and scheduling production are some of the things you will learn during this period. By the end of the first year, you will have learned what worked and have a sense of what you need to do to prevent some of the same problems from repeating during the second year. You may have also learned how much you like running your own business and be enjoying the challenge to improve and expand it. Other people may decide running a business is not right for them and will decide to return to being an employee rather than a business owner.

In the beginning, everything will take longer than you think. You may have trouble meeting deadlines. Your cash flow may be uneven or even below your expectations. There is a reason why the Internal Revenue Service (IRS) allows businesses to deduct losses during the first several years of business. It is a well-known fact that most new businesses lose money in the beginning and the majority fail after the first year. As a result, it is crucial that you have enough capital to see you through possible lean times so that you can stay in business long enough to become self-supporting. Consider obtaining a loan or working part-time to help support yourself as your business grows.

By the fifth year, you will have established your business, learned which markets your work fits into, be good at pricing your work and making a sale, and have perfected your production schedules. You may have hired employees and be learning how to be a supervisor and delegate tasks.

Whether you are in your first year of business, or your tenth, you will always be learning new things and moving your business forward. No matter what stage you're at, there will always be a next one. Even if you knew everything you need to know to run your business, the whims of the market are not within your control and everyone needs to learn to be flexible.

Methods for Measuring Your Success

Most people think of measuring the success of a business by the bottom line or how well the business is doing financially. However, there are other indications of success that are just as important. For example, the satisfaction of working for yourself rather than for an employer, getting your first big wholesale order, or getting accepted into a juried fair are all measures of success of which you should feel proud.

Success is something that can only be measured by you. One way to evaluate your success is to set goals for yourself and your business that are both obtainable and measurable, such as setting a goal of getting into three juried craft fairs in one year.

What are some goals that you would like to set for yourself? Take a few minutes to write down at least three.

Goal #1 _____

_____

Goal #2 _____

_____

Goal #3 _____

_____

How to Write a Business Plan

A business plan should include the purpose of your business, what the value of your product or service is to your customers, why you are qualified to run the business, how you will market your work, what makes your product different from that of your competitors, and financial projections for several years. Use the following outline to formulate and write your business plan:

1. Start the plan with a simple summary of your business.

Write a summary as though you are trying to attract the attention of a potential lender or investor. You want to make it really easy to understand. A couple of paragraphs is all you need.

2. What is your business?

Describe your business and each product or service separately in layman's terms. Tell not only what you make and how it is used, but also whether it is a new product or one already established in the market. You may want to include a few photographs of your work and studio if you are applying for financing.

3. Why are you qualifed to run this business?

Explain how you learned your craft, any business background you may have, as well as workshops you have taken. Attach a résumé, listing of shows and awards, or articles that may have been written about you and your work.

4. Who are your customers?

Refer to chapter 28 on to help you identify and give descriptions of the general types of people who will buy your work.

5. What is the value of your product or service to the customer?

Think about the features and benefits that customers will experience after they buy a piece of your work. Will it bring beauty to their life? Will they be thought of as someone who purchases unusual gifts? Does your piece serve a function? Refer to the section on making sales in chapter 21 for more information on this subject.

6. Where are you located and how does this affect or enhance sales of your work?

Do you travel to market your work at fairs and live in a remote area to keep expenses down, are you located in a retail district, or do you have a showroom open to the public?

7. How do you market your work?

Refer to chapter 17 to help you with this section.

8. Who are your competitors?

Provide a comparison by including some examples of other craftspeople who make similar work, a description of how they market their items, and a list of their prices.

9. How are you different from your competitors?

Give a couple examples of other craftspeople who run a similar business. Is there enough demand to handle both businesses?

10. Include financial information on your business.

If you are writing a business plan to obtain a loan from a bank, try to think of the plan from the lender's perspective. The lender will be attracted by your business but will also be aware of the risks involved in lending you money. The lender will want to know how much money you want to borrow, what you want the money for, when you will be able to repay the money, and what is available to secure the loan if your business has a setback. The lender's concerns have nothing to do with how good your work is or whether or not he or she likes you as a person, but, rather whether or not you can make your loan payments.

To prepare the financial projections for your business plan, you will have to make certain assumptions based on your projected income and expenses. Refer to chapter 8 for a sample budget, income statement, cash flow statement, and balance sheet. These should all be included with the narrative portion of your business plan.

You should forecast your financial situation for the next three to five years in the business plan. The lender or investor wants to know that enough money is being requested to fund the business, and be able to understand your long-term intentions.

Take some time now to review this sample outline and see how much of your business plan you are prepared to fill out. What you already know about your business will be just as informative as the sections you have not figured out yet. You should consider attaching a résumé, brochure, portfolio, recommendations, credit references, and whatever else makes sense. When you have a working draft of your business plan, meet with your accountant, mentor, or bank representative for a preliminary review of your plan. You should revise and add to your plan as you develop your business, using it as a way to measure your success periodically and to aid you in making important decisions.

CHAPTER 7

ORGANIZING YOUR BUSINESS

Organizing your business means not only selecting a name for the business, but also deciding what form of organization best suits your plans and needs. There will be both positive and negative aspects to any form of organization you choose for your business, so this is a good time to discuss your business plans with your lawyer and accountant to see what kind of business organization fits your personal situation.

Selecting a Name

Choosing the name of your business is a very important decision because it will reflect who you are and what you do. Name recognition for your business is something you are going to invest a lot of time and money to obtain, so take as much time as you need to get it right.

When I was thinking about starting ArtBiz, I wanted to incorporate the concepts of both art and business into the name because I was going to teach business seminars to artists and craftspeople. After talking with friends and relatives, the closest name I could come up with was "The Art Business," but it sounded too formal. One day, when I was stuck in traffic, I started thinking about what name I would have if I got a vanity license plate—the name "ArtBiz" was born.

Keep in mind that your business may change over time. For example, if you pick a name like Tileworks and a year later realize that you are no longer going to make tiles, but rather birdbaths, you may be faced with the possibility of renaming your business. Clayworks may have been a better choice in this case.

In the book *The Craft Business Encyclopedia*, written by Michael Scott and edited by Leonard DuBoff, it is suggested that many business owners use a name for public identification that differs from the name of the owner. You may be Sam Jones, but the sign on your door reads Pot Luck Pottery. That's a trade or assumed business name. In some areas, this is known as the fictitious business name. Since trade names can't be legally responsible for anything, it is almost universally required that a trade name be registered with some government authority, often the secretary of state or the county clerk. The initials *d.b.a.* (doing business as) appear on such documents as legal papers and credit reports to tie the trade name to the owner as in "Sam Jones, d.b.a. Pot Luck Pottery." To protect a trade name from unauthorized use, it may be registered with the federal government as a trademark if certain conditions are met.

Business Name Exercise: What Do You Do?

"Believe it or not, naming your business is one of the hardest questions for creative people to answer," says Ilise Benun, owner of the Art of Self-Promotion, in an article titled "Making Marketing Manageable" published in *How* magazine. Selecting a name becomes even more challenging when what you do is varied. If you find naming your business to be difficult, this exercise designed by Ilise may help.

What do you do? (25 words or less) _____

_____

_____

_____

_____

What do you do? (15 words or less) _____

_____

_____

What do you do? (7 words or less) _____

_____

Now look at the descriptions above and write the key elements below to help you pick out a name for your business. Then let your imagination go and start writing down name ideas that come to mind. In the beginning, try not to edit, just keep coming up with names. Show your ideas to some friends and see which best suits what you are planning to do.

Key elements _____

_____

_____

Name ideas:

1. _____
2. _____
3. _____

For example, let's use the fictitious business name "Wearable Weavings for Women." In response to the question What do you do? the owner might have answered that she created handwoven clothing for women using wool from sheep she raised on her farm. The key elements here are: handwoven, clothing, women, and wool. So the name idea, "Wearable Weavings for Women," fits the description. However, if the business was called "Wearable Weavings," the owner would have easily left open the possibility to make clothing for men or children and not have to alter the name. The owner could have also used her own name and medium, for example, "Susan Smith, Weaver," to keep more options open.

Forms of Organization: Sole Proprietorship versus Partnership

Did you know that choosing a form of organization can affect your personal finances? Or that you can be liable for debts made by your partner? In *The Law (in Plain English)® for Crafts*, Leonard DuBoff explains that, since craftspeople must pay taxes, take out loans, and expose themselves to uncertain liabilities with every sale they make, it only makes sense to structure their businesses in such a way as to minimize these worries. Although there are several forms of organization for craftspeople to choose from, I will only outline two here: sole proprietor and partnerships. I have outlined the positive and negatives aspects of each, so you can make an informed decision depending on your circumstances.

Sole Proprietorship

Most craftspeople start their business as a sole proprietor. A sole proprietorship is defined as an unincorporated business owned by one person. As a form of business, it is elegant in its simplicity because it requires little money and work, and legal requirements are few. One area for concern if you are a sole proprietor is that your personal property is at stake. If, for any reason, you owe your creditors more than the dollar value of your business, they can take most of your personal property to satisfy your debt.

Although in some areas you may need to obtain a license to operate, in general, as a sole proprietor, you are in business immediately. When filing for income taxes, you can even use your own social security number. Although you will be taxed on business profits, you may also deduct business losses.

Partnership

A partnership is usually defined as an association of two or more people to conduct a business for profit. It is not an agreement to enter into lightly. Even though it seems like such a great idea to go into business with your best friend, I recommend you think it over carefully, have a serious discussion, and put some things in writing first. What if you don't agree on how to run the business or one of you decides to do something else?

The economic advantages of doing business with a partner are the pooling of capital, greater ease in obtaining credit because of the collective credit rating, and a more efficient allocation of labor and resources. A major disadvantage is that each partner is fully and personally liable for all the debts of the partnership—even if they were not personally involved in incurring those debts.

A partnership does not possess any special tax advantages over a sole proprietorship. As a partner, you will pay a personal income tax on your share of the profits, whether or not they are distributed, and will be entitled to the same proportion of the partnership deductions and credits.

Consider the following before going into a partnership arrangement:
- Choose your partner carefully. Do your skills and personalities compliment each other? Do you trust them to make decisions in your best interests?
- Make sure you are adequately insured to protect both the assets of the partnership and the personal assets of each partner.

- Prepare a written partnership agreement with the help of a lawyer in order to avoid confusion or misunderstandings in the future. Some initial legal fees now could save you costs later on.

Enter into a partnership agreement with your eyes open and your mutual understanding on paper. A basic partnership agreement should include all of the following:

- The name of the partnership
- A description of the business
- How much capital each partner will contribute
- The length of the partnership
- How profits will be distributed
- When you will have meetings
- Who will manage the business
- Terms to end the partnership if the need arises

Many craft businesses start out as a sole proprietorship and later change status if or when it makes sense to do so. While a sole proprietor may put his or her personal property at stake, a partner is responsible for debts incurred by the other partner. When deciding whether you will organize your business as a sole proprietorship or a partnership, you should keep the advantages and disadvantages of each in mind. Remember to find out if you need a license to operate your business, and if you choose a partnership, prepare a written agreement.

CHAPTER 8

FINANCES

Before we talk about the financial aspects of your business, I want to acknowledge that most people find the financial aspect of running a craft business the most overwhelming part. Some craftspeople are very comfortable planning their finances, but many others know that they need to set up systems and plan their finances—yet they just never seem to get around to it until things are at a deadline or crisis stage. However, if you set up a simple system and keep your records current, you will see that the financial aspect of your business is just another planning tool that helps you make and sell your work.

In this chapter, I will show you how to plan a simple budget, suggest several different options to finance your business, help you figure out your hourly labor rate, and price a piece of your work from a cost-based perspective. In chapter 12, I will discuss recordkeeping, taxes, and credit and collection.

It's so easy to keep track of your finances when you keep your records up-to-date. The best advice I can give you can be summed up in the following points:

- Find a financial system you feel comfortable using, whether it is a manual or computer-based system
- Schedule a regular time each week to take care of your finances so that, for example, doing your payables and receivables don't pile up and become a huge task
- Find a financial advisor you can call with questions

- Review your overall financial situation on at least a monthly basis to make sure you are on track

"Most people are afraid to see the real financial situation of their business," writes Lu Bauer, a holistic CPA from Maine, in her column called "Crafts Finance" in the *Crafts Report*. "Afraid if they make money, they will have to pay taxes, or if they don't make enough money to run their business successfully, they will have to deal with the shame of going back to working for someone else again. I suggest rather than having craftspeople design a budget, which most people see as a form of punishment, that they instead focus on looking at what is happening in their business by reviewing their figures monthly to make sense of their business. Most people don't know how to handle the financial side of their business and need to learn how."

Every month you are going to have expenses—such as rent, materials, or shipping costs. You will also, hopefully, have income—such as selling work at a craft fair or filling a wholesale order and receiving payment. A cash-flow projection is a simple way to project your income and expenses for the entire year. If you make more money than you spend, you will show a profit for the year. Likewise, if you spend more money than you make, you will show a net loss for the year.

Designing a Budget

If you are just starting out in your craft business, you may have no idea how to set up a budget or project your income and expenses. In the beginning, your estimations will be based on comparing how much it will cost to produce the pieces, what your plans are to market your work, and what you think you can sell. After the first year, it will be easier to plan your budget because you can look back at the prior year and make adjustments based on what you did that year and what your current plans are for the new budget year.

In his book, *How to Live Within Your Means and Still Finance Your Dreams*, Robert Ortalda Jr. says that many people start their budgeting projects with a weekend-long binge of catching up on a year's worth of accounting. This makes some sense. You have to know, the reasoning goes, where you currently stand before you can start making any changes. However, there is a fatal flaw in this logic: the weekend you spend doing accounting is very likely the only weekend you will have to devote to budgeting. You'll blow all your budgeting time doing bookkeeping. Not a good idea. There are better ways. One alternative is to do no historical accounting at all. Just forget about what has happened in the past, depend on your memory, and dive right into making decisions about your future spending. Because you're making decisions without complete and accurate information, you'll make mistakes. But what the hell—you're going to make mistakes anyway! Your budget is never going to be right! The best you can do with a budget is just get close—maybe real close. Anyone can tell you how to take control of your finances by slavishly spending all your weekends with a quill pen and green eyeshade. But you need a system you can live with. Decision making—not accounting—is the primary purpose of budgeting.

I recommend that you plan your budget based on the calendar year (January to December) and set up your categories to correspond to Schedule C of your income tax return using categories such as advertising, commissions, insurance, legal services, office expenses, mortgage or studio rent, materials, taxes and licenses, travel, meals, entertainment, utilities, and wages. You may also have other expenses such as dues and subscriptions, postage, or showroom expenses. Think of the things that you want to keep track of and make a category for each of them in your budget.

At the end of the year, do a comparison between your projected budget and the actual figures for each line. Then, with this comparison in front of you, it will be easy to see where you need to make changes for the next year by either raising or lowering the figures. On the next page is a sample budget for your review.

Many craftspeople have erratic incomes, subject to extremely lucrative months when they do a fair, for example, and corresponding dry spells between selling opportunities. To build some security into your business and to avoid the need to micromanage your monthly spending, you should establish a baseline budget. A baseline budget is a conservative, estimate of your monthly after-tax income. A baseline budget keeps you from spending your money before you get it or from spending money you hoped to get but never actually received. Once in a while, you will have "extra" money that you will need to decide how to spend.

To figure out your baseline budget, divide your total estimated income (in the example above, $45,000) by twelve months for a baseline income projection of $3,750 per month. Even though you may receive the money erratically, this is the monthly figure you can use for planning purposes.

Sample Budget

INCOME	BUDGET	ACTUAL	DIFFERENCE
Retail Sales	$5,000.00		
Wholesale Sales	$25,000.00		
Shows and Fairs	$15,000.00		
Total Income	$45,000.00		

EXPENSES	BUDGET	ACTUAL	DIFFERENCE
Advertising	$2,000.00		
Commissions	$250.00		
Materials	$5,000.00		
Offce Expense	$300.00		
Wages	$16,000.00		
Payroll Taxes	$2,500.00		
Rent or Mortgage	$6,200.00		
Utilities	$1,200.00		
Insurance	$500.00		
Legal Services	$100.00		
Licenses	$50.00		
Telephone	$1,200.00		
Taxes	$2,000.00		
Sales Expenses	$600.00		
Travel	$3,500.00		
Meals	$1,500.00		
Entertainment	$600.00		
Miscellaneous	$1,500.00		
Total Expenses	$45,000.00		

Income Statement

A summary, figured at least once a year, of the income and expenses during a given period is known as an income statement or profit and loss statement. Net income for the period is determined by deducting the expense total from the income total. If expenses were larger than the income, the statement will show a net loss. You will show a profit when income exceeds expenses. For many craft businesses, it is commonplace to show a net loss for a quarter or more.

Depending on your fair and show schedules, you may make most of your income during an extremely short period, such as the holiday season.

A comparison of your income statement with previous years can be helpful in pinpointing improvements or shortcomings in specific areas of income and expense. The following example is an income statement for an imaginary crafts business. The owner of the business put herself on the payroll for $13,000, which is part of the wages expense. Her total income for the year (wages plus net income) was $22,864.74. A business owner may choose to keep her wages low for cash flow reasons (see next section) and take the cost of her compensation in periodic distributions of profit.

Sample Income Statement

INCOME	
Retail Sales	$7,631.52
Wholesale Sales	$29,943.30
Shows and Fairs	$3,444.76
Total Income	$41,019.58

EXPENSES	
Raw Materials	$7,036.22
Wages	$16,800.00
Payroll Taxes	$2,429.00
Rent	$2,400.00
Utilities	$794.48
Insurance	$479.00
Telephone	$285.36
Sales Expenses	$630.92
Miscellaneous	$379.86
Total Expenses	$31,154.84
Net Income	$9,864.74

Cash-Flow Statement

A cash-flow statement lists your payables and receivables and adds the all-important element of timing. You can only stay in the black if you not only earn money faster than you spend it but also collect it faster than you spend it.

Plan your expenses and income twelve months ahead to see when your strong sales periods are and when you may need to delay a payment or offer an incentive to a customer to pay immediately. For example, your studio rent may be due on the first of the month and a loan payment due to the bank on the fifteenth. Cash-flow needs may also require planning for growth such as buying new equipment or moving to a larger studio.

You may have fixed monthly costs such as rent or mortgage on your studio, utilities, a loan for equipment, and your salary. In addition, you will have other bills to pay such as materials, insurance, booth fees, travel, and advertising. Your income may be derived from sources such as retails sales, wholesale sales, and renting out space in your studio. The income from sales of your work may be sporadic, while the income on renting your studio will be consistent.

Although you would usually plan your cash flow by month, this example of income and expenses is arranged by quarter, just to give you a general idea.

Cash Flow by Quarter

INCOME	1ST QUARTER	2ND QUARTER	3RD QUARTER	4TH QUARTER	TOTAL
Retail Sales	$1,000	$500	$1,500	$2,000	$5,000
Wholesale Sales	$0	$10,000	$15,000	$0	$25,000
Shows and Fairs	$0	$0	$2,500	$2,500	$5,000
Total Income	$1,000	$10,500	$19,000	$4,500	$35,000

EXPENSES	1ST QUARTER	2ND QUARTER	3RD QUARTER	4TH QUARTER	TOTAL
Raw Materials	$4,000	$0	$1,000	$0	$5,000
Wages	$4,000	$4,000	$4,000	$4,000	$16,000
Payroll Taxes	$625	$625	$625	$625	$2,500
Rent	$1,550	$1,550	$1,550	$1,550	$6,200
Utilities	$300	$300	$300	$300	$1,200
Insurance	$125	$125	$125	$125	$500
Telephone	$200	$400	$100	$100	$800
Depreciation	$500	$500	$500	$500	$2,000
Sales Expenses	$300	$300	$0	$0	$600
Miscellaneous	$0	$50	$50	$100	$200
Total Expenses	$11,600	$7,850	$8,250	$7,300	$35,000

Cash-Flow Income and Expenses

STARTING CASH BALANCE: $15,000

	1ST QUARTER	2ND QUARTER	3RD QUARTER	4TH QUARTER	TOTAL
Income Subtotal	$1,000	$10,500	$19,000	$4,500	$35,000
Expense Subtotal	$11,600	$7,850	$8,250	$7,300	$35,000
Difference	−$10,600	+$2,650	+$10,750	−$2,800	$0
Cash Balance + Difference					
Ending Cash Balance	+$4,400	+$7,050	+$17,800	+$15,000	

If you look at the cash-flow income and expense totals in this example by quarter, you will see that in the first and fourth quarters, the cash flow is negative, while in the second and third quarters, the cash flow is positive. The year ends basically breaking even.

In this example, you can see that most of the income for the year is earned in the third quarter from sales for the holiday season while most of the expense was incurred in the first quarter when the raw materials were ordered for production in the winter and spring. Next year this craftsperson could buy materials for the following year in the third quarter to smooth out cash flow. This business had a surplus (cash on hand) to cover the loss in the first quarter or those expenses would have carried over to the second quarter. In that case, business would have run at a loss most of the year. If the craftsperson didn't have a subsistence wage in the expense total, he or she would have had a very tough year financially.

Balance Sheet

Unlike an income statement, which summarizes the income and expenses over a given period, the balance sheet (often called a financial statement) reports the financial condition of a business at a given point, such as on the last day of the year, or on the date of a loan application.

The balance sheet reports the assets (everything you own including receivables) and the liabilities (everything you owe) on a particular date. Subtracting the liabilities from the assets produces a figure that is the owner's equity, or the net worth of the business (which can be positive or negative).

A sample balance sheet for an imaginary crafts business is illustrated on the next page. In this example, the owner finds that the net worth of the business is $15,629.84.

Note: When you produce a balance sheet, always double check that assets equal liabilities and capital. If not, you have made a mistake somewhere.

Financing Your Business

There are several ways to finance a new business or refinance a current one. If you are just starting, you will need a certain amount of start-up money to enable you to have time to establish and expand your business before it will begin to earn income. Some people use their savings. Other options are to write a business plan and apply for a business or a personal loan from a bank

Sample Balance Sheet as of December 31, ___

ASSETS

Current Assets

Cash	$1,843.56
Accounts Receivable	$4,765.50
Raw Material Inventory	$1,216.46
Finished Inventory	$8,075.41
Prepaid Expenses	$350.80
Total Assets	$16,251.73
Less Allowance for Bad Debts	$97.30

Total Current Assets	$16,154.43

Fixed Assets

Building	$14,152.80
Less Depreciation	$2,100.00
	$12,052.80
Equipment	$2,629.44
Less Depreciation	$464.73
	$2,164.71

Total Fixed Assets	$14,217.51

Current Assets + Fixed Assets

Total Assets	$30,371.94

LIABILITIES

Liabilities

Accounts Payable	$1,389.63
Mortgage	$10,400.00
Loans	$2,666.78
Payroll Taxes Payable	$285.69

Total Liabilities	$14,742.10

Total Assets – Liabilities

Net Worth of Business	$15,629.84

or investors or to look for peer-lending programs. Still others keep working at another job to finance their business. The choice is yours.

In their book *Making It on Your Own,* Sarah and Paul Edwards offer the following suggestions to finding a cash cushion while you are growing your business:

- Start your business on the side while you still have a job. When it gets going, leave your job.
- Take a parttime job that will cover your basic expenses while you get your business under way.
- Do temporary work while getting your business under way.
- If you're living with a partner, cut expenses and live off one salary while you start your business.
- Use your savings or other sources of income, like retirement funds, a sabbatical, divorce settlements, or an inheritance, as a cushion.
- Take out a second mortgage on your home or arrange to get a consumer line of credit, such as the kind some banks are offering to very small businesses, which enables you to borrow if, and only if, you need to. These loans are secured with the equity in your home or other assets.

There are also organizations that offer small business—financing programs such as peer lending groups. These groups offer loans of $500 to $5,000 and include extensive training, networking, and support. Call your local bank or the Small Business Administration to find a peer-lending program near you.

If you are applying to a bank for a loan and submitting a business plan, I recommend that you first meet with your accountant to review your application and finances while your plan is still in the draft stage. Then you should make an appointment to meet with a loan officer to discuss your application before submitting it for review. The loan officer may be able to offer some valuable tips that will help ensure approval of your application.

What makes the difference between a No and a Yes when applying for a bank loan? Usually, it is preparation. You can vastly improve your chances of obtaining approval for a loan request with the proper preparation. One of the keys to success is to always be ready to answer objections. Be prepared to respond to the typical objections of a lender to a craft business application listed below:

- We don't make loans this small.
- I don't know enough about you or your business.

- You haven't demonstrated what you need the money for.
- What do you plan to do in the future?
- You don't have enough collateral.
- Your business does not support the loan on its own.

How would you handle these comments and questions? You need to do your homework. Does your bank make loans to small businesses? Check with your accountant and other craftspeople for referrals to banks that work with similar businesses. Call the bank and ask to speak with someone in the loan department before you apply to find out if an application from a business your size is appropriate.

How could you make the lender more aware of you and your business? Have you included a résumé or biographical statement with your application? Did you collect some letters of recommendation or copies of articles that have been written about you?

Do you know what you want the money for and how much you need? Before you submit your application for a loan, you should know exactly how much money you need and what you need it for. Don't make the mistake of asking the lender how much he or she will give you.

Make sure you understand your application and can answer questions about the financials that are included. Review your application with your accountant and perhaps have a mock meeting with a friend posing as a lender who will ask you questions before you meet with a potential lender.

Be sure to ask for enough money. Bankers don't want to lend only enough to get you halfway to where you need to be. Your numbers should always have a small contingency account.

Pricing Your Work

Are you pricing your work for the long-term survival of your business or to sell it for some quick cash now? Do you base your prices solely on what other people are getting for similar work or what you know your work costs to produce plus a profit? The following discussion and exercises will help you learn how to determine your hourly rate and to price a sample piece from a cost-based perspective.

Labor: Your Hourly Rate

I want you to think about what you need to make per hour—whether you are planning on selling your work to make a living or in order to supplement your income. This exercise is for your labor or what you would pay yourself as a salary; not your business expenses like overhead or materials. Before you do the exercise, estimate your hourly rate here: $_____.

Worksheet: Calculating Your Hourly Rate

What do you want to make for an annual salary?	$ _____
Add 30% to cover health insurance and retirement savings	$ _____
Total Salary	$ _____

Next, starting with 365 days in a year, subtract the number of days you will need for days off each week (e.g., weekends), sick days, holidays, vacation, and indirect labor. Indirect labor is usually administrative time, i.e., not working in the studio. Most craftspeople would estimate that indirect labor will account for 20–40 percent of their time.

Number of days in a year	365 days
Number of days per week you want off × 52 weeks	_____
Number of sick days per year	_____
Number of paid holidays per year	_____
Number of vacation days per year	_____
Amount of time spent on indirect labor (in days)	_____
Billable Days (Subtract total days from 365)	_____
Divide your total salary (calculated above) by billable days	_____
Divide this by the number of hours worked per day (8)	_____
This is your hourly rate	= $ _____

How does this number compare with your estimate before you did this exercise?

Example

If you had assigned yourself a $30,000 yearly salary and added 30 percent to cover health and retirement benefits, you would need to earn $39,000 for your labor and benefits. If you worked five days a week, gave yourself ten sick days, ten paid holidays, a three-week vacation, and spent one day a week on indirect labor, you would have 180 billable days left out of the year. Divide your total salary ($39,000) by the number of billable days (180) to determine the amount you need to earn per day ($216.66). Divide this by the number of hours you plan to work each day (e.g., eight hours) for your hourly figure, which would be $27 per hour.

Time Log

In order to figure out how much it costs you to make one of your pieces, start keeping track of how long it takes you to make each piece by keeping a time log. Typically craftspeople do not sit down at 8:00 A.M. and finish a piece at 5:00 P.M. A time log doesn't have to be fancy, a piece of scrap paper will work fine. Just keep your time log next to your workspace and write down every time you do something to your piece, for example, a half hour here, four hours there, and so on. You may discover that making a piece you would have estimated to take eight hours actually took ten hours or more. As you produce more work, you will probably develop ways to make your pieces faster. Also, if you make more than one item, you will need to keep a time log for each item in order to price each work.

For example, one of my students suggested using an electric clock with hands to keep track of how long it takes to make a piece. By starting with the clock at 12:00 and plugging it in each time you start working and unplugging it each time you stop, if the clock says 9:00 when you are finished, you will know it took nine hours to make that piece.

Materials

There are a couple of easy ways to keep track of the materials you use to make your pieces. You can either write down exactly what you used in each piece or come up with an estimate based on the cost of your materials divided by the number of pieces you make. I like the latter method because it includes waste, but either method will do. Try both and see which method suits you.

Overhead

Overhead is fixed expenses such as rent for your studio, utilities, telephone, insurance, and accounting fees. If you have a studio in your house, determine what it costs you or what you would have to pay to rent a similar space in your area. For example, if your mortgage is $1,200 per month and your studio takes up a quarter of your house, then the studio costs you $300 per month. The same goes for utilities. Keeping your overhead low is important in order to keep your pricing competitive. As a general rule, your overhead should be roughly 20–25 percent of your labor and material costs.

Profit Margin

In the cost-based approach to pricing, you need to add a profit margin—which can be anything. This is to ensure that even if you sell all your work at the wholesale price to buyers and gallery owners, you will still cover your costs and make a profit.

Take a few minutes to price a representative piece of your work using the worksheet on the next page. If you don't know what your overhead is because you are just starting your business and don't have any accurate figures to work with, remember that overhead is generally 20–25 percent of labor and material costs. You can probably come up with a labor and materials estimate to get started.

Pricing Example

Let's say the piece you are going to price took ten hours to make and you produce twelve each month. The retail price would be determined as follows:

Labor	=	10 hours × hourly rate @ $27/hour	=	$270
Materials	=	$600/month divided by 12	=	$50
Overhead	=	$1,200/month divided by 12	=	$100
Subtotal				$420
Profit	=	20% (variable)	+	$84
Total		*Wholesale price*	=	$504
		Retail price (Wholesale price × 2)	=	$1,008

Do you think you can sell this piece for $1,000? If not, where can you cut some of your costs? Do you think you can sell it for more than $1,000? This is where the market-based approach (what it will sell for) comes in.

Worksheet: Cost-Based Approach to Pricing Your Work

BASIC FORMULA

Wholesale Price = Labor + Materials + Overhead + Margin

Retail Price   = Wholesale Price × 2

LABOR		MONTHLY		ANNUALLY
Your hourly rate	= $ _____	$ _____	× 12 =	$ _____
Assistant's rate	= $ _____	$ _____	× 12 =	$ _____

TIME LOG

How many pieces do you make?	_____	× 12 =	_____
How long does it take to make a piece?	_____ hours		

MATERIALS (LIST MATERIALS AND THEIR COST)	MONTHLY	ANNUALLY
_____	_____	_____
_____	_____	_____
_____	_____	_____
_____	_____	_____
_____	_____	_____
Total	$ _____	$ _____

OVERHEAD AND OTHER EXPENSES	MONTHLY		ANNUALLY
Mortgage or rent for studio	_____	× 12 =	_____
Utilities	_____	× 12 =	_____
Telephone	_____	× 12 =	_____
Offce supplies, copying	_____	× 12 =	_____
Postage	_____	× 12 =	_____
Insurance, legal or accounting fees	_____	× 12 =	_____
Dues, subscriptions, fees, course fees	_____	× 12 =	_____
Promotional materials	_____	× 12 =	_____
Photography	_____	× 12 =	_____
Other	_____	× 12 =	_____
Total	$ _____		$ _____

PROFIT MARGIN

What percentage do you fgure? _____%

If you need to reduce the costs of your piece because you know it's too expensive for today's market, consider the following options:

- Paying yourself less in the beginning until you are established
- Hiring someone else to help you that you pay less than your hourly rate
- Buying your supplies in bulk with another craftsperson
- Renting out part of your studio
- Finding ways to work faster by making templates or doing several pieces at once

The other aspect of pricing is demand. Your cost-based retail price may be $1,008 but you can sell the piece for $3,000 because of the market value, your reputation, or the fact that the demand for your work exceeds your ability to produce it. The important thing is to make sure you are charging enough for your pieces so you can earn a livable wage and stay in business. It won't help you if you can sell a lot of work but lose money on every sale.

Some General Rules about Pricing Your Work

Your retail price should remain the same.

Keep in mind that whether you sell your pieces directly to the customer at a craft fair or market them through a shop or gallery, your prices should not be affected. While you cannot control the price at which a buyer will resell your work, you can control your own prices and provide a suggested retail price. If a customer or shop owner finds out that you are selling the same work cheaper out of your studio or at a fair, that person is not going to feel good about the price he or she paid for the work. A shop or gallery owner will feel that you are undercutting his or her efforts to sell your work. Remember that you are building a relationship with people—that means being fair.

Be aware of other costs.

Whether you sell your work or someone else does, there are costs incurred in selling—such as booth fees or overhead of a gallery or shop. If a shop is able to sell your work, be happy to give the store its share of the price. After all, you have already built a profit into your wholesale prices.

Determine the right price.

Acknowledge that there are a lot of emotions involved in pricing your work. I've had students who have looked at another student's work priced at $25 and been upset at how low that person priced his or her work. To determine the right price, try some pricing experiments, like raising your prices at one show and evaluating the results.

Feel good about your prices.

You have put a lot of effort into making your pieces and your work is not only good but worth the price. If people aren't willing to pay for it, maybe they are not your potential customers and you are trying to sell to the wrong market. Any ambivalence about your prices will show when you try to sell your work.

This look at business finances has highlighted the key numbers you need to run your craft business. It is important to set business goals, break down your expenses, and analyze your progress. No one is suggesting that numbers tell the whole story. Numbers don't reflect the love, talent, and inspiration you put into your work. But you can only have a long-term career selling your work as a craftsperson if the numbers make good business sense—i.e., charging more for your work than it costs to make it, your income exceeding your expenses, and managing to have cash when you need it.

CHAPTER 9

STUDIO

Anyone can have a problem locating adequate and affordable housing, but it is especially difficult for craftspeople. Most craftspeople cannot afford to pay rent in two places—a studio and a separate home or apartment—during the startup phase of their business. If you are interested in finding a good studio in which you can live as well as work in, you should look for one that is safe, legal, and affordable.

Most craftspeople start out working in a spare room, basement, or garage before obtaining a studio space away from home. Wherever you work, at home or in a rented space, there are several things to consider such as zoning laws, the pros and cons of leasing versus owning your studio space, and contracts or leases.

It's easy to get isolated and discouraged when you are working alone. One way to combat isolation is to rent or buy a studio space in an artists' studio building. Not only will you be surrounded by people with the same goals and dreams, but you can get inspiration, share resources, and gain other valuable tips from each other as well. Call you local craft organization for referrals of studio buildings in your area.

Zoning

If your studio is at home in your garage or basement, be aware that several types of restrictions may apply. For example, the studio may be limited to a certain number of square feet, outbuildings may not be allowed, or the type of equipment used may be restricted. Noise, smoke, and odor restrictions may apply and you may even have to obtain approval from some of the neighbors. Call your local zoning board to find out what the restrictions may be in your area before you set up your studio and business. For example, one potter I know had no problem getting permission to use her kiln in a residential area, but she had to obtain a permit from the local fire department whenever she wanted to do a pit firing to get special smoke marks on her pieces.

Local zoning ordinances can be a significant factor for craftspeople who want to live and work in the same space. Some city and counties prohibit using the same space as a business and a dwelling. In some commercially zoned areas where craftspeople can rent lowcost lofts and studios, it is illegal to maintain a residence in the same space. In residential areas, the craftsperson may have to comply with regulations that require permits and restrict the use of the studio. Check with your local government agency to find out the specific requirements in your area before you sign a lease.

If you do choose to work and/or live in a studio space that does not legally allow you to be there, while these tend to have lower rentals, it may not only make it difficult to obtain insurance, but you may also forfeit other services such as voting privileges, trash collection, and security. Call your insurance agent to find out if your current policy has any restrictions and, if so, what you can do to comply with their policies.

Leasing versus Owning Your Space

Cities around the country realize that the arts and crafts are not only good for business, but also for revitalizing downtown areas. If you are leasing your space, check out the arrangements thoroughly before moving into a new studio. Although you may enjoy helping an area come back to life, without adequate provisions in your lease, you may eventually have to relocate as property values rise. For this reason, I feel that owning a space, whether on your own or as part of a cooperative, is preferable whenever possible.

If individual ownership is beyond your current means, you may find a solution by joining other craftspeople in a cooperative or a nonprofit corporation. As a cooperative or nonprofit group, you may be eligible for private or government funding from individuals, developers, private foundations, corporations, and municipal governments that recognize the special needs and contributions of craftspeople within their community.

Providence, Rhode Island, has put together an unusual plan to revitalize its downtown area by building the local economy around the arts. To my knowledge, this is the first case of an American city using fiscal incentives to lure artists to its downtown area. According to the plan, any artist, writer, or composer who takes up residence in the downtown area will pay no state income tax on any art-generated revenue. Downtown property owners will receive low-interest loans and a ten-year property-tax abatement if they reno-vate their abandoned buildings and agree to lease them to artists at below-market rents. All the landlord has to do to qualify is bring the building up to code.

In the early 1980s, an artists' studio building in Boston called Fenway Studios changed from a place where artists rented studios to a cooperative owned by the artists themselves. Built in 1905, the building was to be sold before the artists got organized and formed Fenway Studios, Inc. After ob-taining a loan from the National Consumer Cooperative in Washington, D.C., and making a 20 percent down payment on their studios, each artist became a shareholder. Now each artist makes a mortgage payment, ranging from $350 to $750 per month, depending on the value of their studio. Although the ac-tual cost of the studio has not changed dramatically, the peace of mind gained by owning their space has been well worth the effort. Finding and keeping a stable studio situation is important because if you lease your studio and have to move, it can take a long time to find a new studio, move, get back to the work, and become comfortable in the space.

Contracts

When you sign a lease for a studio or storefront, you are signing a contract. The contract should spell out the following:
- A description of the space you are renting
- The length of the lease
- If you have the option to renew the lease
- Any restrictions for using the property
- Insurance requirements, security, remodeling, and utilities
- The amount of a deposit and what needs to be done to get it re-funded

No matter what terms you and the landlord agree upon for your lease, get it in writing and keep a copy in a safe place. You should consider the following ten questions before signing any lease:

1. If you are renting a storefront, are you responsible for common areas?

2. Do you pay a flat fee or is your rate based on your earnings at that location?

3. Can you extend your lease with the same terms?

4. Is the area zoned to prohibit certain activities such as using a kiln?

5. Who pays for remodeling costs?

6. If you need special utilities, who is responsible for paying for them?

7. Do you insure your studio only or do you need to insure the building as well?

8. Can you install a security system or is the landlord responsible for providing security?

9. Can you live in your studio legally?

10. If the building in which your studio is located is for sale, does the landlord have to tell you?

Studio Concerns

To solve the problem of adequate studio space, think about what type of studio arrangement will work best for you. For example, if your studio is located in your home, can you work uninterrupted? Conversely, will you be able to separate your work life from your personal life if your studio is in your home—or will you have the tendency to become a workaholic? Can you afford to have a studio away from home? Whether you have your studio in your home or rent or buy a separate studio space, make sure you have all the facts so you can make an informed decision. You need to be aware of the zoning laws, building code standards and consider the matter of insurance.

It is my suggestion that you should own your workplace if possible. However, if you rent or lease a space, review the ten questions mentioned above and have your lawyer review any lease or contract before you sign it.

CHAPTER 10

WORKING WITH PROFESSIONALS

Many craftspeople are skilled at handling their own financial, legal, photographic, and marketing needs. However, whether you are able to do all the work yourself or not, you may not always have the time. Having the advice and assistance of professionals such as an accountant or lawyer can be a smart way to manage your time and get you back to the studio producing your work. After all, isn't that why you went into business for yourself in the first place? Following are some questions to help you evaluate the professionals you hire:

- Do you understand your professional's fee structure?
- Is the person easy to reach and does he or she return messages promptly?
- Does the person spend enough time helping you?
- Is work completed when you need it?
- Does the professional you are dealing with work with other craftspeople and understand your business?
- Does he or she keep up-to-date on laws that might affect your business?

Although finding the right professionals to assist you in running your business can seem overwhelming at first, these questions should help you get started and evaluate their performance over time. If possible, meet with several prospective professionals before deciding which one is right for you and your business. View hiring a professional the same as you would a new employee for your business.

Financial Professionals

When you need help managing your finances, you want someone you can trust, skilled in communications, and able to give advice without making you feel dumb. No matter which type of financial professional you choose to work with, to save time and money, bring only the paperwork and prepared summaries of what he or she needs to see. If you don't know what to bring, ask what kind of documentation is necessary when you make the appointment.

Review the basic descriptions for a bookkeeper, accountant, and tax preparer, which are outlined below, before deciding which type of financial professional would be appropriate for your business.

Bookkeepers

Bookkeepers keep accurate records, keep the books, write checks, and reconcile bank statements. Although many bookkeepers are very capable, you should be aware that they are not trained to be the overall financial manager of a business.

When you first start your business, you may not have enough sales to warrant hiring extra help. If you find that your business has grown to the point where it is difficult to keep up with the recordkeeping yourself, consider hiring a bookkeeper because this is one area where someone else can easily take over. However, just because someone else is keeping your books doesn't give you permission to not be aware of the financial status of your business at all times. You will still need to supervise the bookkeeper's work and use the information provided to make informed financial decisions. See chapter 12 for more information.

Accountants

An accountant can help you set up a recordkeeping system, tell you what is required to put employees on the payroll, prepare tax returns, and answer any questions you might have on financial matters.

An accountant, unlike a certified public accountant (CPA), does not have to pass an examination, meet educational requirements, or continue their education even though they usually have taken courses in accounting or have degrees in accounting. Unless you need the expertise of someone to conduct a formal review or audit, for example, you probably need only the services of an accountant, not a CPA. Each state has different standards for licensing CPAs.

Generally, CPAs need to have a four-year degree, pass an examination, meet a "good character" requirement, and have two years of experience working under a licensed CPA. Then, to maintain their CPA license, they must complete specific requirements of continuing professional education.

Tax Preparers

A tax preparer is someone who helps you prepare your tax returns. You may be surprised to find out that a tax preparer doesn't have to pass a special test or even have a license to prepare tax returns. In fact, there are no requirements to meet before offering such services. This doesn't mean that the person you have hired to do your tax returns is incompetent, it just means that the field is not regulated and you may want to do a little homework before retaining the services of a tax preparer.

Whether you decide to retain the services of a bookkeeper, accountant, or tax preparer, keep in mind your specific needs. It may be wise to use a CPA, for example, who may also offer bookkeeping services and prepare tax returns. There is a nationwide organization called Accountants for the Public Interest that provides free accounting services—such as preparing tax returns or help in setting up a small business—to individuals and organizations that otherwise might not have access to needed professional assistance. You can contact the Accountants for the Public Interest at 1012 14th Street, Suite 1003, Washington, D.C. 20005; (202) 289-2272 to see if you are eligible and for an affiliate near you.

Financial Planners

In their book *Investing from the Heart,* Jack Brill and Alan Reder claim that once you start looking for financial advice, you will notice that it is everywhere and that it comes in a variety of packages. Since there are no government licenses regulating who can offer this advice, anyone can legally call him- or herself a financial advisor, financial planner, financial consultant, or investment advisor. There are also a number of insurance agents, real estate agents, tax professionals, attorneys, accountants, and stockbrokers advertising financial planning services. Some of them may be well qualified to help you, with a broad base of experience and knowledge behind their claims. Others are simply offering an auxiliary service to their clients that come to them for their primary area of expertise.

Find out how your advisor is compensated because the type of advice you receive may be directly related to the ways financial advisors make money. There are commission-based advisors, fee based advisors, combination fee/commission advisors, and discount brokers. Commission-based advisors only get paid when you buy a product from them so their advice is free; fee-based advisors charge a basic or hourly fee for their advice; combination advisors charge you hourly for advice and credit commissions against your account; and finally, discount brokers purchase stocks and bonds at a discount, but do not offer any advice. In order to help you select a financial planner, consider this list of questions to ask prospective planners.

- How are you paid?
- What is your training?
- How many years have you been doing financial planning?
- Are you an official representative for any particular products?
- May I have some references to contact?

In addition to inquiring about the credentials and references of your financial planner, you need to feel comfortable enough to share the financial details of your life with this person. Does he or she seem knowledgeable and display integrity?

Lawyers

A lawyer can help you with the legal aspects of running your business such as reviewing a lease or contract for a studio space or with a gallery; helping you incorporate your business; handling copyright issues; drawing up a partnership agreement; estate planning; and writing a will. Finding and establishing a relationship with a lawyer allows you to rely on his or her guidance, often preventing legal problems before they have a chance to arise.

All lawyers are licensed so you are basically looking for someone you trust. Ask other craftspeople to recommend someone they have found to be satisfactory and talk with several lawyers before selecting one. If you have a problem that requires specialized legal experience, call your local bar association to recommend a lawyer. Do not hesitate to discuss fees with a lawyer. Fees usually depend on the amount of time and research involved in a case. Fees for simple matters such as incorporating a business or drawing up a will can easily be determined. More complicated cases may require an estimate.

The Volunteer Lawyers for the Arts (VLA) was founded in New York

City in 1969 to provide artists and arts organizations with the legal assistance they required but were not able to afford. VLA chapters provide educational programs, newsletters, accounting, and business advice to artists and craftspeople either free of charge or at discounted rates for those with limited means. You can contact Volunteer Lawyers for the Arts at 1 East 53rd St, 6th Floor, New York, NY 10022, (212) 319-2787; *www.vlany.org* to find the chapter nearest you.

Bankers

Most craftspeople don't think about establishing a relationship with a bank until they need some money. However, most small businesses will need financing at some point and your local bank will probably be the first place you contact. Your relationship with your local bank may start by opening a business checking account, establishing a line of credit, applying for a charge card machine, or even requesting a loan to start your business. Craftspeople often complain that bankers don't understand the nature of their business and, to a certain extent, they are right. But that doesn't mean you can't qualify for a loan.

There are two types of banks: commercial banks and savings banks. Commercial banks deal primarily with business transactions such as checks, credit cards, and automobile loans. Savings banks deal primarily in a variety of savings accounts and long-term loans such as mortgages. Although banks are regulated by state and federal agencies, the specific services offered may vary from state to state. In some states, for example, commercial banks can offer savings accounts and savings banks can offer checking accounts.

Shop around and compare rates of interest and fees before opening an account. For example, some banks may have a charge per check written while others may have a monthly fee. When looking into loans, you should get several quotes before you sign an agreement because the difference in the interest rates can add up to a lot of money over time. Bankers are in the business of lending money so make it easy for them. Many banks are very interested in small businesses and anxious to help you establish yours. You just need to find out what information they need and provide it in an organized and concise manner. If you are applying for a loan, for example, know how much money you want to borrow and be prepared to submit a business plan (see chapter 6). Ask questions, get information, and make the right choice for you and your business.

Photographers

You may need a photographer to take slides of your work for a juried craft fair, black-and-white photographs for a brochure, or photographs of yourself for publicity. While many craftspeople are good photographers, when you are ready to sell your work, you need to have the best quality images you can afford. After all, you won't be there to explain to a juror, for example, that one of your pieces is really a brighter blue than the slide illustrates or that if you had owned a different lens, he or she could really see the detail in that piece of jewelry. The craft world has become a very competitive place and you need the best quality photographic images possible in order to let your work speak for itself.

When you need a photographer, look for one who is experienced photographing crafts. Ask other craftspeople about photographers who have done satisfactory work for them for referrals. When you contact a photographer, ask to see his or her portfolio. Good photographers enjoy a chance to show their portfolios because they know that quality work sells itself. Look at the portfolio to see how the photographer has handled crafts similar to your own. If the photographer has no portfolio, you should probably look for someone else who does. You should address the following issues when you are hiring a photographer:

- Why you need the images (e.g., a juried fair application, publicity purposes, or a brochure)
- How many slides or photographs you need
- Ask for price estimates before the work is done—does the photographer charge an hourly fee plus the costs of the film and processing or by the job?
- Request a simple written contract covering the work to be done
- Find out if you can be present during the session or if the photographer prefers you to leave your work
- Give the photographer a deadline for receiving the images that allows enough time for a reshoot
- Ask if he or she has experience photographing crafts
- Ask to see a portfolio
- Ask for a couple references
- If the photographer doesn't think he or she is the right person for your needs, can he or she recommend someone else?

I know someone who paid a professional photographer to shoot several different pieces who didn't explain that she needed the slides to apply to a juried show. Although she received beautiful high-quality slides, each image had a different background. Individually, they were fine, but together they did not look like a cohesive body of work. Discuss how the images will be used to prevent misunderstandings with your photographer before the session begins.

Do you know that both the photographer and you own a copyright for the pieces? The photographer holds a copyright for the photographic image and you hold the copyright for the actual design of the piece. For this reason, consider using a simple agreement to give the photographer credit whenever your publish his or her image and have the photographer agree to limit the use of reproducing the photograph according to your specifications.

Knowing that you are getting the work done professionally—working with an financial professional, lawyer, or photographer—can make your job a lot easier. Choose your professionals carefully and supply them with the necessary information to do their jobs well and in a timely manner. After doing research and getting referrals, meet with several professionals before retaining their services. Once you have retained the services of one or more professionals, be sure to keep them informed of your activities so they can service you better. With their help, you can spend more time in the studio making your crafts rather than in your office doing paperwork.

MANAGING YOUR CRAFTS BUSINESS

CHAPTER 11

SETTING UP
A COMPUTER SYSTEM

Why have a computer and how do you select one? A computer is the single most versatile and valuable piece of office equipment you can own because it can be a secretary, bookkeeper, receptionist, file clerk, business consultant, financial analyst, tax preparer, graphic designer, and print shop in one. A computer set up properly and kept updated can transform your office management duties into simple and cost-efficient tasks.

Before selecting a computer for your craft business, think about how you are going to use the computer. Will you be sending out letters, using forms, keeping a mailing list, publishing a newsletter, keeping track of your inventory of supplies and finished work, or posting your checkbook register on your computer? Will you have an e-mail address, a Web page, and use the Internet? For more information about the Internet, see chapter 28.

Once you have made a list of the kinds of things you plan to use your computer for, review the types of software discussed below and start looking at the programs you may want to use. The software you choose may influence the type of hardware you need to purchase. After you have reviewed the basic computer terms and concepts included in this chapter, use the Selecting Software, Computer, and Printer worksheet to prepare for purchasing your computer. If you still feel lost, visit some other craftspeople or small businesses that use computers; see what they use the computer for, and what types of programs they use. Ask them what they do and do not like about their systems and why.

To run a small craft business, you will probably need a computer in order to use a word processing program (to write letters and make forms), a database (to keep track of your mailing list and inventory), and a spreadsheet program (to produce lists and reports). In addition, you may want to have a graphics program that will allow you to do your own desktop publishing, so you can lay out newsletters or other camera-ready pieces. Finally, it is advisable to have a program to keep track of your finances.

There are many different computers on the market and software programs to choose from. You can spend as little as a couple hundred dollars for a good used system or as much as several thousand dollars for a deluxe new system. Keep in mind that computers depreciate just like any other equipment and you will probably want to upgrade your system every few years or so as the technology improves. To give you an idea of what you may be able to afford, I've included three sample configurations in different price ranges: budget, mid-range, and deluxe.

There are desktop computers and laptop computers. Do you need to be able to easily take your computer with you or will you only use it in your office? While laptop computers are attractive because they are so compact and lightweight, they tend to be considerably more expensive than desktop computers of equivalent power and capacity and have smaller viewing screens.

When it comes to printing, there are ink-jet printers, laser printers, and dot-matrix printers. Dot-matrix printers take longer to print, are usually noisy, and have poor print quality. However, for certain uses—such as printing drafts, labels, or reports—dot-matrix printers can be fine. Ink-jet printers have nearly the same quality as laser printers, print fairly quickly, and are much less expensive. Laser printers are the best quality and print very quietly, but they tend to be the most expensive. If your budget is small, you may want to start out with an ink-jet printer and upgrade later to a laser printer.

These days there isn't much of a visible difference between Macintosh ("Mac") computers and X86 computers ("PCs") running Windows. The programs are very user-friendly and you can either use the pull-down menus or memorize the commands, whichever you prefer. Most computers today use 3½-inch disks with the option to add a Zip drive, which holds a lot more information than a standard disk.

You can order a computer through the mail, on the Internet, or through a computer store. If the computer doesn't come all set to go, ask if someone can set up the computer and install the software for you. Check out *How to Use Your Computer*, by Lisa Biow. Whether you have a PC or a Mac, this book will answer all your questions about the basic functions of your computer. Alternately, many adult education programs offer good basic courses in how to use different computer systems. Such classes may save you some of the time it takes to learn a new program on your own using a manual.

Types of Software

Your basic software is likely to include an integrated program, a personal finance program, and a personal information manager. These three programs will cover a surprising portion of your daily business tasks.

Integrated Programs

Considered the Swiss army knife of software, one of these programs is usually installed on a new computer. This type of software is versatile because it includes word-processing, spreadsheet, database, and other programs. Because the programs are integrated with one another, you can easily transfer information from one program (e.g., your database of contact information) to another (e.g., your form letter in your word-processing program). Examples of an integrated program are Microsoft Works and ClarisWorks.

Personal Finance Programs

Quicken, the leading personal software finance program, is a very good tool for many small businesses because it is inexpensive and relatively easy to use. Another example is Microsoft Money. See chapter 12 for more information on recordkeeping.

Personal Information Managers

These programs function like an electronic day planner and they include an address book, calendar, and phone book. You can use this to automatically remind you of approaching deadlines. Examples of this type of program are Sidekick, Lotus Organizer, DayTimer, Claris Organizer, Now Contact/Now Up to Date, or Time and Chaos (available as shareware).

General Tips for Purchasing Software

Try before you buy.

You may be able to download a trial version of a program you are consider-ing buying, which operates for a limited time or has some of the functions disabled.

Use the simplest tool to do the job.

Don't feel that you have to invest in fancy programs when your word-process-ing program is sufficient for your needs.

Consider shareware.

Many fine programs are available through Shareware (*www.shareware.com*) for downloading from the Internet. If you commit to using a shareware program, you are expected to register it and pay a small fee. Shareware publishers are the struggling craftspeople of the software industry.

Commit to a program and learn to use it thoroughly.

Read the manual and take a course if necessary. The biggest cost in software is the time spent learning how to use the program, so resist the temptation to switch programs every time something new comes on the market.

Think before you upgrade.

Just because some companies release a new version of your program every year doesn't mean that you have to buy it. Purchase every second or third upgrade to save time, money, and space in your computer.

Sample Computer Configurations

Budget System

In this price range, consider secondhand, factory refurbished, or end of life (new but obsolete) equipment. Make sure you have adequate return and war-ranty coverage. You should be able to get a 486 or a slow Pentium or 68K Mac or early Power Mac. Favor equipment that is basic but high quality over flashier noname products. This price range should include a computer, monitor, modem, ink-jet printer, and works and finance programs. A good book to check out is Bill Camarda's *Cheapskate's Guide to Bargain Computing*.

Mid-range System

In this price range, you can look at all new equipment if desired or an even more powerful refurbished unit. You should be able to get a fast Pentium or Pentium clone (over 200 MHz), 32K RAM (random-access memory), multimedia, a 56K modem, and software programs. This is the most you will have to spend for strictly business use.

Deluxe System

It is not difficult to spend a lot of money on computer equipment. In this price range, the CPU (central processing unit) will be faster, e.g., the Pentium II class, with better graphics, more RAM, a bigger hard drive, and a larger monitor. The only reason to spend this much money is if you are doing advanced Web and multimedia work, are addicted to computer games, or are in need of a tax deduction.

Worksheet: Selecting a Computer, Software, and Printer

Name of store _____

Telephone _____

Salesperson _____

Reasons why I am buying a computer:

1. _____

2. _____

3. _____

My budget to buy a computer is: $_____

SOFTWARE PROGRAMS	FEATURES	PRICE

COMPUTERS	FEATURES	PRICE

PRINTERS	FEATURES	PRICE

Does the store have a service department?   ☐ Yes   ☐ No

If not, where does it refer customers?

Is any training available to learn how to use my computer?   ☐ Yes   ☐ No

Other:

CHAPTER 12

PRODUCTION AND OFFICE WORK

Whether you are selecting a computer, using form letters and premade forms to expedite a task, scheduling production and office work, or shipping your work to a shop or gallery, understanding basic office procedures will save you time and money.

Letter Formats

When you are running a craft business, having sample letters and forms will save you time because many of the tasks you do will require the same information. Why reinvent the wheel every time you take an order, for example, and risk not getting all the information you need the first time you talk with the customer? I have supplied some suggestions for letters and forms that you may need. You can alter them to fit your needs, but once they are in your computer, it is easy to add a personal line or change a paragraph when necessary. Below are three sample letter formats for your review.

Inquiry Letter

This type of letter is sent when you are inquiring about having your work shown at a new craft shop or gallery. Before sending the letter, I would make a quick phone call to check the address and find out the name of the person you should contact, as well as what he or she prefers to see when initially reviewing new work—such as slides or a brochure.

Date

Company Name

Attn: _____

Address

City, State, Zip Code

Dear _____:

State how you found out about the shop or gallery, mention the name if someone referred you, and state that you are inquiring about having your work sold or shown there and would like more information.

Give a brief description of your business and describe your products. Note that you have enclosed some information such as a résumé, brochure, postcard snapshot, or slides, for their review—whatever format you were told was preferred.

Mention that you will be calling soon to make sure the package was received and to check on the status of your inquiry. Thank the person for his or her time to review your material. Enclose an SASE if you want your material returned.

Sincerely,

Name

Prospective Commissions

This type of letter is sent to supplement an order form when someone commissions or has expressed interest in commissioning a custom piece.

Date

Company Name

Attn: _____

Address

City, State, Zip Code

Dear _____:

Thank the person for their interest in your work and remind him or her how you met.

Outline what the person asked you to make, what materials would be used, the dimensions of the piece, and the date the piece could be ready if the person places an order and pays a deposit by a particular date.

Outline the financial agreement, noting that an order form is attached and requires a signature. Tell the person that the form specifies the total cost for the piece, when the deposit is due and for how much, and when the final payment is due. Note that if the person requests any changes to the final piece, there will be an extra fee of so much per hour.

If the person wanted to see a model before you make the final piece, specify when it would be ready for review and quote the fee to cover the cost of making it. Next, specify how the piece will be shipped and what the shipping cost will be.

Thank the person again for his or her interest and express your interest in making a piece for him or her. Ask to have the order form returned by a certain date with the person's signature and a check for the deposit so that you can proceed with the work in a timely fashion.

Sincerely,
Name

Receivables Letter

You should send a letter like this one to a customer from whom you are having difficulty receiving payment.

Date
Company Name
Attn: _____
Address
City, State, Zip Code

Dear _____:

First, thank the person for his or her order of your pieces.

Then state the date the pieces were shipped and when an invoice was sent. State the date when payment was due. State your payment policy and the fact that interest is being charged per your policy.

Ask the person to make payment by a new date. Tell the person that if this is not possible, he or she should contact you to arrange for a payment plan.

If you can't work something out, tell the person you will have to take further action.

Thank the person for their cooperation.

Sincerely,

Name

Forms

Forms can be very useful in helping you run your office efficiently by making sure you get consistent information each time you do a particular task. In this section, I have included samples of the following forms:

- A purchase order form to keep track of the materials you have ordered
- An inventory form listing finished pieces
- An order form
- A packing slip to go with orders shipped
- An invoice to send to buyers

Although you can buy preprinted forms in an office supply store, you can also make forms that are customized to your needs by using your computer, printing them on letterhead, and running off copies as needed.

Purchase Orders

A purchase order (PO) assigns an identifying number to every order you place. A PO needs to include the name and address of the company you are ordering from, your company name and shipping address, the date the PO is sent, the date the items are required, the items ordered, the quantity, the cost, payment terms, and how you would like your order shipped. There must be a signature on the PO approving the order.

Inventory Forms

You should regularly check your inventory of materials as well as finished pieces in order to know what is available to produce work, to ship out in response to orders received from buyers, or to take to sell at a craft show. Having inventory records from the prior year can be a useful planning tool when

Sample Purchase Order Form *(Print on letterhead)*

Purchase Order # _____ Date _____

To: _____

_____

_____

_____

Telephone _____

Date Required _____

Shipping Method: ☐ UPS   ☐ Federal Express   ☐ Other _____

Payment Terms: ☐ Bill me   ☐ Check enclosed   ☐ Mastercard/Visa

Card # _____ Expiration Date

Signature _____

QUANTITY	ITEM #	DESCRIPTION	UNIT COST	TOTAL COST

Subtotal $ _____

Sales Tax $ _____

Shipping $ _____

Total Cost $ _____

Order approved by: _____

figuring out what materials to order and your production needs for the following year. In addition, inventory records are necessary for determining where you stand financially on financial reports such as your balance sheet.

An inventory should include the date the inventory is taken, a list of the materials and finished pieces you make and the quantities on hand, their wholesale and retail prices, and the ideal quantity you always want to have in stock. With this information, you can easily see how much material you need to order, how many items you need to make of an item that is selling, as well as which items and materials you may want to discontinue or put on sale.

Sample Inventory Form *(Print on letterhead)*

☐ Materials Inventory   ☐ Finished Pieces Inventory

Date _____

ITEM #	DESCRIPTION	QUANTITY	# NEEDED	WHOLESALE $	RETAIL $

Total Value $_____ $_____

Order Form

An order form should always be used to get the information you need in a consistent manner, whether you are taking orders at shows, over the telephone, or in your showroom. An order form should include the following information:

- The date the order is taken and due
- The company name, shipping/billing address, telephone number, and name of the buyer
- The items ordered and their quantity

- The wholesale and suggested retail prices you quoted for each item (Depending on the size of the order, you may have different prices according to quantities ordered)
- The method of shipping
- A purchase order number
- Payment terms
- The total amount due
- A space for notes
- The source of the order (used to track which marketing efforts generated this order)

Packing Slips

The primary purpose of a packing slip is to give the person unpacking the box basic information such as where the order came from, if the order was complete or partial, and a reference to a purchase order number (PO #) so that he or she can check the items and let purchasing and accounts payable know the order was received. A packing slip does not need to have financial information on it. Some print shops make forms in triplicate consisting of the order information on the top page, the packing slip (without the financial information coming through) in the middle, and the bottom copy for your records.

While some shops and galleries are small enough that the same person will make the order, unpack the boxes, and send your payment, you still want to make processing your order as easy as possible by giving him or her the necessary information. For example, the buyer may order from you more than once or perhaps for a special customer. A packing slip serves as a reminder of what or who this order is for. In a larger company, it is not uncommon that at least three people will process your order: the buyer who ordered the work, the person unpacking the box, and the person who pays the invoice.

Sample Order Form *(Print on letterhead)*

Date _____ Date Due _____

Company _____

Billing Address _____

_____

Shipping Address _____

_____

Contact/Buyer _____

Telephone _____

Shipping Method: ☐ UPS   ☐ FedEx   ☐ Other _____

Purchase Order #

Payment Terms: ☐ COD   ☐ Net 30   ☐ Other _____

                   ☐ Mastercard/Visa   ☐ Other _____

           Card # _____ Expiration Date _____

           Signature _____

QUANTITY	ITEM #	DESCRIPTION	WHOLESALE $	RETAIL $	TOTAL $

Subtotal $ _____

Sales Tax $ _____

Shipping $ _____

Total Due $ _____

Notes _____

_____

_____

Source of order: ☐ Ad   ☐ Show   ☐ Referral   ☐ Word of mouth   ☐ Other:

Sample Packing Slip *(Print on letterhead)*

Date _____ Date Due _____

Company _____

Billing Address _____

_____

Shipping Address _____

_____

Contact/Buyer _____

Telephone _____

Shipping Method: ☐ UPS   ☐ FedEx   ☐ Other_____

Purchase Order # _____

QUANTITY   ITEM #   DESCRIPTION

_____

_____

_____

_____

_____

_____

Invoices

You should create a simple invoice form that is saved in your computer. You can merge your database with the form to speed up invoicing tasks. An invoice should include the following information:

- The date
- An invoice number to help buyers keep track of your invoice(s)
- Purchase order number, if used
- The name, shipping and billing address of the company you are invoicing
- The quantity and descriptions of the products ordered
- The unit and total price, sales tax, and shipping costs
- The payment terms or when payment is due
- Your policies regarding payment (e.g., charges for overdue payments or incentives for early payments)

Sample Invoice *(Print on letterhead)*

Date _____   Date Due _____

Invoice # _____

Company _____

Billing Address _____

_____

Shipping Address _____

_____

Contact/Buyer _____

Telephone _____

Purchase Order # _____

Payment Terms: ☐ COD   ☐ Net 30   ☐ Other _____

QUANTITY   ITEM #   DESCRIPTION   UNIT COST   TOTAL COST

_____

_____

_____

_____

_____

_____

_____

_____

_____

_____

	Subtotal	$ _____
	Sales Tax	$ _____
	Shipping	$ _____
	Total Cost	$ _____

Policy on payments:

(1) Payments received within ____ days will receive a ____ % discount.

(2) *Late payments.* Payments not received in a timely manner in accordance with the payment terms agreed upon above, will be charged ____% interest. If you anticipate a problem with payment, please call to discuss the matter and work out a new deadline or solution.

Thank you for your order.

Scheduling Production and Office Work

Are you working more than forty hours a week? Nights and weekends? When was the last time you took a vacation? Do you feel you have to do everything yourself or can you delegate some things? Although there may be times that will require you to put in extra effort, you should be able to organize your production and office tasks so that you can meet your business obligations and take time off to enjoy the other aspects of your life.

Set up a schedule for yourself that reflects your best working patterns and energy levels and stick to it. Just like an exercise program, running a business and selling your work requires a time commitment, discipline, as well as days off to recover. It is a well-known fact that running a craft business means spending between 20 and 40 percent of your time doing administrative tasks, leaving only 60–80 percent of your time in the studio.

One solution may be to block out chunks of time in your calendar for different tasks. For example, schedule a day each week to do bookkeeping, ordering supplies, and running errands, another day to do marketing, and keep three days to work in the studio. Or do paperwork, errands, and marketing in the morning and work in the studio each afternoon. Or work in the studio until 3:00 P.M. and spend the last hour or two working in your office. Find a schedule that works best for you.

Scheduling the production of your pieces is very important. For example, if you sell your work to buyers, you will need to be able to ship work when you say you will in order to build a positive ongoing relationship and receive payment for your work. If you anticipate not being able to make a deadline, call and discuss solutions with the buyer so he or she can make other plans, if necessary. Although some craftspeople choose to only do retail shows so that they do not have to worry about filling orders and can sell what they make, most craftspeople sell their work through a combination of both wholesale and retail sales and need to plan production accordingly.

Review the exercise of keeping a time log in chapter 8. If a piece takes you five hours to make and you spend three days a week in the studio, you can easily produce 5 pieces per week, 20 a month, or 250 a year. Knowing how many pieces you can realistically produce is very helpful information in accepting orders and putting together your production schedule. As you get used to filling orders or producing inventory for a show, you may be able to produce more than when you first started out. If you are filling an order for

20 pieces, you will begin to find ways to make them en masse in less time than it takes to produce them individually.

In their book, *The Craft Business Encyclopedia,* Michael Scott and Leonard DuBoff suggest you've got to have rhythm! The secret of the well-organized crafts producer is that the production steps follow in logical sequence. The very nature of the craft dictates much of this. A piece of pottery, obviously, can't go into the kiln until it's been glazed, and it can't be glazed until it comes off the wheel. But in production crafts, the important question becomes one of how many steps should be performed at the same time. Who would dream, for example, of making a single mug, glazing it, and then firing it? That would be a clear waste of time and money. It would also seem laborious to make a mug and attach a handle, make a mug and attach a handle, make a mug and attach a handle. Getting two dozen mugs off the wheel and then attaching two dozen handles expedites the process, reduces the production time, and thereby increases the profit. Care must be taken, of course, to avoid boredom and, in turn, the potential decline in craftsmanship that can result from repeating the same step too many times before going onto something else. Achieving the right combination is a matter of individual style and experience.

How do you plan a production schedule? Break each finished piece or product down into steps and assign a time needed to complete each step. This will also be a helpful training tool for new employees as well as a valuable pricing and planning tool. Once this is done, if you have an order for one hundred mugs, for example, and you know it takes you ten hours to make twenty mugs from start to finish, then to make one hundred mugs, you will need fifty hours or two weeks.

Here are a some tips to help you run your office efficiently:

- Make your office easy to use. Have a permanent place for your office equipment, an extra table to spread out office projects, and everything you need within easy reach.
- Put things away when you are finished using them.
- Set up a simple filing system and file things immediately instead of making piles.
- Keep message pads, order forms, and pens next to the phone for taking orders.
- Get a telephone answering machine. Instead of being interrupted constantly, return all your calls once a day.
- If you can afford to, buy a copy and fax machine and have a second

Production Schedule

Product Line _____

STEPS TO PRODUCE   TIME NEEDED

1. _____
2. _____
3. _____
4. _____
5. _____
6. _____
7. _____
8. _____
9. _____
10. _____

Total time needed to make _____ pieces = _____

Notes _____
_____
_____

phone line installed so that your answering machine can still take messages when you are on the phone. You can also use your second line soley for your fax or Internet connection.

Think of the primary activities you carry out each week and create a workspace where you keep all the materials and supplies related to that activity in that same work area. This could be nothing more than a specific drawer or shelf, or depending on how much material and activity is involved, it could be an entire table, separate desk, or even a portion of the room. For example, have a space where you write checks and pay bills, that has a calculator and file drawer for recordkeeping.

Shipping

Shipping is something for which you bill your customers in addition to your regular prices. This is a good example of an activity that needs to have a space of its own for efficiency. Create a space that includes a large table, packing materials, boxes, bubble wrap, shredded paper, tape, labels, a scale, and marking pens. If you use UPS, have the UPS book handy and the rates posted for easy review.

Do all your shipping at one time, usually at the end of the day or first thing in the morning, depending on your pickup time or when your time to do errands is scheduled. Take the time to research how long it takes to ship to different parts of the country and compare costs between carriers.

Here are a few questions to consider before shipping your pieces:

• Does the method you use insure your product?
• Does the shipper have tracking systems if something gets lost?
• Are there any weight or size restrictions?
• What will it cost to ship your work?
• Will the shipper pick up or deliver the work?
• How long will it take to arrive?

Shipping your work is something that many craftspeople don't think about until a deadline is looming or they have sold a piece and haven't charged for shipping. Know the approximate cost to package and ship a piece, and offer the information to customers when they buy or place an order for one of your pieces.

The important points to remember about your production and office work is finding ways that make your tasks efficient and suit your personal style of working. Set up a production and work schedule that is realistic and efficient—then stick to it. Make sure to schedule time off. Draft sample letters, make forms, and always use purchase orders to keep track of orders. Keep track of your raw materials and finished pieces by updating your inventory often. Use order forms effectively, include packing slips with your orders, and send an invoice for timely payment. It is worth it to research shipping alternatives and pick the best method for your customers. When you have your computer set up, sample letters and forms ready, your production and administrative work scheduled, and a place to easily ship your pieces, managing your crafts business should be an easy—not daunting—job.

CHAPTER 13

KEEPING THE BOOKS

Accurate bookkeeping is a very important aspect of your business. Before you start keeping records for your craft business, I recommend that you keep your business finances separate from your personal finances by doing the following:

- Open a business checking account at your local bank.
- Get a charge card that you will use only for business purposes. Even though you can use your personal charge card and reimburse yourself, with so many no-fee credit cards available, why not have another card and keep your business and personal finances separate?
- Apply for a charge card machine so customers can put their purchases of your work on their charge cards. Although you have to pay a small percentage of each sale to the bank, it will make the payment process much easier for your customers. You wouldn't want to lose a sale because someone wanting to buy one of your pieces doesn't have cash or a checkbook with them?

Recordkeeping

Pick a recordkeeping system that is well suited to you and your business that you like and that you will use. You may want to discuss options with your accountant. Choose a system that makes recordkeeping easy so that you can keep the system updated with minimal effort. A recordkeeping system should provide information about your finances so you can make informed decisions about your business on a monthly basis.

Here are some sample questions to ask your accountant or tax return preparer regarding recordkeeping:

- Which recordkeeping system do you recommend for my business?
- What income and expense categories should I use?
- How will I record items I buy with cash instead of using a check? Or items I buy for my personal use and the business using the same check?
- How should I handle expenses with my car?
- How can I use my recordkeeping system to better manage my business?

"For craftspeople just starting a business, I recommend a program called Quicken if they have a computer," says Lu Bauer, CPA. "If they don't have a computer, I recommend the One Write System. I suggest they open their mail right at the computer every day and enter each bill immediately. They can also assign a payment date, which will create postdated checks. Using the check-writing capability of the program is easy to use, requires less paper handling, and although the checks are more expensive, doing it this way saves time."

One Write System

The One Write System is an excellent manual system for keeping track of the financial side of your business. The One Write System is aptly named because when you write a check, the carbon backing transfers the transaction to a ledger page—so you only need to make the entry once. By eliminating the transfer of information from your checkbook to a separate set of books, this not only saves time, it saves you from making mistakes.

After you write the check, you need to record the amount in the appropriate column or category on the same ledger page. At the end of the month, simply total the columns and enter them on a summary page. Then, at the end of the year, your summary page is ready for when you do your taxes.

Safeguard and McBee are national distributors of the One Write System. Call your local bank for information or look in the yellow pages for your local representative.

Quicken

Quicken is a software program available in any computer store. Quicken manages your check register, keeps track of your income and expenses, makes reports and graphs to show you where your money goes, has special accounts for different kinds of transactions, and makes balancing your checkbook easy. You can write and print checks; track your credit cards, assets and liabilities, and investments; and set up amortized loans. Quicken also helps you prepare your income taxes.

I use Quicken for ArtBiz and have enjoyed how simple it is to get financial reports. It has not only made balancing my checkbook easy, but I have found the reports have helped immensely with planning my business.

Quickbooks

Although similar to Quicken, Quickbooks has several additional features that you may find valuable. For example, Quickbooks will help you prepare invoices, track your inventory, do payroll for several employees, and track sales tax. Another version, Quickbook Pro, will also track your income and expenses by customer or job as well as create estimates for project costs.

What Records Should You Keep?

In addition to keeping the books, you need to keep records of the following:
- Bank statements and canceled checks
- A file of the bills you paid (arranged by year, usually in alphabetical order by vendor)
- Unpaid bills (accounts payable) arranged by the month they are due to be paid
- The invoices customers have paid
- The invoices customers have yet to pay (accounts receivable) arranged by the month they are due to be paid
- Credit card statements
- Insurance policies
- Contracts
- Deeds or lease agreements
- Copies of correspondence, such as those mentioned in chapter 12

Save calendars, appointment books, business cards, press releases, awards, marketing plans, customer lists, résumés, professional organizations to which you belong, an auto-log recording business travel, and anything else that seems appropriate. If you are ever audited, you will need these records to prove that you were in business.

Set up a simple filing system that makes sense to you. For example, you might have a section for the financial records mentioned above, another section by customer name, another for fairs and shows, and another for suppliers and inventory records. Files can be arranged alphabetically, by month, or by category—whatever makes sense to you.

How Long Should You Store Records and Where?

In addition to recordkeeping systems, there is the question of how long you need to keep records before throwing them away. For example, how long do you need to keep bank statements? Receipts from purchasing equipment for your studio? Or tax returns?

In general, in case of an audit of your federal or state tax returns, you should keep financial records for seven years. This means the tax returns as well as the supporting documentation such as credit card statements, bank statements and canceled checks, receipts for major purchases like equipment, and accounts payable records. After seven years, you can throw everything away except the receipts for large purchases. Keep those until you no longer have the item.

In addition, have a safety deposit box to store copies of your most critical business records. For example, a set of original slides and backup disks for your computer should be stored off-site in case of fire, water damage, or a computer virus. Copies of important contracts, insurance policies, and deeds would also be well stored in a safety deposit box.

In order to keep track of your work and sales records, set up a database to record the date the work was made, price, item number, description of the work, name and address of the buyer, sale date, and any other information that seems relevant to you. This database might be merged with your order or invoice forms to generate invoices, or you can keep track of where your work is in case you want to put together an exhibit at a later date.

Taxes

It's always an interesting experience to mention the word "taxes" to a room full of craftspeople taking one of my seminars and notice the silence that follows. The fear of filing and finding out exactly how much (or how little) you are really making from the sales of your work can be a sobering experience.

I remember asking a friend of mine who had started a craft business what type of bookkeeping system she used and how she figured out how to pay her taxes. She pointed to a shoebox and told me she dropped all her receipts in it and when it was time for her to file her tax return for the year, she sorted the box and filled out the tax forms. Although she kept her receipts, figuring out where she stood financially was always an unpleasant task that she liked to avoid for as long as possible.

How often each year do you examine complete information on your sales, expenses, and inventory? One of the most important reasons to keep financial records is to compare this year's business activity with last year's or to see how close your estimates match your actual figures. Good records help you make sound business decisions. Many craftspeople focus only on the requirements of the Internal Revenue Service (IRS). That is, just like my friend, recordkeeping is only done as often as we need to do our tax returns. For some, that means once a year on April 14. What good is having information three and a half months after the end of the year? Not much. You should be reviewing your financial status monthly, if not more often. Use your computer to keep track of tax-deductible expenses.

Here are some expenses that may be deducted from your income and thereby reduce the taxes that you need to pay:

- Commissions to agents and managers
- Dues to professional organizations
- Periodicals, books, and research materials
- Special clothing worn solely for your work and the resulting laundry/cleaning bills
- Business meetings
- Supplies and materials
- Postage
- Publicity photos, materials, and fees
- Business stationery, letterhead, and cards
- Rent on your studio or workspace
- Depreciation on workrelated equipment

- Utilities and upkeep of your studio or workspace
- Work-related hotel, taxi, and travel expenses
- Business calls
- A percentage of health insurance premiums
- Copyright registration fees
- Training to maintain or improve your skills
- Entertainment related to your profession such as museum entrance fees

Taxes are part of your costs. However, within the limits of the law, you should attempt to minimize what you pay. Holding on to the money you earn is as important as earning additional income. This list indicates only some of the deductions you may be overlooking by not keeping adequate records or the fear of finding out where you stand with your business. The following is an example of a craftsperson who learned the importance of not overpaying taxes by keeping good records in order to minimize taxes:

There was a weaver living in New York City who was not able to support herself solely by her weaving, although, during the past couple of years, she has begun to sell more work. Only in the past two years has she come to recognize the importance of keeping the receipts and canceled checks of her craftrelated expenses. She consulted an accountant and learned how critical it is to pay all her major expenses and deposit her income through a separate checking account as well as to generate financial reports to review her situation. In the past, she had taken no deductions whatsoever for the considerable expenses she incurred as a craftsperson, so she had paid more in taxes than she should have. She now regularly uses an accountant to help with her income taxes. She claims that not only is the accountant's fee far less than the amount she saves in taxes, it is also tax deductible.

Have you missed some business calls that you might have made from your home phone? Do you get receipts for tolls, parking costs, and other small expenditures? Are any of your subscriptions or book purchases useful in your work? Did you take any courses? How about local travel such as to the post office or the bank? Without maintaining a small logbook or keeping receipts (noting on them what you bought), it is easy to forget about the mileage for all those trips to the post office as well as the items you bought with cash when you forgot your business checkbook. Keeping good records will enable you to get all the deductions to which you are entitled.

Whether you are meeting with your accountant or are doing your own tax returns, prepare summaries of your information for easy access. If you have Quicken, print out a transaction report, or if you are using the one-write system, pull out your ledger sheets including the summary sheet. If you forget something or your accountant requests further information, send what is asked for and nothing else as soon as possible.

Tax Forms

As a self-employed craftsperson, the Internal Revenue Service (IRS) is asking you to be your own employer and withhold wages to be paid as taxes as if you were employed by someone else. In addition to filing Form 1040: U.S. Individual Income Tax Return, as a self-employed person, you will need to file the following forms with the IRS:

- *Schedule C: Profit (or loss) from business or profession.* Schedule C is used to itemize your business expenses and includes the income from your business.
- *Form ES for your self-employment taxes.* According to the law, anyone who earns more than $500 not subject to withholding tax must file Form 1040 ES. Form ES consists of an estimated tax worksheet and four declaration vouchers. The first declaration voucher reports the amount you think you'll owe in taxes for the current year and may be paid in full or in installments. Or, if you are unable to estimate your taxes, you can simply pay installments in an amount equal to 100 percent of the taxes you had paid by January 15 of the previous year. Even if this amount falls below the taxes you actually owe, the IRS will not penalize you. Of course, you would have to make up the difference when you submit your return on April 15.
- *Form SE for social security withholding.* This allows you to contribute toward social security, also known as FICA.

Tax Audits

There is no way of being sure that your federal income tax return won't be audited. Some returns are pulled out by random selection, others are chosen by IRS computers because medical expenses, contributions, or property taxes represent an unusually high percentage of the taxpayer's income, the figures on the return do not agree with other information received by the IRS, or because of tips provided by tax informants.

If you receive notice that you are going to be audited, gather all your records for the period specified and meet with your accountant. If the IRS can show that you did not pay the right amount of taxes, you will be billed for that amount plus interest and possibly penalties.

Sales Tax

Another type of tax you may have to pay is sales tax to the state for sales of your work directly to retail customers. When you sell your work wholesale to buyers who will resell the work, they do not pay sales tax because the customer will pay the tax and it would be taxing the item twice.

Call your state department of taxation for information and forms. You will be assigned a resale number and will be required to pay either monthly, quarterly, or annually, depending on your sales volume. If you sell your work at fairs or shows out of state, you are also required by law to obtain a resale number from that state if it has a sales tax.

A resale number will also allow you to buy supplies for your work without paying the sales tax. Again, according to law, sales tax can only be charged once. Just show the clerk your resale number and you will not be charged sales tax for materials to make your work.

Credit and Collection

Someone wants to buy your work but asks if he or she can be billed instead of paying you right now? To whom do you extend credit, what do you do if the person doesn't pay you in a timely manner, or never pays you at all?

It is challenging enough to make sales without worrying about collection problems. However, not everyone will pay before receiving the work so you need to have policies in place to prevent collection problems. The general rule when making a sale is that payment is due upon delivery of the item being sold unless an arrangement has been made between the buyer and the seller that would allow the purchaser to delay payment. For example, a buyer places an order and expects to be sent an invoice.

When you are making sales directly to customers such as at a craft fair, payment is generally due at the time the customer purchases the piece. What forms of payment will you accept? What do you do if someone writes a check and the check bounces, or charges the purchase on a credit card and the card is refused for authorization? What do you do when a buyer wants to be billed for a purchase and then you never receive the payment?

If someone wants to write a check, make sure the person's telephone number is on the check and ask for two pieces of identification—one with a photo. Compare the signature on the check with the signature on the ID and do not take checks for more than the sales amount or cash a third-party check. Your policy on checks should be posted. For example, do you charge a fee if a customer's check bounces? You are a craftsperson selling your work—not a bank. Even when you have taken all these precautions, there is still the possibility that a check will bounce.

If someone wants to charge a purchase on a credit card, call for the authorization right away. Purchase a system that allows you to check the card before the customer leaves. With the authorization code in place, you are guaranteed payment even if the person stole the card or has reached his or her spending limit.

If someone asks to be billed for a purchase, hold the work until the buyer can pay for it. Ask for a deposit up front and the balance later. What if the person changes his or her mind and you miss another sale because you are holding the piece for them?

What about when you sell work to a wholesale buyer? If you sell your work through a shop on consignment, you will not be paid until the piece is sold. Or perhaps your work has been bought by a buyer who wants to be given an invoice payable in thirty days. What do you do if payment isn't received in a reasonable period of time?

Before you offer to send someone an invoice, you should ask the buyer to supply three references, perhaps from a bank and suppliers or other craftspeople. Contact the three references to do a credit check before you ship the work. Tell the buyer that it is your policy to send work COD the first time a shop places an order and that you can set up a Net 30 account for subsequent orders. Consider offering a cash discount to give buyers an incentive to send their payment early. If it is a large order or they are going to order with you over a period of time, they may be interested in saving even 2 percent of the overall order.

If the payment is late, charge interest or penalties. If you do decide to charge interest for late payments, remember to note this on all correspondence including the invoice so that the buyer knows up front. I always suggest that before you send late charges or start some sort of legal proceedings, call and talk to the accounts payable department or the owner to find out what the problem is and see if you can work out a payment plan. If the payment never comes, you can choose to do nothing and write it off as a bad debt, pursue collection, or even initiate a lawsuit. It's up to you.

What do you do if the gallery goes bankrupt? Craftspeople who have work on consignment in a shop or gallery will be among the creditors if that business goes bankrupt. Surprisingly, many craftspeople do nothing when they receive the required notification from the bankruptcy court. Take the time to reply to the request for information from the bankruptcy trustee and to appear at any creditors' meetings. Get together with other craftspeople who are owed money and consider appointing one person to appear at the creditors' meetings as a representative, or pool your resources and hire a lawyer to represent you. Although this will cost some money, if the amount at stake is large, it may be well worth it. If the amount is small, it may not make economic sense to pursue the matter. You will have to decide.

Keeping good, accurate records is vital for the success of your business. Financial reports can help you stay in touch with the health of your business and make the necessary adjustments to keep moving in a forward direction. When tax time comes around, accurate records make it is easy to fill out the required paperwork and not pay any more taxes than you really owe. When it comes to collecting payments from customers and buyers, accurate records and good policies help you stay on top of a situation before it gets lost in the shuffle. Set up systems you will use, and keep them updated so that the task does not become overwhelming. Organize your recordkeeping system to comply with tax keeping requirements and contact your state tax office for resale number. Decide what forms of payment you will accept and set up policies and procedures to help ensure payment, like penalties for late payments and returned checks, and incentives for early payment. Finally, use the information you have! Review your records periodically to help you make important decisions.

CHAPTER 14

INSURANCE

This chapter outlines the basic information essential to making informed decisions about your insurance needs such as health, disability, product liability, or studio and property insurance. Use the questionnaires provided when you call insurance agents for information so that you can select the best insurance choices possible for your health and your business.

Health Insurance

What is health insurance? Health insurance is an agreement between you and an insurance company under which the insurance company agrees to pay for some or all of the costs of healthcare provided. Although the insurance company assumes financial risk in issuing a policy to you because the actual cost of your care may exceed the premium amount, there are many instances in which the company makes a profit because the income from the policy exceeds the cost of care.

The crafts community has known for years that many craftspeople across the United States have no health insurance. Even those who consider health insurance a high priority find the prices so high that they tend to give up on obtaining insurance. They simply can't afford it—along with everything else. To address the need for artists and craftspeople to find affordable insurance, a new organization is being formed called the Artists' Health Insurance Information Center through the National Endowment for the Arts (NEA). The center will offer basic insurance information, information specific to the state you live in, and a series of questions to help you determine what type of coverage you need, through both an Internet site and a toll-free number. Call the NEA for details at (202) 682-5400.

The types of health insurance plans are changing. According to Lenore Janecek in her book *Health Insurance: A Guide for Artists, Consultants, Entrepreneurs, and Other Self-Employed*, in 1984, 96 percent of Americans were covered by comprehensive major-medical fee-for-service plans. By 1991, only 28 percent remained on this type of program. It is estimated that by the year 2000, only 20 percent will be insured in this way. Managed-care plans focus on preventative care, offering comprehensive services while keeping costs low. They also offer lower co-payments, no deductibles if you use their doctors, and lower premiums. These plans are the wave of the future. On average, healthcare costs over $3,000 per year for each person living in the United States, and many patients are unable to pay for their care. About half the country's healthcare spending, or $350 billion, is related to lifestyle factors such as diet, lack of exercise, smoking, and substance abuse. More dollars are spent on treating our illnesses than in helping us prevent them. Through managed care, this situation is changing. Managed care balances the cost and the quality of healthcare.

There are basically two types of health insurance plans: managed-care plans, and traditional major-medical plans. Managed-care plans include preferred provider organizations (PPOs) and health maintenance organizations (HMOs). A major-medical plan offers you the freedom to choose any doctor. When considering a major-medical plan, remember that you will have to pay a deductible before the insurance company pays a percentage of the bill. After the deductible is met, you will pay a percentage of all costs up to a predetermined amount (after which the insurer will pay 100 percent up to a maximum limit).

As a form of managed care, PPOs provide discounted services to receive more patients. If you use doctors within the network, you will receive greater benefits than if you choose to have services provided by doctors outside the network. You can still choose your doctor, but will be rewarded by getting better benefits or a higher percentage of coverage if you use those doctors in the network.

Another form of managed care, HMOs offer comprehensive preventative care. However, you must use HMO doctors and hospitals if you want your insurance to cover the costs. You must select a primary-care doctor— from a list of participating physicians—who will provide your basic medical care. They can also makes referrals to other doctors if the need arises.

There are two HMO models to choose from: a staff model (where you visit doctors at a centrally located health center) or visiting a doctor in private practice who receives a monthly payment from the HMO. There are no maximum benefit limits with an HMO.

How can you find health insurance? Call your local craft organization to see if they offer a policy for their members. If not, call the Visual Artists Info Hotline at (800) 232-2789, to be sent a list of organizations that offer group health insurance plans to artists and craftspeople. For example, members of the American Craft Council are eligible for group health insurance. In addition, you can call local insurance agencies for information on plans such as Blue Cross and Blue Shield. I recommend that you call at least three insurance agencies and ask the following questions so you can make an informed decision about which company to use.

Questions for Insurance Agencies Concerning Health Insurance

Company Name _____

Contact Person _____

Telephone _____

Type of plan: ☐ Major Medical ☐ Preferred Provider ☐ HMO

What is the lifetime coverage amount?

What is the out-of-pocket maximum that I will have to pay?

What are my choices for deductibles?

Is there a waiting period before an illness is covered?

Can I choose my own physician and hospital?

What percentage does the policy pay for hospital services? Medical and surgical?
   Emergency care?

Do I need approval before I have a procedure done in order to be covered?

Are routine exams and physicals covered?

Are prescription drugs covered?

What about coverage for mental health expenses such as counseling?

What about coverage for maternity costs?

Rate quoted = $_____ with $_____ deductible.

Notes _____

   _____

   _____

   _____

Disability Insurance

If you lose the ability to earn your living from making and selling your craft due to a long illness or an accident, what will happen to everything you have worked so hard to attain? Disability insurance policies offer coverage to help you in case you can no longer work. The policies are based on the amount of income you need to replace, the length of time you will need the income, and your occupation or the type of duties you perform on a daily basis. Although an insurance company will offer you disability benefits between 60 and 70 percent of your annual income, because you are a self-employed craftsperson, it will require financial records from your business to determine your yearly income.

When applying for benefits, you should consider the elimination period (the amount of time you have to wait until your benefits are paid) and the benefit period (how long the benefits are paid to you). Other important factors are the amount of your monthly payment, your age, and whether or not you are a smoker.

Social security disability insurance is available if you have a condition that has prevented you from working for the past year and the condition will make you permanently disabled. Call the Social Security Administration at (800) 772-1213 for information.

Product Liability Insurance

Product liability insurance offers protection when a product that you produce injures someone. For example, if a chair you made breaks when someone sits in it and the person is injured, your product liability insurance comes into effect. Check with your insurance agent to make sure that this is included in your business insurance policy. In general, approximately $100,000 of liability insurance will cost $100 annually.

According to Leonard DuBoff in *The Law (in Plain English)*® *for Crafts,* in every product liability case, the plaintiff must prove that: (1) some injury occurred, (2) the injury was caused by some defect in the product, and (3) the defect was present in the product when the maker had control over it. Once individuals obtain your product, you will not be able to stop them from injuring themselves, but you can make sure that any item that leaves your studio does not contain a defect.

What should you do to prevent injuries to people who buy and use your products? To prevent mechanical defects, you need to test your products, record the results, keep records of the materials you have purchased to make the products, and devise some way to check any premanufactured parts. Although courts tend to apply common sense criteria regarding design defects, you should make yourself aware of consumer protection laws to make sure the design of your piece is not in violation of these laws.

On- and Off-Site Coverage: Property and Studio Insurance

Most insurance companies have a form of studio insurance that provides protection for the physical structure of the studio as well as for the equipment, materials, and work in the studio. Many craftspeople do not carry insurance coverage because they can't afford the premiums, have been turned down by local agents for working in an older building, or work with flammable or costly materials. Affordable insurance policies are available to safeguard your property and studios for as little as $250 annually for basic coverage. Insurance may seem like a luxury when you are looking at your checkbook balance, but you really should view it as a necessity.

You may be thinking that your homeowner's insurance policy will cover your studio since it is located in your home. Call your insurance agent right now to determine if this is true before something happens and you find out differently. Although homeowner's insurance will often cover all your insurance needs if you consider yourself a hobbyist, that may change as soon as you begin selling your crafts and making a profit. Once you start selling, your work now has provable value and should be insured for loss. In addition, if you make sales from your studio, you need to be insured in case people injure themselves on your property.

A copy of your insurance policy, records of sales, an inventory list of pieces with values, backup disks for computers, and slides, photographs, or videos would be best stored off-site. Even with a good insurance policy, the burden of proof will be yours regarding the value of any items on a claim you submit.

The Crafts Emergency Relief Fund (CERF)

Although it should not be viewed as a replacement to having adequate insurance coverage, the Crafts Emergency Relief Fund (CERF) offers no-interest loans of $2,000 and more to professional craftspeople devastated by a catastrophic event such as a fire, flood, or earthquake. CERF also offers discounts on supplies and equipment as well as fee waivers for booth spaces at participating shows. For more information, contact CERF at P.O. Box 838, Montpelier, VT 05601; (802) 229-2306; *www.craftemergency.org*.

I recommend that you call at least three insurance agencies to ask the following questions so you can make an informed decision about which agency to use.

Questions Concerning Property and Studio Insurance

Company Name _____

Contact Person _____

Telephone _____

What are your policy rates?

How often do you expect them to increase?

What is the deductible amount that I would pay before my policy would pay for losses?

What would be protected under a basic policy?

What things should I add to a basic policy to cover my specifc needs?

Does the policy cover replacement costs or fair market value?

If someone gets hurt while making, selling, or handling my work, would I be protected from liability? What are the liability limits?

Does the policy cover transporting goods or items displayed on a consignment basis or in an exhibition or craft fair?

What kind of records should I be keeping in case I need to submit a claim?

Can you send me some information?

Rate quoted = $_____ minus $_____ deductible.

Notes _____

_____

_____

Although many craftspeople do not currently maintain insurance covering health, disability, product liability, and studio and property, you would be wise to call today for quotes and sign up for the appropriate policies. Every couple years, get new quotes to make sure your agency is still competitive. Insurance is a cost of doing business and should be built into your pricing just like rent or wages. An unexpected event such as a fire or theft could wipe you out completely, with very little hope of being able to gather the funds necessary to start over again.

CHAPTER 15

EMPLOYEES

Are you thinking of hiring some help to get ready for a show, to assist with office work, or to fill a large order? Going from working by yourself to having employees is a step that you should consider carefully before you start hiring. Having employees will mean you are now a craftsperson and a supervisor who has pieces to produce, a payroll to meet, people to train and direct, and legal requirements to follow.

One craftsperson told me that it really wasn't worth having employees until there were at least ten. When she had five employees, her business could produce more work but she spent the majority of her time managing the staff. Moving up to ten employees allowed the employees to manage themselves and the owner to get back into the studio. Another craftsperson said she had grown her business to the point where she had two showrooms and several employees. She had become a manager instead of a craftsperson. When we sat down to review her status, we found out that she wasn't making any more money with several employees than she had with just one. Although she had enjoyed the recognition of increasing her business, she decided to gradually scale back her business to just one showroom and one employee to simplify her life.

Subcontractors versus Employees

Before you decide to take on the responsibility of hiring employees, consider hiring subcontractors to get the help you need until you are ready to start hiring employees.

Although you are running your own business, you don't have to do everything yourself, even if you can't afford to hire full- or part-time employees. Most of your time-consuming tasks can be done by outside help on a project-by-project basis, such as bookkeeping, public relations, filing, mailing list management, newsletter preparation, and housecleaning.

Although people frequently tell me they can't afford to hire outside help, sometimes you will actually save money by hiring someone else rather than trying to do everything yourself. I know that when you are starting a business, you may have more time than money to spend on hiring help—but in the long run, subcontracting could save you time *and* money.

You may find that you work more productively if you take time off, let other people handle some of the routine matters of running of your business, concentrate on the parts that require your input or skills, and not drive yourself crazy working night and day doing things that you could have delegated. Can you afford not to hire the help you need?

Subcontractors or independent contractors are people you hire to work for you on an as-needed basis. Although you pay them for their work, they remain their own bosses. If you occasionally give some of your work to another craftsperson to sell on consignment at a craft fair or hire an accountant to go over your records, they are independent contractors, not your employees. When you use a subcontractor, you do not have to pay social security taxes, withhold income taxes, or observe other rules that you would if they were your employees.

When you hire subcontractors to help you with your business, you need to discuss their fees as well as what materials or directions they will need from you to do their assigned duties. A timeline for completing the work should be agreed upon and to prevent misunderstandings, put your agreement in writing.

Employees are people you hire to work for you on a regular basis, whether full- or part-time, year-round, or seasonally. You pay employees hourly wages or a salary and withhold taxes including social security. Employees can be terminated by you or can give you notice at any time. You might hire an employee to help you produce work in the studio, make sales in the showroom, accompany you to shows, or to be your office manager.

Hiring employees is a very important decision that will not only affect your work environment but the way your business is viewed by your customers and your other employees. Although you can train employees in methods and procedures, there are some things you can't teach them. You should recognize that sometimes you will make a poor hiring decision and will need to let someone go. To prevent this, you should do some simple planning before making a job offer. Think about the type of skills, duties, and responsibilities required for each position you wish to fill and based on these needs, write a job description. Use the job description to draw up a list of interview questions to ask each potential candidate.

There are certain questions that you should not ask someone in an interview situation, such as the person's age, marital status, or religion—these questions could be considered discriminatory. You can ask questions about prior work experience, why the person is interested in working in your business, why they left their last job, and to provide references. A good candidate should have questions for you as well. If you are interested in a candidate, call his or her references *before* you make a job offer.

If you have never interviewed anyone before, remember that most people tend to be nervous when they are being interviewed for a new job and, as the interviewer, you need do what you can to make them feel comfortable. This is also their chance to check out you and your business. Put some effort into conveying an honest depiction of the position and the current state of your business.

It's up to you if you want to discuss the wage or salary range before, during, or after the interview. It can save valuable time for everyone if the potential candidates know this information up front because if someone will choose not to work for the amount you are offering, then why should you both spend the time in an interview?

When you are ready to offer someone a job, make the offer over the phone or in person, explain their duties and responsibilities again, and outline the salary as well as any benefits you offer. Be prepared for the fact that the person may want to think about the offer or discuss it with someone else overnight. Establish when you want him or her to start. If the person accepts the job, put the offer in writing in a simple letter and keep a copy for his or her personnel file.

What if you do a search and don't come up with any good candidates for the job? Should you advertise again? Make some phone calls to generate some referrals? Perhaps there is someone in a similar job that may be interested in making a lateral move to work for you or who is in a junior position that is interested in a step up the career ladder? Use your contacts to help you get the word out about job opportunities.

In addition to doing interviews when you hire new employees, I suggest that you do exit interviews when employees leave. This gives you an opportunity to get their suggestions for ways to improve the position and business. They may be willing to return to help with training their replacements if you think this would be helpful.

For easy reference, make a simple form (such as the one that follows) to keep in each employee's personnel file to keep track of who to call in case of an emergency, annual reviews, and days off, for example.

Employee File Form

Name _____

Address _____

Telephone _____

In case of an emergency, contact:

NAME	TELEPHONE	RELATIONSHIP

1. _____

2. _____

Social Security # _____

Job Title _____

Job Description _____

_____

_____

Date Hired _____	Starting Wage or Salary: $ _____
Review Date _____	Wage or Salary Increase: $ _____
Review Date _____	Wage or Salary Increase: $ _____
Review Date _____	Wage or Salary Increase: $ _____
Review Date _____	Wage or Salary Increase: $ _____
Benefts _____	

_____

Vacation Days	EARNED	TAKEN	REMAINING
Year 1	_____	_____	_____
2	_____	_____	_____
3	_____	_____	_____
4	_____	_____	_____
5	_____	_____	_____

Policies

Once you have hired an employee, you will need to be familiar with general employee practices as well as those particular to your business. What policies should be in place for employees and supervisors? How will you evaluate an employee's performance if there isn't a job description? Will employees know what they should do if there is a problem with another employee or with

Sick Days	EARNED	TAKEN	REMAINING
Year 1			
2			
3			
4			
5			

Personal Days	EARNED	TAKEN	REMAINING
Year 1			
2			
3			
4			
5			

Exit Interview   Date _____

Reason for Leaving _____

Suggestions _____

Available for Training Replacement? _____

Notes _____

_____

_____

_____

_____

_____

_____

_____

you? How are raises determined? These things and more should be spelled out in a simple and straightforward handbook or personnel manual. It doesn't have to be fancy—a few typewritten pages will do just fine. All your employees should be given a copy and each of them should sign a simple form stating that he or she has read the manual and understands it. Put this signed form in the employee's personnel file.

I recommend including job descriptions for every position (including your own) and an organizational chart (if size warrants) in your handbook. A company handbook should include the following:

- An equal opportunity statement
- Basic policies regarding employment such as hiring procedures, probationary period, and types of employment (e.g., part- or full-time)
- Working hours and policies such as flexible time, overtime, and taking time off
- Salary and wage information such as paydays, overtime, and deductions
- Employee benefits such as vacations, holidays, sick days, personal days, maternity or paternity leave, leave of absence, and discount policy, if applicable
- Insurance such as medical, life, disability, unemployment, and workers' compensation
- General policies such as telephone use, travel, smoking, dress code (if there is one), safety rules, use of equipment, breaks and lunch hours
- Performance and salary reviews
- Problems such as grievance procedures and warnings
- Resignation, retirement, and termination policies

Wages and Benefits

There are many reasons why people stay with an employer over a period of time. The most obvious reasons, of course, are because they enjoy the work and/or they are satisfied with the wages and benefits. Other factors can also be important.

When you write a job description for each position in your business, you should not only assign an hourly wage or salary, but a range as well. For example, if you are hiring an office manager at a starting salary of $10 per hour or $20,000 per year, what will you pay this person after a favorable first annual review? Or in five years if the person is still working for you? You need to establish a wage range for each position in the beginning so that wages are fairly distributed and you can plan ahead when budgeting.

In terms of raises, there are cost-of-living increases as well as merit increases. A cost-of-living increase in usually based on a percentage such as the rate of inflation or perhaps 4 percent. A merit increase is based on how well someone does his or her job and how much it is worth to you.

The job market is very competitive these days and treating your employees well is an important task for an employer who wants to retain them. It's not what you can afford to pay your employees, but what you can offer them in addition to wages or a salary that will provide incentives to reward and keep valuable employees. Think about the costs incurred when someone leaves your business in terms of not only the actual costs of advertising, but the time spent hiring, training a new employee, as well as the loss of productivity.

In an article titled "Compensation for Today's Employees" in the October 1997 issue of the *Crafts Report*, Bill Pearson states that creative, nonmonetary compensation, or "psychic income" has become very visible in the personnel marketplace. These techniques can give you a meaningful edge in hiring and retaining employees. In addition to a competitive salary, Bill suggests you consider the following ideas:

- Medical insurance
- Health club membership
- Paid parking
- Higher employee discount
- One three-day weekend each month
- Market trips twice a year
- A gift certificate for a manicure or pedicure
- An extra vacation day
- Theater or movie tickets
- Gift certificate for a tape or CD
- A gift certificate for ten cappuccinos
- A monthly lunch with a guest

Whether this list is more or less than what you are doing is not the issue. Excluding the health insurance, the value of these "perks" is far greater than their cost. Today's employees respect and appreciate this type of creative compensation. Loyalty, after all, should be mutual. Put your creativity to work to come up with some benefits that you can offer your employees to reward them and to retain them.

Supervisory Skills

Very few people are taught how to be good supervisors. Usually, someone is doing a good job, his or her boss leaves, the person is promoted, and voilà!— he or she becomes a supervisor. Not only do supervisors need to be aware of the policies and procedures outlined in your handbook, but they must de- velop a method of training, communicating effectively with their employees and evaluating their progress.

If you want to develop a loyal, hard-working staff, you should set an example by being a positive role model. Let your employees know that you are always available for questions and suggestions and make it clear that good performance will be rewarded whenever possible. Saying thank you for a job well done lets your employees know that you appreciate them. Even a quick handwritten note speaks volumes to your employees. Remember, mom was right: be nice and say thank you. It's important and employees value it.

What should you do if a problem arises with an employee? Consider adopting the following procedure:

1. Talk with the person as soon as you become aware of the problem.
2. If necessary, give him or her a verbal warning with a timeline for correcting the problem.
3. If the problem persists, give the person a written warning with an- other timeline.
4. If it is not corrected by the end of the written time period, you may want to consider giving them an extension or even firing them if the problem is serious enough.

A good supervisor lets employees know when there is a problem, works with them to find a solution, gives them several chances to correct the prob- lem, and decides what to do if they don't remedy the situation. You are now the boss.

For example, say an employee is chronically late. You might first remind him or her of the scheduled hours and ask if they have a problem adhering to those hours. It may turn out that a slightly different schedule is needed because, for example, the person needs to wait until his or her children are on a school bus. If you can, revise the employee's schedule. If you cannot afford to do so, tell the person that it is a problem for you if he or she is not at work on time and to make other arrangements for their children and the bus. If the problem is not corrected within the agreed-upon time frame, give them a written warning with the time they are being given to solve it. If the problem is still not corrected, you may want to consider terminating their employment. Although firing someone can be upsetting, it may be the lesser of two evils if you keep a problem employee.

As the supervisor, you are responsible for scheduling an annual review time for your employees when you sit down with each one individually to review his or her performance and salary. Use the person's job description as a starting place and go over his or her performance item by item. Note areas that need improvement as well as those that have been done well. Ask the person for feedback. Rate your employees on things such as how well they understand their job, their productivity, quality of work, attendance, and creativity. If an employee's duties have changed, maybe his or her job description needs to be revised. This is also the time to discuss either a cost-of-living increase or raise.

On a simple review form, note the employee's suggestions and feedback, insert comments, and sign it. Have the employee sign it as well and give him or her a copy. Keep the original in the person's personnel file. This creates a record for future reviews as well as a means to refresh your memory later on if you should be called for a recommendation after they leave.

Legal Requirements

There are other issues you should consider when hiring an employee that fall into the realm of accounting or bookkeeping responsibilities. Consult with your accountant regarding the following:

- *Workers' Compensation* This is a policy for your employees in the event of an on-the-job injury. State laws vary on the minimum number of employees an employer must have before obtaining a workers' compensation policy. Find out the requirements in your state.
- *Withholding Federal, State, and Local Taxes* Here, too, the laws vary, and you will need to find out what is required in your area.
- *Social Security* (FICA) Contact your local Social Security office to determine what the requirements are for your business.
- *Federal and State Unemployment Insurance* This includes certain requirements for subcontractors.
- *Health and Safety* You should know both the federal and state regulations for your business and your obligations to your employees.
- *Municipal Taxes*

- *Employee Benefits* Examples of these are insurance coverage (medical, dental, legal), parking, and retirements benefits.
- *Union Requirements* You or your employees may be subject to union contracts.
- *Wage and Hour Laws* Make sure you know the federal and state laws concerning payment of your employees, including minimum wage and overtime requirements. In some states, the law regulates with-holding and vacation requirements, as well as the method of paying employees during employment and upon termination.

As already noted above, the requirements of these laws may vary dramatically from state to state, and you should discuss them with your accountant.

When you hire someone to help you, you have entered a whole new phase in your business. The moment you become an employer, you assume responsibility for meeting a payroll; payment of social security, workers' compensation, and unemployment insurance; collecting and paying withholding taxes; the payment of time off (e.g., holidays and vacations); and a variety of other managerial functions—not to mention the added paperwork. All this is worth the effort, of course, if what your employees produce is worth more than what you pay them in wages and fringe benefits. After all, you have hired your employees to help you make a better profit.

CHAPTER 16

RETIREMENT PLANNING

Do you want to retire? Are you willing to do the necessary steps to ensure that you will be able to choose the kind of lifestyle you live as you grow older? You will need to plan your investments now to maximize returns later and be able to supplement your income if necessary. You will want to prepare your estate to benefit those people and places that you care about after you die.

Some craftspeople don't plan on retiring, others want to achieve financial independence in midlife, while still others plan to have a small retirement income supplemented by selling their crafts part-time. Although there are plenty of good role models of craftspeople who are in their eighties and older who still work in their studios every day and continue to sell their work, retirement isn't always a voluntary decision. A medical reason or some other unforeseen event can force you to stop working before you are ready. Being self-employed also means that you won't have any investment income when you retire unless you have planned for it.

The time to begin planning for your retirement is now. The example below is calculated based on your saving $200 per month at a 9 percent annual rate of return for either a twenty-, thirty-, or forty-year period:

LENGTH OF TIME	ACTUAL MONEY SAVED	W/ COMPOUNDED INTEREST	DIFFERENCE
20 years	$48,000	$133,577	$85,577
30 years	$72,000	$366,149	$294,149
40 years	$96,000	$936,264	$840,264

As you can see in this example, although you would have saved twice the amount of money at forty years than you would have in twenty years, the amount of return would be almost ten times as much. The sooner you begin to invest, the more money you will have when you reach retirement age.

Lifestyle Issues

What does being retired mean to you? Are you looking forward to not having to work? Do you want to travel more or less than you are now? Will you sell your city place and move to your country house full-time or vice versa? Is this a chance to give back to the community and do volunteer work or become a mentor? Or do you want to continue at the same pace at which you are currently working? Now that you may have the opportunity to fill your days any way you please, what do you really want to do?

Figuring out the lifestyle you want to have in retirement will determine how much you need to save today. Instead of thinking of this as retirement, why not look at it as achieving financial independence, a chance to do some of the other things you have always wanted, or perhaps make crafts that you don't have to be concerned with selling. Financial independence is defined as having enough money to support your lifestyle and living expenses without having to earn money other than the earnings from investments.

Supplementing Your Income

Do you have enough money invested to be comfortable in your retirement or do you need to supplement your income? How do you know if you will have enough money? You need to figure what your income needs for retirement are and what financial sources of income you may already have in place. Calculating your monthly income during retirement means starting with the income you're earning now and making adjustments for the changes in your spending habits after you retire. For example, if you are currently spending $500 a month on a mortgage that will be paid off by the time you retire at age sixty, your expenses for your residence will drop $500 a month. However, if you are also planning to travel more once you are retired, then your expenses for travel will increase.

Try filling out the following cost comparison chart. Then, compare your needs in retirement with your projected income in the next section on investment planning.

Cost Comparison Chart for Personal Expenses
Current Needs versus Retirement

ITEM	NOW	RETIREMENT
Rent/Mortgage	$ _____	$ _____
Taxes	$ _____	$ _____
Utilities	$ _____	$ _____
Food/Dining Out	$ _____	$ _____
Insurance	$ _____	$ _____
Retirement Savings	$ _____	$ _____
Telephone	$ _____	$ _____
Vacation/Travel	$ _____	$ _____
Car/Transportation	$ _____	$ _____
Entertainment	$ _____	$ _____
Education	$ _____	$ _____
Hobbies or Sports	$ _____	$ _____
Debt Payments	$ _____	$ _____
Miscellaneous	$ _____	$ _____
Monthly Need	$ _____	$ _____

Investment Planning

Diversification in your investment planning guards your finances against being wiped out by a single investment going sour and protects you against fluctuations in the economy. It also allows you to take some calculated risks without endangering your overall financial plan.

When planning your investments, consider how readily they can be converted into cash if the need arises. A savings account is easy—just take the money out of the bank. A stock may increase or decrease in value and you may not be able to sell when you want to without taking a loss, but it is still considered relatively liquid. Used equipment may be difficult to convert into cash, and property can take time to sell. As a result, it's important to have a balance between investments that can be easily converted into cash as well as those that may take a little longer to convert into cash should the need arise.

If you have already been investing your savings for your retirement and want to project the value for your retirement:

1. Add up the current value of your savings $ _____
2. Multiply by a reasonable rate of interest (8 or 9 percent) $ _____
3. Divide by 12 $ _____

This is how much your current investments may be able to contribute toward your monthly retirement need. If your potential investment and savings income is not as much as your monthly need total in the cost comparison chart, you may have to rethink your investment plan or scale down your needs. If your potential income is higher than your monthly need, you may want to start planning some extras!

Income from Investments for Retirement

ITEM	ANNUAL INCOME	MONTHLY INCOME
Social Security	$ _____	$ _____
IRA	$ _____	$ _____
Keogh or SEP	$ _____	$ _____
Investments	$ _____	$ _____
Annuities	$ _____	$ _____
Rentals	$ _____	$ _____
Other	$ _____	$ _____
	$ _____	$ _____
Total Income	$ _____	$ _____

Now compare your projected monthly expense needs in the cost comparison chart with your monthly projected income in the income from investments chart and see if there is either a positive or negative difference. If there is a negative difference, you need to cut your expenses, figure out a way to save more money, or plan to supplement your income in some way. Could you still run your business part-time? Work for somebody else part-time? Rent out your studio? Sell your house and move to a smaller place?

There are different types of investments: annuities, individual retirement accounts (IRAs), Keogh and SEP plans, mutual funds, the stock market, bonds, certificates of deposit (CDs), as well as tangible items that you can sell or collect ongoing income from, such as antiques or real estate rentals.

Tax annuity plans offer a way to help accumulate money that will provide you with income for a certain period of time or even for the rest of your life. Although there are several different types of annuities, the most common for retirement planning purposes is called a deferred annuity, which allows you to have tax-deferred growth over a period of time. You can choose to receive the money in one lump sum or as monthly income, either for a specified amount of time or for the rest of your life.

Individual retirement accounts (IRAs) were created in 1975 by the federal government to help people save for retirement. An IRA is a retirement account to which up to $2,000 may be contributed annually and the investments accumulate tax free until withdrawn. You must keep your money in an IRA account until age fifty-nine and a half or pay a penalty plus income tax. In addition, you must begin to receive money by age seventy and a half.

According to Jack Brill and Alan Reder in their book *Investing from the Heart*, any company or self-employed person (including the part-time self-employed) may set up something called a money-purchase or profit-sharing plan (formerly known as a Keogh plan), or a combination of these plans.

Under a money-purchase plan, you can set aside up to 25 percent of earnings, up to a limit of $30,000 annually per participant. You inform the IRS of the level you choose, and the plan stays at that level until you specify a change. The catch here is that once you have initiated a money-purchase plan, you must fund it every year thereafter.

Profit-sharing plans, conversely, can be funded or not after the first year, entirely at your choice. However, the set-aside range is less than for money-purchase plans—up to 15 percent of profit; the maximum per participant still being $30,000. You can change the percentage level of a profit-sharing plan without notifying the IRS, so there is less administrative overhead cost than with a money-purchase plan.

Some companies or self-employed individuals choose a third option: a combination money-purchase/profit-sharing plan. Set-asides in this arrangement are limited to a maximum of 25 percent of the earnings or $30,000 per participant, whichever is less. The maximum set-aside for the profit-sharing side of the plan is still 15 percent of profits. Thus, 10 percent money-purchase/15 percent profit-sharing is a popular combination.

Another option recommended to serve the needs of self-employed persons (including the part-time self-employed who report self-employment income to the IRS) as well as owners and employees of small companies is an SEP IRA. As a self-employed person or small business owner, you may set aside about 15 percent of profit for a SEP IRA according to a formula. You are allowed to set aside profits one year and not the next. For example, if you don't have business profits the year after you begin your plan, you do not have to set aside any money in your account that year or contribute to employee accounts. A maximum of $30,000 can be set aside in any SEP IRA participant's (employer or employee) account.

If you are interested in buying mutual funds, stocks, or bonds, you can go through a financial planner or stock broker, or sign up with a discount broker such as Charles Schwab to make your own investment decisions. Whatever you do, consult your investment advisor or accountant for more information.

Estate Planning

There are different opinions about how to plan your estate. Some people want to leave a legacy while others follow a new philosophy of going to the grave penniless—that is, giving away all their assets while they are still alive.

In an article called "Estate Planning for Artists" in the August 1997 issue of the *Crafts Report*, Robert Louis explains that estate planning is simply a process by which people determine what will happen to their property after they are gone, and attempt to minimize the "bite" of taxes imposed by the federal and state governments. Some people avoid preparing wills because it makes them think of unpleasant (but inevitable) events. The same people insure their homes against fire and their cars against accidents. Some people say, "I'll let my kids worry about it. They can pay the taxes. I won't be around anyway." These people are placing a needless burden on their children and making an often avoidable payment of taxes to federal and state governments. Estate planning also concerns providing for disability or incapacity, or for problems arising from serious illness. Planning how to accumulate and maximize wealth is a lifelong process, and it's important to consider how to pass it on at appropriate times and at the lowest possible tax cost.

To figure out what your estate is worth and how much will be taxable at both the federal and state levels, total all your assets including real estate, investments, life insurance policies, as well as the value of your art or craft work. This process is similar to doing a balance sheet for your business, but with your personal property and finances included as well. Then subtract any debts that will persist, such as mortgages or funeral expenses. For federal taxes, subtract the $600,000 exemption allowed by law. Whatever is left over will be taxed and payable nine months after your death. In addition, your estate may be subject to a state inheritance tax. This varies by state, so find out what the laws are in your state.

As part of estate planning, you should have a will drawn up that specifies the property and items you want to leave people and organizations, and also names a guardian for your children who are minors. You should also sign a living will stating your wishes should you become terminally ill and are being kept alive by artificial means. Finally, after consulting with your lawyer, you should assign a power of attorney to someone who you wish to act for you if you are unable to handle your own affairs.

If you are a craftsperson and own a collection, you need to get organized by preparing and maintaining detailed information about the work you have created and what has been purchased. You may want to hire an appraiser for this step. Lastly, you should obtain advice on how to dispose of your estate in accordance with your wishes with the best possible tax consequences.

Planning for retirement is up to you. Nobody is going to require you to do it. As a self-employed craftsperson, you must prepare for your retirement needs by looking into savings and investment options and deciding what sort of lifestyle you want to maintain. Figure out how much you need when you are retired (using the cost comparison chart) and compare the amount with your projected savings (using the income from investments chart). Make sure that the types of savings or investments plans you are using fit your needs. Determine what you wish to have done with your belongings at the time of your death and do not put off writing a will and signing a living will. If you have people to whom you intend to leave money or your possessions, you will probably want to handle your affairs in such a way as to make things easier for them.

MARKETING YOUR CRAFTS

CHAPTER 17

MARKETING PLANS

Did you know that creative people tend to make something they like first and then try to find a market for it rather than first finding out what needs exist in the market and then designing a product to fill those needs? Either way, craftspeople who wish to sell their crafts should put together a simple marketing plan. Set aside some time on a regular basis to focus on planning because if you don't, you will always be running after your business rather than being the driving force behind it.

A marketing plan does not have to be a thick official-looking document that takes months to produce and then is filed away. It can be a simple one-page plan or a series of strategies that are a way for you to design the future of your business, take steps to accomplish your goals, and keep track of your progress. A marketing plan is like a mini business plan that focuses on increasing sales. A business plan is a road map for all aspects of your business.

Designing a Marketing Plan

In an article titled "The Doable Marketing Plan" in the winter 1995 issue of the *Art of Self-Promotion,* Ilise Benun asks, How many times have you wanted to create a marketing plan but just didn't take the time to sit down and do it? Or maybe you've started the process but never finished it? The truth is, you don't need to have a plan. It is possible to run, and even grow, your business without one—most people do. However, without a plan, your marketing is probably haphazard, scattered and slipshod. A marketing opportunity pops up—maybe an ad in a special section of the local paper or a trade show you

weren't planning to exhibit at—and you jump at it because you've been meaning to do some marketing. So you create an ad or promo piece to hand out at
your booth. But because everything was done at the last minute, there was no
time to proofread and there are a few typographical errors, or maybe you
forgot to include your phone number. But at least it's done—and you go back
to doing your work and wait for new customers to come knocking on your
door, which could happen, I suppose. That's one option. If, on the other hand,
you had a marketing plan into which you had fit that ad or trade show, you
would have allotted the time necessary for preparation, executed your plan,
and followed through in a methodical way.

A simple marketing plan can help you locate the right craft fair to sell
your work to potential customers, find a shop or gallery to buy or showcase
your work, connect you with an interior designer that uses crafts, or get an
article written about your business. It's up to you to set the goals, break them
down into steps to accomplish them, and then take the time necessary to reach
your objective. Marketing is an ongoing process that permeates all levels of
your business.

At right is a sample marketing plan form you can use to help you get
started.

Sample Marketing Plan

1. What do I want to do?

   *My goal is to locate three craft fairs where I can sell my furniture in the
   Northeast and make sales of approximately $15,000 each or $45,000 total.*

2. What resources will I use to help me?

   *I will buy a guide listing craft fairs, look in magazines such as the Crafts
   Report for ideas, call my local crafts organization for referrals, and ask other
   craftspeople for suggestions.*

3. How will I contact people or places for information?

   *I will make introductory phone calls to show promoters, attend fairs, and do
   follow-up calls with exhibitors. I will research fairs by requesting applications,
   speaking with a show producer on the telephone, attending several craft fairs,
   and calling up exhibitors with questions after the show.*

4. How much time and money can I spend?

   *I can spend three hours every week for the next two months and spend $500
   on books and magazines, phone calls, as well as on travel to visit fairs in my
   region.*

Marketing Plan Form

1. Determine what you want to do by setting a specifc goal.

   Goal: _____

   _____

2. Make a list of potential resources.

   a. _____
   b. _____
   c. _____
   d. _____
   e. _____

3. Figure out how you will contact people or places for information.

   ☐ Telephone calls   ☐ Letters   ☐ Visits

   ☐ Other _____

4. Allocate how much time and money you can spend to accomplish your goal.

   Amount of Time: _____ Daily   _____ Weekly   _____ Monthly

   Amount of Money: $ _____

5. Establish a timeline for accomplishing your goal, preferably in a week-by-week format.

   Week 1 _____
   Week 2 _____
   Week 3 _____
   Week 4 _____
   Week 5 _____
   Week 6 _____
   Week 7 _____
   Week 8 _____

6. Evaluate what you have done and repeat the process.

   _____
   _____
   _____
   _____

5. What are the steps I need to take?

WEEK 1 *Buy crafts fair guidebook and issues of magazines with fair listings.*

WEEK 2 *Call my local crafts organization and other craftspeople for ideas.*

WEEK 3 *Call show producers for applications and deadline information.*

WEEK 4 *Review applications, call with questions, and ask for suggestions.*

WEEK 5 *Visit a fair and speak to exhibitors after the fair.*

WEEK 6 *Visit a fair and speak to exhibitors after the fair.*

WEEK 7 *Visit a fair and speak to exhibitors after the fair.*

WEEK 8 *Submit applications to my top three fair prospects.*

6. *I will do the crafts fairs I am accepted into, evaluate the results, and continue this process until my sales at three fairs meet my marketing goals.*

Measuring Results

Let's say you have completed a marketing plan and executed it. Do you know how well it worked? It is important when you are writing a marketing plan that you not only establish clear and measurable goals, but keep track of the results in order to know if you have been successful.

For example, say you want to locate three craft fairs at which to sell your furniture and make (as in the sample plan above) $45,000, and you located ten fairs and earned $15,000 each—then you have succeeded far beyond your intentions. However, if you found only one fair, you have fallen short of your goal.

A lot of people have trouble making not only initial cold calls on the telephone, but follow-up calls as well. If you are calling to request information or to check on the status of an application you submitted, you can say things like: "I'm interested in finding out about how woodworkers do at your annual craft fair," or "I'd like to check on the status of an application I sent about participating in your annual craft fair."

Remember that what they *say* and what you *hear* may be two different things. The important thing is to discover what they really mean and figure out what you should do next. For example, if you call to check on the status of your application and the person tells you they haven't had a chance to look at it yet, you may feel that they are avoiding you. However, they really may not have had time to look at it yet. Ask the person when a decision will be made and mark your calendar to check with them again at that time.

Marketing plans should be used as simple tools to help you stay focused and can help you measure your success in your efforts to promote and sell your work. Whenever you have an idea, take the time to devise a simple marketing plan. With an idea in writing that you can refer to, the task may not seem quite as overwhelming.

Keep in mind that the lead time for getting business can vary considerably—from several weeks up to several years—depending on the type of business you do, especially if you're working with large companies that must go through layers of decision making. If you need business fast and don't have time to wait for the normal marketing process to unfold, I suggest that you get on the phone and call current customers and buyers, make a special offer, or offer a pricing incentive. You can always do some subcontracting work. Call other craftspeople and offer to do the work they can't get to. These are "emergency measures." If you keep up your ongoing marketing efforts, however, you won't have future emergencies.

CHAPTER 18

YOUR IMAGE ON PAPER

Whether you get new customers through referrals, by having your work seen in a shop or gallery, or as a result of an advertisement, your first contact with potential customers may be on paper rather than in person. An introduction to your business may come in the form of your logo or business card, a letter sent on your stationery, a hangtag attached to a piece, a copy of your brochure, or even your résumé. Your printed materials should consistently reinforce your image. Your crafts have a recognizable style and your image on paper should too.

Whatever format you choose to use to promote your business on paper, remember to ask customers how they heard about you and keep records. You want to know what does and does not work, so that you can get the most response for your time and money.

Logo Design

What is a logo and why do you need one? A logo is a recognizable symbol or image that projects what you do and the quality of your business. A logo helps you to build visual recognition for your products and compliments the name of your business. Used consistently, people will begin to identify your work and style with your logo.

For example, my ArtBiz logo above is very simple, black and white, and uses a positive and negative design. I chose this logo because I want my potential customers to know that although art and business are usually thought of as opposites, they really go side by side.

You will use your logo on all your printed materials. Take the time necessary to get the logo right by using the services of a graphic designer or a printer to help with the design. Just like the name of your business, your logo is an important marketing tool.

Brochures

A brochure is a printed statement that uses information and pictures to help you sell your work. Although the thought of producing a brochure may be overwhelming, keep in mind that someone is interested in your work and wants to know more about it. The great thing about a brochure is that it lets you respond easily to inquiries while communicating consistent information about your work to a potential customer.

Craftspeople put a lot of planning and time into the production of their pieces and need to do the same with their printed materials. While putting together a brochure does not have to take a huge amount of time, it does require planning, writing copy, designing a printed piece, working with a printer, allocating a budget, and deciding how to distribute it. Think of it as another way of presenting your work.

If possible, after you send a brochure, schedule a time to follow up requests with a quick phone call, preferably after a week. Plan to send several mailings for each inquiry you respond to. Decide how many pieces you are willing to send a potential customer before you remove them from your mailing list. Keep track of how many contacts you have with a person about your work before it turns into a sale. Sometimes it may take several contacts with a potential client before he or she is ready to commission or purchase your work. The object here is not to get a big mailing list, but to keep potential customers informed about your work until they have a reason—and are ready—to buy.

How can you communicate your work and the type of image it conveys through the design, typeface, color, and paper used? For example, is your product highly sophisticated or folksy? Would a four-, two-, or one-color brochure be more appropriate? Will handmade or recycled paper convey the proper image? Are you trying to change your image to attract a different market? Make a conscious decision about how to project your unique image on paper through your brochure. Your customers are buying from you, a craftsperson, instead of a large corporation, so be creative and let your unique personality shine through.

If you are new to promoting your work, you may not be sure what your image should be. Look at samples of printed materials used by other craftspeople to see how they present themselves. Decide if the way the competition presents itself is appropriate for you or if you need another approach to differentiate your work from theirs. Put together a couple of sample brochures and get some feedback from other craftspeople. Before completing the brochure worksheet in this chapter, consider the following questions regarding the design of your brochure:

Who are your customers?

Are your customers interior designers? A corporation buying your work for their conference room? Another craftsperson? A homemaker who is redecorating? Or all of the above? Do the customer profile worksheet in chapter 29 to help you figure out the profiles of your potential customers.

When a potential customer sees your brochure, what do you want them to do next?

For example, will the brochure include an order form to make it easy for customers to place an order, generate a phone call for more information, or prompt a visit to your studio? What kind of information would customers need to know in order to buy one or more of your pieces? Do they need a brochure or do they really just need a business card with an address and phone number on it? Try to anticipate your customers' response and design your brochure accordingly.

What kind of budget do you need to spend on your brochure?

Even if you don't have a lot of money to spend on a brochure right now, there are so many ways you can convey quality through simple designs and the use of different papers. One of the most attractive brochures I have seen simply used a bold graphic design on a colored paper with one ink color. It was printed on standard-sized paper to save a cutting charge and was folded as a self-mailer to save on buying and stuffing envelopes.

How many brochures do you need to have printed?

Before you take your brochure to the printer, you need to decide how you will distribute it. Will this be a piece to hand out upon request? Something you will be sending out as a direct mailing? To hand out to anyone who is interested in your work at a craft fair? Or do you just need a few to give to people as a follow-up? Make a list of your marketing plans for the year and estimate the number of brochures you may need so you can have one larger printing done rather than several smaller ones. You will save time and money in the long run if you do this.

Do you need one brochure or should you design several different pieces that go together?

If you have more than one product line, you may want to think about having several printed pieces available to send. For example, if you make furniture and picture frames, or clothing and handbags, you may want to have a different brochure for each product line.

Will you be including visuals such as photographs or drawings?

Visuals help people to remember you and your work. They can be black and white or color, depending on your budget, ink choices, and the work you produce. Include drawings or photographs of you working in your studio as well as your work. See chapter 20 for more information.

What kind of paper, inks, and typeface will you use?

If you want your brochure to double as a self-mailer, you may want to choose a heavier paper. If your work is very colorful, budget enough money to incorporate the same color sense and palette into your brochure. Perhaps you have found a typeface that seems to work well with your image. Remember to make the type large enough to be easily read.

Can you afford to hire a graphic designer, will you work with a printer, or do it yourself?

A graphic designer as well as your printer can help you make decisions about what is possible technically, in addition to what your ideas cost. Many printers have staff to typeset your brochure and help you with its layout and design. I suggest you get three estimates from different designers and printers after checking the quality of their work. Ask to approve the final copy before the piece is printed to avoid costly errors.

What about including prices in your brochure?

Unless you have budgeted to reprint your brochure whenever you change your prices, a separate price page should be designed to be inserted into your brochure. With a separate price page, you are not stuck with a brochure that has last year's prices on it and can change prices easily and inexpensively. Consider having separate retail and wholesale price list inserts if you sell your work to buyers from shops and galleries.

What about using dates in your brochure?

Although it is helpful for buyers who keep brochures and price lists on file, if you use dates in your brochure, it may make it seem obsolete to the reader if you plan to have this brochure last several years. Consider putting a date on the price page.

What should you say in the brochure?

When you write the copy to be used in your brochure, think about what makes your business and products unique. The copy need not be extensive, it just needs to be long enough to adequately describe your work. Save the specifics for your sales pitch or follow-up mailings.

Who are you, why do you do what you do, and who collects or shows your work?

Craftspeople need to educate their buyers by articulating their passion for their work and why their work is different from mass-produced or imported pieces. People want to know where you studied, why you make what you make, and even who else has sold or purchased your work. Your customers are buying not only your creative work, but a story about you as a craftsperson that they can tell when they show your work or give one of your pieces as a gift. Sometimes it is helpful for customers and buyers to see where else you sell your work or a client list. It may impress them to see who else has purchased your work or give them extra confidence that if your work sold in a certain shop, it will sell in their shop as well.

Brochure Alternatives

Do you really need a brochure? Would something else be more appropriate? Postcards, newsletters, and fact sheets are good alternatives as well as complements to a brochure.

Brochure Worksheet

Product Description

_____

_____

_____

Artist's Statement

_____

_____

_____

Biographical Statement

_____

_____

_____

Client List

_____

_____

_____

Testimonials

_____

_____

_____

Photographs

1. Product Shots _____

_____

_____

2. You in Your Studio _____

Contact Information

Logo/Business Name _____

Address _____

Telephone _____

Fax _____

E-mail _____

Web Page _____

Map/Directions

_____

_____

_____

Distribution Plans

_____

_____

_____

Number of Brochures   _____

Type of Paper   _____

Ink Color(s)   _____

Budget $_____

Deadline   _____

Printer Estimates

NAME   TELEPHONE   ESTIMATED PRICE

1. _____

2. _____

3. _____

Additional Information

_____

_____

_____

_____

_____

_____

_____

_____

Postcards

Postcards are a wonderful printed piece to hand out to potential customers, use as a follow-up to send to someone you just met, or announce a show to your current customers. They are relatively inexpensive, can include a four-color image of your work, fit into index file boxes for buyers and curators to store for future reference, can include contact information, and are an instant visual reminder of your work.

There are several good printers around the country who will print five hundred postcards for under $100 if you supply them with a quality slide and the information you want on the back. Try Modern Postcard in California at (800) 959-8365, *www.modernpostcard.com,* for samples and pricing information. Also try calling your local printer for estimates.

Fact Sheets

A fact sheet is usually a simple one-sided, one-page printed piece that tells about your business in a style that is easy and quick to read. In some ways, it is like a résumé for your business instead of a résumé about you. Important information that a fact sheet might offer would include: how long you have been in business, how many clients you have, what regions of the country you sell in, what products you sell, how much they cost, who buys them, and what the function is of your products. You get the idea.

Stationery, Business Cards, and Hangtags

Other methods of putting your image on paper include stationery, envelopes, business cards, and hangtags. When you send an inquiry to a shop or gallery, for example, you will probably be sending a letter printed on your stationery, along with a business card, brochure, résumé, and a sample, if possible, in an envelope or box.

Stationery

Stationery usually includes your logo, business name, address, telephone number, as well as an e-mail and Web page address if applicable. Just as you put thought into your brochures, think about the design of your stationery, the quality of the paper, how many you will need to have printed, and the ink color—each factor is a reflection of your image. Alternatively, you can scan your logo into your computer and use it to print out your letters every time.

Envelopes

The first impression made by your envelope may actually influence whether or not your package is opened or circular filed. Think about a gallery owner, for example, who gets hundreds of inquiries from craftspeople interested in having their work shown at that gallery. They may quickly scan packages to decide whether or not they want to take the time to open them. I actually open my mail next to a wastebasket and it's not unusual for me to throw away unopened mail or quickly scan something to see if I want to follow up or toss it. How can you make your envelope or package stand out so that you can encourage busy people to take the time to open it and look at what's inside?

If you can afford it, consider having envelopes and mailing labels printed to match your stationery—this keeps your image in front of people. Eventually, people who get your mailings may see the logo on the envelope and eagerly open the envelope wondering what you are sending this time.

Business Cards

Business cards come in handy when you meet a prospective customer and are easy to carry with you at all times. After all, you never know when you will need to give someone a business card so he or she can get in touch with you again. Even if your business is listed in the telephone book, how will they get in touch with you when the need arises if they forget your name?

Business cards are usually printed in boxes of five hundred and can be one or more colors. Some people I know practically make their business cards into mini brochures by including photographs, listing the type of work they make, and maps to their studios.

Sometimes, when I later refer to a business card I have been given, I cannot remember if the person was a potter or a weaver or anything about them because the card has only a name and address. You should try to give a clue, such as a sentence to describe your work in addition to your business name and logo. For example, in addition to the name of my business, ArtBiz, my services are listed on my card: business seminars for artists and craftspeople, career counseling, and books for sale. That way, if someone thinks ArtBiz is an artist's studio business, I have taken away the guesswork. Consider putting an extra line or the short version of what you do on your business card to clearly convey your business or product.

Hangtags

Hangtags are the identification tags that are attached to your work when you sell it. Sometimes the information on this tag may be the only thing a customer ever reads about you. Be sure your hangtags include your logo, a sentence about your work, and care instructions for the piece, in a style that reflects your image.

Some people advise that you have two sets of hangtags, one to use when you are selling your work retail and another when you sell your work wholesale. When you sell your work retail from your studio or at a crafts fair, include your address and telephone number. When you sell your work wholesale to a buyer, include your business name but leave off the contact information. Some customers try to bypass the shop or gallery thinking they will get a better deal by contacting the craftsperson directly. If they don't know how to contact you or if you make it a little harder for them by leaving off your contact information, they will not be able to easily do this. This is part of establishing a good relationship with the people who sell your work.

Résumé and Biographical Description

Why do you need a résumé or biographical statement and when would you use one? For most craftspeople, it's a concise way to show someone your background and achievements, whether it's a gallery owner, collector, sales rep, someone reviewing a proposal or grant, or a banker. Write a résumé and a biographical statement before you need it so they are ready when an opportunity presents itself.

If a craftsperson is self-taught and has not had much formal training or recognition in crafts, I usually recommend a biographical statement instead of a résumé. A biographical statement is a way to show how you learned your craft, started running your own business, and began selling your work. In addition, many people will find it interesting to learn of your other career before you started selling your crafts, so don't leave it out because you feel it isn't relevant.

The layout of a résumé or statement is just as important as the content because if people reading it can't find the information quickly, they probably won't take the time to look at it. Use bullets, lots of white space, and an easy-to-read typeface. Too many people try to squeeze in too much information and make the typeface so small that it can be difficult to read.

Make a list of all the jobs you have ever had, the dates you worked there, as well as your education, exhibitions, awards, and publicity. You may want to keep what is called a curriculum vitae: a résumé that lists every job and everything you ever did in chronological order. This way—no matter what the opportunity is—you can easily pull together the pertinent facts to customize your résumé to the purpose it is needed. I have separate sections that I add to my basic résumé depending on what I am applying for, such as listing my exhibitions, courses I have taught, or a list of references.

On the other hand, you can make several résumés for different purposes. For example, I might send a different résumé to a place where I want to teach an ArtBiz business seminar than I would to a gallery where I am trying to get my work exhibited. For the seminar opportunity, I would stress all the places I have taught, while for the gallery, I would still list ArtBiz on my résumé but would emphasize my background as an artist and the other shows I have done.

Don't worry if you don't have a lot of things to put on your résumé yet. As you get your work out there and take advantage of different opportunities, you will eventually have the problem of what to leave off your résumé rather than what to put on it. Proofread your résumé or statement several times to make sure there aren't any mistakes or typographical errors. Try to keep your résumé at a length of one or two pages and include your name, address, and telephone number at the top of each page, in case the pages get separated.

If you choose to write a biographical statement, write it using short, concise paragraphs. You are telling your story. Include how you learned your craft, any workshops you have taken, people you have studied with, shows you have been in, and memberships.

To help you get started, use the applicable categories listed below. Try presenting them in different sequences until you are happy with the results.

- *Education* List any degrees earned, schools attended, or workshops taken, and include the names of your teachers. If you have a degree in English but are a self-taught weaver, state that here. If you just graduated from craft school, you probably should consider listing this category first on your résumé.

- *Employment History* List any jobs you have had that pertain to the opportunity you are going after as well as other positions. You should include dates, your job title, and name of the business. Consider putting your jobs in categories like Craft-Related Positions and Other Positions, if it makes sense. List your duties and responsibilities plus any achievements. If you are applying for a bank loan to start your own business and you worked for another craftsperson or small business, you should list the experience prominently or mention it in your cover letter.

- *Exhibitions* Use this section if you have been in group shows or have had any solo exhibits. List the most recent and upcoming exhibitions first. If you have been in a lot of exhibits, you may want to put this section on its own separate page.

- *Collections or Client List* Use this section if you have had some of your work purchased by individuals or companies.

- *Commissions* Use this section if you have made custom work for individual customers, public buildings (such as through the Percent for Art program), or corporations.

- *Awards and Honors* Use this section if you have received an award at a craft fair or some other honor.

- *Teaching and Lecturing* Use this section if you have been an artist-in-residence in the schools, taught workshops or courses for credit, or given lectures or slide presentations to groups.

- *Professional Memberships* I like this section because even though you can't always control whether or not you get in a juried exhibit, you can always pay a fee and join an organization that reflects your interests and intent. If you serve on any committees or volunteer, include that information as well.

Your image on paper is almost as important as the work itself. Your logo, brochures and their alternatives (i.e., postcards, newsletters, and fact sheets), business cards, hangtags, and even your résumé are important selling tools. With all these complementary pieces ready, you will convey a professional image consistently, no matter what the opportunity.

CHAPTER 19

DESCRIPTION OF YOUR WORK

Sometimes you only have a few seconds to engage a customer's interest—meaning you need a good, short description of your work. Other times, you may be asked to address a group for twenty minutes—and you can't imagine talking for that long about your business! For a variety of situations and lengths of time, you need to be able to describe your products and your business, verbally or on paper, in a clear, concise, and interesting way.

In addition, describing your work in a way that will protect your designs and image is important for retaining ownership of your ideas. You have put a lot of work into your business and wouldn't want to have someone else capitalize on your efforts. Using the legal system to copyright your designs and trademark your products is something you should seriously consider before it is too late.

Product Descriptions

How would you describe your work to someone who has never seen it before, who may not be familiar with the process you used to make it, or the materials? When you need to describe your work, whether it's for a promotional piece, in person, or to fill out a copyright application, think of what distinguishes it from other pieces and explain it as if you are talking to a novice.

Following are some examples of business and product descriptions from the 1997/98 issue of the *Maine Cultural Guide* published annually by the Maine

Crafts Association. Notice that after reading these examples, you have a strong image of the work in your mind.

- *Unity Leather:* "Classically styled, functional, multicompartmented soft leather handbags of top quality, full-grain cowhides, suede lined, some with textured leathers, some exotic trims."
- *Kathy Woell Garments:* "Handwoven and knit garments in rayon chenille yarns for women interested in luscious color with classical styles."
- *John McAlevey:* "Contemporary furniture designed and made from North American hardwoods using traditional joinery and oil varnish finishes."
- *Laurie V. Adams:* "Wheel-thrown and handbuilt porcelain pottery glazed in subtle colors, embellished with oriental brush designs."
- *Elan Bindery:* "Fine binding and restoration of books, custom wedding and anniversary albums, unique portfolios for artists and photographers, personalized yachting log books, archival library-style cases and folders, limited editions. Custom handwork our speciality."
- *Spare Moments:* "Contemporary fused, slumped, and leaded art glass. Specializing in limited-edition fused plates and platters. Unusual candleholders. Glass flowers and fall leaves. Stained-glass windows for home, business, and church. Restoration and repair services."

For each product that you make, write a short description below.

1. _____
   _____
   _____

2. _____
   _____
   _____

3. _____
   _____
   _____

Use these descriptions in your promotional materials, for your sales pitch, or to submit with a copyright application.

Copyright

If you talk with enough craftspeople, you may hear stories about other craftspeople copying their work. Although craftspeople do have the option of copyrighting their designs as well as taking legal action if someone copies their work, how many take the time to submit the required paperwork and fees? Although it's useful, a copyright is not foolproof because it often isn't enough to deter people. Even if you find out that your work is being copied, will you take the time and money required to take legal action and protect your work? You need to decide if getting a copyright for your designs is important to you and what you would do if you found out someone had stolen your designs. When you are in business selling your crafts, having someone copy your work can have a big impact on your potential sales and income.

What is copyright? A copyright gives the owner of the copyright the exclusive rights to reproduce, sell, distribute, display, publish, and make other types of work from the original. A copyright also prevents anyone else from doing these same things. When you sell your work, you still own the copyright to the piece unless you specifically sell that along with the actual piece, stated in a written document. Remember, copyright isn't just about artistic rights, it's also about who earns money by selling copies of a piece of work.

If you want to copyright your work, you should routinely mark all your finished pieces with the word "copyright" or the copyright symbol ©, your name, and the year it is made. Take photographs of the front and back of each piece to document it visually. If you are interested in formally registering the work, you will need to contact the Library of Congress for the proper forms and fees.

Although you do not have to formally register your work for it to be protected, do so as soon as possible. If you later find that someone has copied your work, you will have to register the piece before you can file a lawsuit. Registering your work before a problem arises shows a level of seriousness on your part that will only help when the time comes to defend your designs.

If you find out that someone has copied your work, you should try to deal with the problem informally at first. Talk to the person and let him or her know that you believe he or she has copied your work. It is best to see if you can work out an agreement before taking any other type of action. If that doesn't work, speak with your lawyer and send the person a letter on your lawyer's stationery stating that further action may be taken if he or she continues to produce the pieces in question. Then discuss with your lawyer how far you want to take this. Do you want to file a lawsuit and take the person to court? Can you reach a financial settlement out of court? Or do you just want to get back to your studio and let it go? You need to decide what this situation is worth to you. Ask your lawyer how long lawsuits like this usually take, how much they cost, and decide if you can afford to lose the time from working in your studio.

In an article titled "Copyrighting Your Designs: Is It Worth It?" in the October 1995 issue of the *Crafts Report,* writer Karen Aude interviewed copyright attorney, Marya Lenn Yee on the difficulties of copyright law for artists. "We all know that the most expensive part of doing battle is assessing how much is owed to the artists," says Yee. "Each infringement [on any design] is assessed at anywhere from $20,000 to $100,000 and the judge sets what he or she thinks it is worth." Yee's point about registration is simple. She explains, "When lawyers [for the infringer] see the first letter complaining about the infringing act and that the [original] work has a registered copyright, they know what they are exposed to and they know it's a good idea to settle. They ask themselves, 'Why expose my clients to statutory damages that might be higher than the profits?'" Yee points out that when you register your work, what you get is, quite simply, "a lot of clout without a lot of wrangling."

What about students or former employees who copy your work? Is the copyright owned by the employer or the person who physically made the piece? There is a section in copyright law called the "works-for-hire doctrine." Employers are granted the copyright in works created by their employees if it was created within the scope of the employee's job and the employee was paid a salary. For example, if you work for a jeweler and make his or her designs as a paid employee, the copyright of the jewelry belongs to the jeweler. You should discuss this with your employees.

Whether the work-for-hire doctrine is applicable is based on several factors—that the work is produced for the employer under his or her direction and the employee is paid for the work.

Another interesting aspect of the copyright law includes the photographs or slides taken of your work by a photographer. Do you own the copyright to those images or does the photographer? Technically, you have the copyright to the work, and the photographer has the copyright to the photograph of the work. When you have a photographer shoot your work, you need to sit down and discuss your rights and how you plan to use the photographs as well as the photographer's rights and how he or she plans to use the photographs. If the photographer wants to use the photographs in advertising, for example, you must give your okay. You must make it clear to the photographer how you will use the images as well. There shouldn't be any problems as long as you keep communication lines open. Usually, all a photographer wants is a credit when you use the photograph, and you would want to know if the photographer were planning to use your image for another purpose. Ask the photographer how he or she would like to handle the copyright to the photographs to avoid problems. Many will turn his or her copyright over to you except in rare circumstances. Do what you can to protect yourself and your art by copyrighting your work.

For more information, contact the Copyright Office at the Library of Congress, Washington, D.C. 20559; (202) 707-3000 for information on the laws and procedures or call (202) 707-9100 to receive the necessary forms; or go to *www.copyright.gov.*

Trademarks

According to Leonard DuBoff in his book *The Law (in Plain English)® for Crafts,* although modern trademark law is a relatively new development, its historical antecedents date back to medieval England. In those days, certain craft guilds often required their members to place their individual marks on the products they produced so that in the event that a product proved defective, the guild could trace its origins to a particular craftsperson and impose appropriate sanctions. As such, the marks enabled the guild to maintain the integrity of its name. Moreover, merchants would often affix marks to their products for purposes of identification. If the product was stolen or misplaced, the merchant could prove ownership by virtue of the mark. Of course, merchants quickly realized that there was easy money to be made from the use of another's mark, or one confusingly similar. The shoddy craftmakers could readily sell their products by affixing the marks belonging to the quality craftmakers. It was in response to this problem of consumer deception that the first trademark laws were later developed in the United States.

A trademark is a design, word, or symbol used by a manufacturer to identify the source of a product. By using a trademark, you give people a way to recognize and distinguish your products. By registering your trademark, you are trying to prevent someone else from cashing in on the recognition and reputation that you have developed for your product. It is different from copyrighting the design of your work because trademarks are used primarily for company names, logos, or product names. For example, the *Crafts Report* and *WOODSHOP News* magazine titles are registered trademarks. Manufacturers benefit by using the trademark as a marketing and advertising tool.

Registration of a trademark is evidence of the registrant's right to the exclusive use of the mark and may deter others from using it. Once a trademark is registered, the owner is allowed to use the symbol ® to show that the mark or name is a trademark (and therefore protected by trademark law). Talk with your lawyer about the process, the length of time necessary, and fees associated with registering a trademark.

For more information, contact the U.S. Patent and Trademark Office at 5 Clark Place, Arlington, VA 22202; (800) 786-9199.

It is not enough to be able to describe your work for promotional purposes. The use of copyrights and trademarks helps identify and differentiate your work and business, while also providing you with legal protection.

CHAPTER 20

YOUR PORTFOLIO

A portfolio is another selling tool that shows your work to a potential buyer, customer, or jury. A portfolio should be used to impress the viewer with the quality and presentation of your work, yet many craftspeople make the mistake of having portfolios that show a mixture of styles, use photographs or slides of poor quality, or fail to edit work that does not fit into a consistent presentation. While it is important to keep a record of your past work, for example, a portfolio that you are using to sell your current work should show the viewer a cohesive body of current work. Craftspeople that work in different styles or mediums may choose to have more than one portfolio.

Portfolios come in many shapes and sizes, from small albums using standard-sized snapshots to large carrying cases. I recommend using a three-ring binder because it can show different formats such as slide pages or photographic prints, as well as résumés and other printed pieces, in transparent pages. The sturdy cover provides protection from damage especially during shipping, it's easy to carry, and it projects an image of a professional, organized craftsperson. You can also ensure the viewing sequence of the pieces whether you are present or not because it functions like a book.

Although it will be an expensive investment, consider having at least ten sets of your portfolio ready to go at any time. There will be times when you will have several portfolios out and another opportunity presents itself. You don't want to be caught shorthanded and miss out on something because you didn't have enough copies made of your portfolio.

In order to be prepared, consider having the following items:

- Color slides of your work. These should include shots of your pieces that fill the frame (for craft fairs), shots showing a detail of the piece, shots of the piece displayed or being used (for catalog purposes), and shots for scanning into the computer (for a Web page).
- Black-and-white photographs. These are used for publicity purposes, a one-color brochure, and also for scanning into the computer for a Web page.
- A photograph of you—preferably working in your studio or a head-and-shoulders shot. This is important for publicity, a brochure, or a Web page.
- A photograph of your booth display. (Applications for juried fairs sometimes require this.)
- A copy of your brochure, postcards, fact sheet, and/or newsletter.
- Articles that have been written about you or by you.
- Your résumé or biographical information.
- A client list of the people who own or sell your work.
- Anything else you think is pertinent.

You should have representations of your work available in different formats, such as slides or photographic prints, so that you will have the appropriate material and format ready to send out at a moment's notice. Be sure to label everything in your portfolio with your name, address, and telephone number in case it gets separated during viewing. Include a self-addressed stamped envelope to help ensure the return of your materials.

Steve Meltzer, in his book *Photographing Your Craftwork,* suggests a unique portfolio sequence. The opening pages can show a photo of you working on a piece in your studio, giving the viewer a feeling for the investment you have in your tools, that you are a professional and this is your work, not simply your hobby. Opposite this picture you might place a shot of the piece on which you are working in the first photo to make the connection between the place where you work and what you are capable of producing there. Turning the page, the viewer comes to a medium-distance image of you working with a special tool or process. This can be a very dramatic shot or at least a dramatically lit shot. Again, the piece you are seen working on in the "dramatic" shot should be seen in its entirety in an accompanying shot. Now you have shown who, where, and what, and you have hooked the viewers into your story. They are curious and really want to look at your portfolio. Next, you move in closer still. A tight closeup shot shows the care with which you work and should illustrate your skill. Again, a photo of the completed work, accompanying the close-up, will connect process to product. If you show in galleries or sell at fairs, you might want to illustrate this next. This tells the viewer why you do what you do, and again speaks for your professionalism. Follow up the gallery or fair photos with perhaps six to ten additional pictures of your recent work to complete your story.

This portfolio example shows the viewer not only the work, but also the process of making the pieces. It is a lot more exciting than just showing your work in chronological order without any shots of you working in your studio. In this competitive career, feel free to let your creativity loose in your portfolio. You may be surprised at the reactions and interest that results.

Developing a Body of Work

Before you can put together a portfolio, you need to develop a body of work. Although a body of work can be made up of any number of pieces, as a general rule of thumb, you should have at least twenty pieces of work that have a consistent, recognizable style. This doesn't mean that you can't work in different mediums or in different styles; just that each body of work needs to look as if the same person made them. For example, if you are a functional potter and a sculptor, you may have one body of work of your pottery and another of your sculpture.

Everyone has different methods of creating a body of work. Some people start out with a concept or idea for a series and go about methodically making the pieces one after another. Other people work more spontaneously, first on one piece and then another, making something entirely different each time until they realize later on that a pattern has been emerging and decide to expand on it. Either way, both approaches can develop into a body of work.

If you are just starting out, you may not have a cohesive body of work yet. Take the time necessary to develop your work and learn your craft, always paying attention to quality. Although everyone's work can go through different stages, once you are earning money from selling your crafts, people will expect you to present a unified style that they can depend on receiving, time after time.

Probably one of the hardest aspects of selling your work is that while you are selling one line, you need to be thinking about creating, producing, and marketing new work. The needs and desires of customers, buyers, and collectors will push you into developing new lines, whether you are ready or not, just to keep up with their demand.

When You Will Need a Portfolio

Depending on what your marketing goals are for your work, you may never need a portfolio. If you only plan to sell your work once in a while, either out of your studio or at small nonjuried retail craft fairs, you may not need a portfolio. However, if you want to apply to juried craft fairs and shows, or have your work in a shop or gallery, you are going to need to show other people what you do, and a portfolio is a professional way to present your work.

If your plans include applying to juried craft shows and fairs, you will need three to five slides of your work, depending on the show's requirements. Some shows will require a slide of your booth display as well, to help them ensure consistency in presentation. (Craft fairs are discussed in more detail in chapter 22.) In the case of craft shops and galleries, you will have to find out what format is desired. Each shop or gallery is set up differently to review work. Some will prefer slides and others will want to see a simple snapshot of your work or even actual samples. (See chapter 21 for more details on galleries.)

If your plans include getting publicity in a newspaper or magazine, chances are the publishers will use black-and-white photographs of your work or of you working in your studio—even though most publications are in color. (See chapter 21 for more details on press releases and publicity.)

Photographs of your work for a catalog will differ from the type you would submit for a juried show. The images must be interesting visually as well as show how your work is used or displayed in a real-life setting. Although you may have wonderful portfolio shots, they may not be usable in a catalog. For example, a typical catalog shot of a dresser would not emphasize the wood but might show how much clothing can be stored in a drawer or what kinds of items would be displayed on top.

As you make each piece, whether it is part of a body of work or a single, unrelated piece, you should get in the habit of documenting your work by taking photographs and slides. You never know when the opportunity to sell something may present itself and you may later regret not having a slide or photograph of the piece.

Slides

Slides are a very important marketing tool for a craftsperson and should be considered an important investment. Consider having a professional photographer who has experience photographing crafts like yours take your slides.

Caring for your slides is also important to keep them dust- and scratch-free as well as maintain their color. Invest in slide boxes or plastic slide sheets to store your slides. You can also buy individual slide protectors as well as glass mounts to protect them further.

Try to purchase plastic slide sleeves that do not contain polyvinyl chloride (PVC) which can cause chemical damage to the slides over time. Always pick up slides by the mount, not the film, wearing white cotton gloves if necessary. No matter how well you take care of your slides, they will eventually fade because color processes, unlike black and white, are still not permanent.

Did you know that it is less expensive and the slides will be of better quality if you take more original slides than have duplicates made from original slides later? Have ten to twenty sets made or as many as you can afford during the photo session. Keep a set of your original slides in a safe place off-site in case of fire or other disaster.

Think about the ways you will want to use the slides before you snap the shutter. Are these slides going to be sent to a juried craft fair or put in a slide presentation? Will they be used in a brochure or for publicity purposes? Are you giving a slide talk on your work? Your best bet is to take slides for every possible purpose so that you will be prepared when your needs or opportunities change.

If you are taking slides for a juried fair that accepts only five images, they should look like a family. Make sure that the quality of your work is evident in the slides, that the background is simple and consistent among the slides, and that each slide shows a single piece. Usually, all your slides will be projected at once so you may also be given the opportunity to specify the sequence that the slides are viewed, whether they are shown side by side in a line or a few up and a few down.

There has been a lot of controversy and discussion about how to label slides. It seems that every time you submit slides for something, the organizers ask you to label the slides differently than the last place you sent them to. While there is still not a uniform way to label slides, basically you want to include your name, address, telephone number, title of the piece, year made, size, as well as an indication as to which side is the top of the slide. A simple arrow or dot will do to mark the top. Include whatever is necessary to help the person loading the slide carousel prepare your work so that it is viewed the way you intended it to be.

Some places want you to use slide labels and others forbid you to use labels because they can jam slide projectors. Invest in a good fine-point permanent marker, buy some empty slide mounts so you can remount your slides if you need to, or look into one of the many slide-labeling services available that will print your information right on the slide mount.

In addition to labeling each slide, you can submit a separate page that lists your name, address, and telephone number, and the descriptive information for each slide (e.g., title of the piece, dimensions, year it was made, and price, if applicable).

Photographs

There are many reasons to have photographs, black and white as well as color, as part of your portfolio. Photographs can help generate publicity, be used in a brochure or on a Web page, or easily show your work to a prospective customer without the need for special equipment.

A couple of years ago, I helped organize a regional juried craft fair with over eighty craftspeople who all made their living from selling their work. In addition to their slides, they were asked to submit black-and-white photographs to be used for publicity purposes. In addition to the poor quality, I was amazed at how few people actually had any black-and-white photographs to submit. The fair, as well as the individual craftspeople who didn't submit photographs, missed out on several good chances for free publicity because of the lack of photographs. The photographs that were submitted were sent out with press releases and, in several cases, received valuable coverage in the newspaper.

Although some newspapers are now using color, most still rely on black-and-white photographs. It is a known fact that if you send in a black-and-white photograph with a press release, you have a better chance at getting your event or story covered in the paper.

I recommend reading *Photographing Your Craftwork*, by Steve Meltzer, available through the *Crafts Report* by calling (800) 777-7098, to learn not only about how to do your own photography, but to help you be better informed when you are ready to hire a professional photographer.

Although you don't have to have a portfolio to sell your work, you may miss out on some lucrative opportunities or a chance for publicity because you don't have the right materials or they are out-of-date. When you update your portfolio, it is best to hire a professional photographer. You should always have color slides, black-and-white, and digital photographs of your work, your booth, and yourself available, as well as a brochure, postcards, newsletter, résumé and client list prepared. Whether putting together a traditional physical or digital portfolio, pick a format that meets your needs, and consider the sequence of your images. Label everything. While it seems more logical to let your needs dictate the kind of promotional materials you invest in, it pays to be prepared for every kind of opportunity.

CHAPTER 21

GETTING THE WORD OUT ABOUT YOUR WORK

You've got everything ready—your marketing plan is in order, you have put together your portfolio, and you have perfected your image on paper—now what?

You need to get the word out about your work—place advertisements, get valuable publicity, do a direct-mail campaign, and write a simple newsletter. You want to keep valuable customers and media contacts posted on what's going on in your business, but how do you know what will work—and where do you start?

Advertising Campaign

What is an advertising campaign? An advertising campaign is a plan that you design and pay for that uses advertisements in places such as a newspaper or magazine, in a sourcebook or directory, on radio or TV, or even on the Internet, to get exposure for your products to a particular market. How much money can you allocate to the campaign? How many responses must you get from this campaign to make it seem worthwhile to you? How do you know if you made a sale as a result of an ad? The most effective campaign is one to which you make a long-term commitment by allocating time and money, set goals, and measure the results.

The beauty of placing a paid advertisement in your local newspaper, in a national magazine, or on the radio or TV is that because you paid for it, you have the ability to not only control the size or length of the ad, but the frequency and copy as well. It is very easy to spend a lot of money on advertising and not see any results. Before you write out a check, design an ad, and mail it in to the sales department, review your customer profile in chapter 29. Will your customers read this newspaper or listen to that radio station or buy this directory? How do you find out?

Newspapers, magazines, and radio and TV stations have all done their own marketing surveys in order to sell advertisements, and know exactly who reads or watches them. Call up and speak to someone in the sales department and ask to be sent rate information, profiles on customers, and the response rates of some of the other advertisers who sell a similar product. Most places should be able to tell you that their readers fit specific profiles and be able to give you statistics and data so that you can make an informed decision about whether or not this is a good place for you to advertise.

For example, you may find out that the average reader of a particular magazine is a college-educated woman, age forty-seven, who lives in an urban area, earns $77,000 annually, and spends $4,000 on gifts, $1,500 on decorating her home, and $2,000 on clothing each year. Does the profile of this reader fit your customer profile? If it does, you have found a good match and should consider including this publication in your advertising campaign. If not, unless you are trying to change your market, why would you pay to advertise in a publication that doesn't cater to your customer profile?

Running an advertisement once is probably a waste of time and money because it is repetition that usually works in an advertising campaign. It takes a number of contacts through advertising before a new customer will purchase a product, so you need to be prepared to do this more than just once or twice.

According to Ilise Benun, in an article titled "Does Advertising Work?" in the winter 1996 issue of the *Art of Self-Promotion,* the first rule is this: Once is not enough. In fact, once is a waste. The chances that your prospect will just happen to see your ad the one time you advertise are very slim. You have to start small, go slowly, and give it a chance, which means you must run your ad at least six times, or even over the course of six months. During that time you can change a word here or there to test its effect on response. Or test three versions of one ad in three different media and see if the differences affect response. Using this strategy, you'll be able to track the results and you'll have the time to get a sense of which ad is more effective.

Following are some suggestions for get started on an advertising campaign:

1. Call a number of publications you think might be a good fit, review their information, and narrow it down to a number of good prospects. These prospects might include your local daily newspaper; two national magazines published monthly for buyers, such as the *Crafts Report* and *Niche;* two magazines likely to reach customers, such as *Downeast Magazine* and the *New Yorker;* your local public radio station; and an annual sourcebook, such as *The Guild,* which is read by architects and interior designers.

2. Fill out a copy of the advertising campaign form included in this chapter for each of these places and make a separate file for each one for easy access. Note their telephone number, mailing address, contact name, size of ads available, rates, discounts for frequency, and a space to project results, record responses, and track sales.

3. After reviewing your proposed budget and marketing plans, decide which places you want to start placing ads. For example, if you are having an annual studio sale, a good place to start might be your local newspaper. If you are accepted into a juried national fair, the showcase section in the *Crafts Report* or an ad in *Niche* magazine noting your booth number at the upcoming show might be an appropriate way to attract buyers to your booth. If you are interested in breaking into the interior design field, an ad in *The Guild* sourcebook may be the way to go.

4. If you aren't good at graphic design and writing or can't take the time, hire someone to work with you to design the ads and write the copy. An ad projects your image on paper to potential customers. Their first contact with you will be by seeing or hearing your advertisement, rather than meeting you or seeing your product. Use your logo and write the copy as if you are talking to your potential customer, not just anyone. Think back to your product description in chapter 19 and use that as the basis for the ad.

5. Find out if any of the magazines have issues that are put together around a theme. When you call for rate and profile information, ask to be sent information on the themes of upcoming issues. For example, if the June theme is weddings, you can write your copy and highlight a piece that would make a great wedding present.

6. What do you want the people who see your ad to do and how will you know if the orders or calls you receive are a result of the ad? Sometimes it takes months before you hear from people who clipped

your ad. One way to determine if someone is responding to your ad is to include a department code in the return address so you will know by looking at the envelope or when the caller requests a certain person or department. When you get a piece of mail or a phone call requesting that department, you will know it was in response to your ad. Get in the habit of asking everyone who calls how they heard about you and develop a system to note their responses. You may be surprised at the results. Or offer a special ad that requires clipping a coupon, for example. Every time you get an order with the coupon, you know it was in response to a particular ad.

How will you know if your advertising campaign is successful? If an ad campaign in one magazine costs $1,800 a year and you get twenty responses that generate five sales at $1,000 each, was the ad worth it? What if you get two additional sales the next year from the twenty original responses? One metalsmith I know advertises regularly in the *New Yorker* with just a small display ad that she says costs around $800 to run once, but because she receives twelve to fifteen orders each time, it is well worth it.

Many businesses fail because they don't spend enough money on advertising. Others spend too much, or buy ad space that doesn't match their customer profiles. Even if you get a great deal on advertising, it won't generate sales if the people who see your ad aren't likely to be interested in your product.

Public Relations Campaign

What is a public relations campaign and how is it different from advertising? The main difference is that publicity is free and advertising is not. Therefore, good publicity carries more weight than a paid ad because the newspaper, magazine, or TV station is in effect endorsing you and your product. On the other hand, you have no control over when or how often the information will appear (if at all), and what it will look or sound like if your information is used.

A successful publicity campaign finds a way to keep the media informed so that they can use the information as a story tip. For example, publicity might generate a profile on your business, include your studio sale in the calendar section of the paper, or prompt writers to call you for a quote as an expert in your field when they are doing stories on a topic related to your business. Publicity can also come in the form of a letter to the editor, being

Advertising Campaign Form

Company Name _____

Telephone _____ Fax _____

Address _____

_____

Contact _____

Customer Profle _____

_____

☐ Daily ☐ Weekly ☐ Monthly ☐ Bimonthly ☐ Quarterly ☐ Annual

Deadlines _____

SIZE OR LENGTH OF ADS   RATES

_____ $ _____

_____ $ _____

_____ $ _____

_____ $ _____

Discounts for Frequency

Total Cost: $ _____ × _____ issues = $ _____

Size Ad Placed _____

Issues/Dates 1._____ 2. _____ 3. _____ 4. _____ 5. _____ 6. _____

Copy _____

_____

_____

Photographer Credit _____ Department _____

Designer _____ Telephone _____

Quote for Design $ _____ Designer Deadline _____

Projections

Telephone Calls _____ Written Requests _____

Responses

Actual Calls _____ Actual Requests _____

Sales _____

Notes _____

_____

(Attach sample ad for reference on the back.)

included in a list of resources, tips about caring for your product, or an article written by you with a byline.

The most important thing to remember about publicity is that you are building a relationship with the media. You can help by providing interesting story ideas and they can help you by providing you with free publicity. It's a two-way street.

In her book *Bulletproof News Releases*, Kay Borden says that the media needs you as much as you need them, because although editors may use only one in every 10 releases received, survey results show unsolicited news releases occupy 19 percent of editorial space. And it's not at all unusual for the people you read about to have actually written the articles. Businesses receive publicity because they actively pursued opportunities for it. Think of it as a bartering arrangement, editors have empty space to fill, and you have a perspective on business uniquely yours to offer in trade.

Your planned schedule of newsworthy releases will build credibility for news value with the editor, and he or she will begin to recognize your envelope and look forward to seeing what you have to offer. Contributing journalists are more likely to base their decisions about running a particular news release on their familiarity with the reputation of the submitting person or organization. A full 33 percent said their choice was very often based on previous knowledge, while another 32 percent said familiarity was sometimes the deciding factor.

Before you write a press release, put together a press kit, or figure out who to put on your mailing list, think about designing a simple publicity campaign. Just like a marketing plan, a publicity campaign starts with a goal, budget, and deadline. Your goal is broken down into steps and the results are evaluated. Publicity is a simple process that is carried on continuously as time and budgets allow, and, like advertising, needs to be done on a regular basis.

When I first started ArtBiz, I designed a publicity campaign that not only included traditional media such as newspapers, radio, and TV stations, but also schools, individual artists and craftspeople, and membership organizations. As a result of my publicity campaign, during the first two years of running my business, I got three radio interviews, numerous listings in resource and calendar sections, a couple of articles published in craft organization newsletters, and a profile as a new business in both my local newspaper and the *Crafts Report.* I wrote all the copy, made follow-up calls to see if the editors needed any other information, sent more press releases, and when the time was right, I got great coverage from the media.

Unless you ask every customer how he or she found out about your business, publicity is very hard to trace. Many times people will just say they know about you through word of mouth or they won't be able to remember. Just because you got some publicity doesn't mean the phone will start ringing off the hook, but publicity will increase your name recognition and eventually help to generate sales.

Sample Publicity Campaign

Your first publicity goal is probably having your business profiled in your local newspaper within three months. What do you need to do?

1. Figure out what would make your business newsworthy from the media's point of view. Is it a new business located in the area the paper serves? Is it creating new jobs in your area? Have you just received an award? Are you part of a growing trend of some kind? Are you planning an upcoming event such as a studio sale?

2. Set a budget and plan a schedule for the campaign. Can you spend money on several mailings, including photographs, as well as the time to make follow-up phone calls? If you don't get any results from your first efforts, will you continue to dedicate the time and resources to continue your publicity campaign?

3. Call the newspaper to find out to whom you should send your press kit, verify the mailing address, and find out its deadlines. Sometimes the person you need to send your information to is located in a different place. After you mail your information, mark your calendar to call them the next week to make sure they received your package, find out if they need any other information, and see if they have any suggestions for you. You might also invite them over to your studio for a quick tour and personal interview.

4. Keep your media contacts on your mailing list so that every time you send out another mailing, they will get it. You are building name recognition. Over time, as you are building your relationship with your media contacts, they will find an opportunity to include your business in their publication. Also, your business will come to mind if they are working on a story that might require a quote from an expert like you, even if it is about another business or topic.

5. When you get an article written about your business, send a short thank-you note to the media contact. Publicity is like a gift received.

6. Take advantage of any articles you generate by having high-quality copies made to have available to send to the rest of your media list, your customers, and buyers. Publicity gets publicity. Display an enlarged copy in your booth at fairs and shows, and, of course, put a copy in your portfolio. Publicity is a very valuable part of your overall marketing efforts.

Publicity Campaign Form

Media Name _____

Telephone _____ Fax _____

Address _____

_____

Contact _____

Customer Profle _____

_____

_____

☐ Daily ☐ Weekly ☐ Monthly ☐ Bimonthly ☐ Quarterly ☐ Annual

Deadlines _____

Publicity Goal _____

Press Kit Sent _____

Date Sent _____ Follow-up Call _____

Publicity Received _____

Thank-You Note Sent _____

Press Release Topic _____

Date Sent _____ Follow-up Call _____

Publicity Received _____

Thank-You Note Sent _____

Press Release Topic _____

Date Sent _____ Follow-up Call _____

Publicity Received _____

Thank-You Note Sent _____

Press Kits

A press kit is like a portfolio to show editors or news directors to spark their interest in your business and generate an article or interview.

Usually a press kit is in the form of a folder with pockets and includes the following:

- A cover letter
- Press release
- Your business card
- Your brochure or flier
- Photographs of you working in your studio as well as of your work
- Résumé or biographical description
- References (if applicable)
- SASE (if you want your kit or photographs returned)

Your cover letter should tell editors what is in the press kit. Note that you are available if they need any further information and that you will be calling to make sure they have received the press kit. Thank them for reviewing your materials ahead of time.

The availability of good, usable photos or illustrations sometimes influences the decision of an editor to run a news release. Send black-and-white photographs to newspapers and color transparencies to magazines that use color. Check first to find out what they require.

If you are interested in renting a mailing list of publications, for example, you can do so by contacting ArtNetwork at P.O. Box 1360, Nevada City, CA 95959; (800) 383-0677, (530) 470-0862; *www.artmarketing.com.*

Press Releases

Keep your writing simple. The only person you need to impress is the editor who may assign a reporter to follow up on you. Nobody else matters. The editors may not be familiar with the type of work you do, so you need to keep your descriptions in layman's terms. Have someone proofread the release and give you constructive feedback, before you mail it.

Make sure there are no typographical errors, that the copies are of high quality, and that the release is on your stationery. Neatness counts.

When you make a follow-up call, keep it brief. Identify yourself and ask if they have a minute to talk, and if they have received either your press kit or your most recent press release. If they haven't or it is lost on their desk, offer to send or drop off another copy. If they have seen it, ask if they need any further information, and if they think they might be able to use it. You may want to invite them to your opening or studio. Finally, thank them for their time and hang up. Period.

You will find over time that editors remember you when you call and you may even feel as if you are talking with a friend. When they can use your information, they will.

If you are interested in having a show of your work reviewed in the paper, consider sending the editor three mailings and follow up with a phone call as outlined below:

- Two months before the event, send a press release.
- A month before the event, send the editor a personal invitation.
- Two weeks before, send a postcard as a reminder.
- Call and invite them for a personal tour of the exhibit if they can't attend the opening. If they aren't there, leave a message.
- If you are featured in an article, send a brief thank-you note. Make copies for your portfolio and to distribute.

On the opposite page is a sample press release format to help you get started. Type it double-spaced, if possible, and leave wide margins, to make it easy for an editor to read.

Mailing Lists

Before you start asking people to sign their names on a piece of paper to be on your mailing list, put some thought into how you may use the list. The purpose of a mailing list is not to have a huge list, but to have a list of qualified leads and current customers, the names of editors, shop and gallery owners, and organizations that may have an interest in your work.

Will you send everyone on the list, regardless of whether or not he or she has already purchased one of your pieces, an invitation to your studio sale? An announcement and the location of your booth at a juried craft fair? How many mailings will you send to a potential customer before you decide the person is not going to become a customer and remove them from the list? You will need to keep records in order to base these decisions on facts. For example, if you send a potential customer a mailing five times a year, for two years, and the person never places an order, when would it make sense to

---

Sample Press Release Format

[Date]

For Immediate Release

Contact: [Name]   [Telephone/Fax Number]

[Title of Press Release]

The frst paragraph usually includes an overview of the topic or event including answers to the who, what, when, where, and why questions.

The second paragraph gives background information or might include a quote from an expert. The expert could be you or you could call someone that seems appropriate and let him or her know you are asking for a direct quote for a press release—perhaps the owner of the gallery where you have shown your work, a customer, or even one of your teachers.

Use additional paragraphs to give more general information about your business, such as your hours or directions to your studio.

Note that photographs are available upon request.

End with the ### symbol.

---

remove his or her name from your mailing list? After two years? Five years?

After the first couple of years running my business ArtBiz, my mailing list contained several thousand names. Who were these people and how did they get on my mailing list? Luckily, I had kept track, so I knew whether someone had attended one of my seminars and when, if the person bought a book or had just expressed interest when he or she saw my booth at a fair, and if the person fit my customer profile of people that I thought should know about my services. I also had names on my mailing list of media as well as places that I was courting to offer one of my seminars. Having knowledge makes it easier to not only remove obsolete names, but also to sort the list to do a special targeted mailing.

Make a list of the things you would like to know about the people on your mailing list so that you can get the information you need to put them on (or take them off) your list. The following are some things you might want to keep track of on your mailing list:

- *Name* You may want to keep track of each name in two ways on the computer so that if you later merge your mailing list with a letter, you will not only have, for example, Ms. Susan Joy Sager for the address, but Ms. Sager or Susan (depending on how well you know her), for the salutation.
- *Business name* (if applicable)
- *Address* If you are going to buy a bulk-mail permit, you will want to separate the zip code for easy sorting, or for doing a targeted mailing to a particular geographic area.
- *Telephone number, fax number, and e-mail address* Even though we are talking about a mailing list here, you may want to give some customers a follow-up phone call at some point. And in this day and age, you may also want their fax numbers and e-mail addresses as well.
- *How did the person find out about your business?* For example, list the ways you advertise and assign codes to each category, such as newspaper ad, magazine, radio, word of mouth, sign, or directory.
- *What category is the person?* For example, if someone simply inquires about your product, is he or she a customer, buyer for a shop, gallery owner, or editor? Again, assign a code to each. Then, if you just want to do a mailing to buyers, you can sort the list.
- *Date entered on mailing list* This will be helpful later on when you are trying to clean up your list and reduce its size. For instance, if someone hasn't purchased anything in three years, maybe it is time to remove his or her name.

Keep track of anything else that makes sense to you or is unique about your business. For example, you may want to note what items were purchased (do you have a numbering system or code for your pieces?) or the dollar amount spent. You are probably asking yourself, How am I supposed to keep track of all this? If you set up some simple systems and maintain them, this is not rocket science. If you have a computer, you can easily track your mailing list information by using a database with fields. If you don't have a computer, you can make a simple form or card for each person on your list and keep them in a box or file.

So, instead of having people sign their names on a piece of paper one right after the other—and eventually having a mailing list of thousands of unknown names—at your next fair, have interested people fill out the top section of a simple form or card. Every time someone calls on the phone, have blank forms next to the phone (or your computer turned on) so that you can record the data right away, always asking the same questions and getting all the information you need.

As previously discussed, to keep track of the success of your advertising and publicity campaigns, you want to keep track of how people found out about you, to see which parts of your marketing efforts are working. A detailed mailing list takes this one step further by including information like when sales were made or the dollar amount spent to help you make informed decisions.

One of the things that is so nice about using a computer to maintain your mailing list is you can merge the information with a letter to personalize it, print labels or envelopes, as well as sort the list. For example, if you are doing a fair in Philadelphia, you may want to send an announcement only to those customers, buyers, and media contacts within a certain radius of Philadelphia rather than to your entire mailing list. With a computer, it is a matter of a simple sort. Although it can be done with a manual system, it takes much more time.

Your mailing list is a valuable sales tool. If it is on the computer, make sure to keep a hard copy of the list and backup disks in a safe place off-site.

Direct Mail

Direct-mail marketing can be a very effective self-promotion tool. However, if you approach it without careful planning, it can turn into a money pit. Direct-mail marketing can include sending postcards, personalized letters, brochures, fliers, or a newsletter.

Take the time necessary to write the copy and design the piece so that it not only reflects your business image, but is easy and quick to read. You are trying to get some type of response from a mailing, not teach someone how you make your work. Use some drawings or photographs, some simple copy that is bulleted or broken into small paragraphs, and keep it to one page, if possible.

Whatever form your direct-mail pieces take, be sure to include some way for the customer to get in touch with you easily. Are you trying to generate a phone call, a visit to your studio or booth, or an order sent by mail? Whether it's a toll-free number, a return postcard, directions to your studio sale, an invitation to a craft fair with your booth number noted, or even returning an order form you included with a letter, think about the type of response you want.

How will you know if your direct mailing was successful? If you send out two hundred pieces and you get two responses, was it successful? Or will you measure the success of the piece in terms of the dollar amount it generates. If those two responses totaled $1,000 in sales and the mailing cost $500, was it a success? Generally speaking, a direct mailing usually only results in a 2–5 percent response rate unless you do something additional, like make follow-up phone calls. Can you offer any incentives in your direct-mail piece such as something that is discounted or even free, if customers place an order? Will you put a time limit on your offer?

As discussed earlier, one of the biggest challenges you will face is having someone actually open the envelope and take the time to read your piece. Look at your envelope carefully. Would you want to open it? What might make it stand out? Can you take the time to address the envelopes by hand? Is there a type of label or typeface that seems more personalized? Some people even believe that using postage stamps instead of a postage machine can make a difference in getting an envelope opened. Figure out a way to keep track of the results of a direct mailing—assign a code, advertise a special, or provide some other type of incentive you can track.

Newsletters

Why publish a newsletter? Do you want to educate your customers? Keep in touch with them on a regular basis? Or enhance your credibility? Think about how many times a year you might be able to handle publishing a newsletter. Would twice a year be good? What about quarterly, or even monthly? How much time and money can you commit to this? Who will write the copy, design the layout, pick any visuals you might want to include, decide the quantity you need to have printed, and spend the time to address them?

If you have a computer, you will be able to easily produce a basic newsletter yourself. Or you may want to get quotes from your local printer or graphic designer. Again, just like with a brochure, you need to think of how many newsletters you want to mail and have on hand to give out, how much you can spend on both printing and mailing costs, and what you want to include in each issue. It can be something you do on an annual basis or several times a year. Make a list of possible topics you could include in a newsletter.

When I first started ArtBiz, I used to send out simple one-page newsletters twice a year that included my schedule of business seminars, my availability for career counseling by appointment, and a list of titles and prices of the books I sold. I sent it not only to people who had expressed interest in my services, but to those who had taken a seminar, stopped to talk to me at my booth, the media, as well as lists I purchased of artists and craftspeople I thought should know about me. Several organizations inserted my newsletter in with their own (for a fee) and I left others at schools and stores where I thought my customers would shop. So, even though my mailing list may have had five hundred names, I might have two thousand printed to be distributed in these other ways.

Use the sample form below to help you put together a simple newsletter.

Newsletter Worksheet

Name of Newsletter _____

Date _____

Front-Page Article _____

Visuals _____

Page 2 Article _____

Visuals _____

Page 3 Article _____

Visuals _____

Back Page _____

Self-Mailer _____

Quantity Needed _____ Budget $ _____

Printer _____

Telephone _____

Paper and Ink Colors _____

Folded _____

In summary, the important thing to remember when spreading the word about your work is that none of these methods works well in isolation, but rather as part of an overall marketing plan. Research places to find the types of media that your customers read, listen to, or watch. Your media mailing list should be appropriate to your type of business. Allocate a budget to your advertising, publicity, direct mail, and newsletter plans because these methods are best applied over a long period of time—and repeatedly.

For example, say people see your ad or read about you in the local paper, then call to inquire about your product. You send them your brochure and call a few days later to see if they are interested in ordering. Then you put them on your mailing list so they receive direct-mail pieces such as a postcard inviting them to your next event or a newsletter. After one or even several contacts, they may purchase a piece. If they don't purchase after a predetermined amount of time, you remove them from your list. Set goals for each of your efforts, track the responses, and evaluate the results. Over time, you will know what percentage of inquiries turns into orders and how many people reorder as the result of your advertising, publicity, or direct-mail campaigns. They all work together.

CHAPTER 22

CRAFT FAIRS

How do you know if craft fairs are the right market for your work? Do your customers shop at craft fairs? Should you do wholesale or retail fairs? What does a jury look for when selecting work? How do you design a great booth? Or make a sale? Craft fairs can be a great way to get the word out about your work, try your pricing, get feedback on a new product, as well as get some valuable tips from the other exhibitors. Each weekend, hundreds of craft fairs take place across the United States offering the country's more than 10,000 fulltime craftspeople the opportunity to make a living from their craft. How do you find the right fair for you?

Finding the Right Fair for Your Work

Before you try to find the right fair for your work, decide if your potential customers do their shopping at craft fairs. If you aren't sure, do the sample customer profile worksheet in chapter 29. If you discover that your potential customers only shop at the mall, doing a craft fair is probably not worth your while unless it is a wholesale show geared to buyers from gift shops that are located in malls.

Keep in mind that there are different types of craft fairs that cater to different types of clientele. For example, a free craft fair at your local school will draw a different crowd than a juried fair in a rented hall with an entrance fee. There are local fairs in which anyone can participate, juried fairs that are very competitive, and every type of fair in between.

No matter what type of craft fair you do, how will your potential customers hear about it? Will they see an ad in the local paper, hear about it on the radio, see a TV commercial, or receive an invitation in the mail? Is it an annual event that they mark on their calendars where they plan to do their holiday shopping? Finding out how well a fair is advertised and the type of people who attend are very important factors to help you decide whether or not to participate.

There are several ways to research fairs and make an informed decision about which fairs are the best for you to attend. Before having your slides updated, writing a check for the application and booth fee, and sending in your application, do a little research and consider doing the following:

- Subscribing to a magazine that lists and reviews fairs, such as the *Crafts Report* or *Sunshine Artists*.
- Purchasing a directory, such as *The Art Fair Sourcebook*, (800) 358-2045, *www.artfairsource.com*.
- Calling your local or state craft organization for suggestions of fairs in your area.
- Asking other craftspeople for ideas—many craftspeople not only have firsthand experience doing fairs, but will share valuable tips and information with someone just starting to do craft fairs.
- Visiting the fairs you are interested in. Keep a copy of the fair's advertising book so that after the show you can call the promoters and a few exhibitors with a few questions. Although a fair may be good for one exhibitor, it may not be as good for another, so you will need to draw your own conclusions. Use the sample questions included in this chapter for promoters and exhibitors as a guide.

Before you call promoters or exhibitors for information, make sure you can briefly describe your work and your customers. Remember to thank them for their time. Once you have done some research on fairs, it will be clear which fairs are right for you.

Basically, there is only one question you need to ask exhibitors, Will you exhibit in this fair again? If they say yes, then you can assume that it was a profitable show for them or at least good enough for them to try it again next year. If they say no, ask why.

Questions for Fair Promoters

What type of people come to this fair? _____

_____

How do customers and buyers fnd out about the fair? _____

_____

Is the work usually contemporary or traditional? _____

What is the booth fee? $ _____ Are there other fees? $ _____

Can you tell me what the average sales are for exhibitors in my medium? $ _____

What price range seems to sell best? $ _____

How are exhibitors selected? _____

Is there an application deadline? _____

What is the notifcation date? _____

How many applications do you usually receive for this fair? _____

How many booth spaces are available? _____

How are space assignments made? _____

Is this an indoor or outdoor fair? _____

If an outdoor fair, what is the policy for inclement weather? _____

What is the average attendance? _____

Do you have volunteers to help? _____

Do you send exhibitors information about lodging, restaurants, and directions? _____

Do exhibitors need a special sales or tax license? _____

Where do I call? _____

Do you have any suggestions for me? _____

_____

Thank you for your time.

Wholesale versus Retail Fairs

In order to decide whether you want to do wholesale or retail fairs, or both, think about the type of interactions with people you want to have and whether or not you want to fill orders. Do you want to sell your work directly to the customer at fairs designed for the retail public only or do you want to sell your work to buyers who will place orders at wholesale fairs? Some fairs are designed for both retail and wholesale buyers.

Retail fairs are an event that shoppers look forward to because they get a chance to meet the maker of the pieces and learn the story behind the work.

Questions for Exhibitors

Will you exhibit in this fair again? _____

Who are your primary customers at this fair? _____

_____

How many times have you exhibited in this fair? _____

Have sales been consistently good? _____

What are your impressions of the promoters? _____

Is the fair well advertised? _____

What other fairs do you do? _____

_____

Do you have any suggestions for me? _____

_____

Thank you for your time.

Retail fairs give you the opportunity to meet the people buying your work, find out what they like and don't like, and cash to take home at the end of the fair. You may be surprised to find out that some customers will not only collect your work, but will refer other people to you as well.

Wholesale fairs give you a chance to meet and develop a relationship with buyers from shops and galleries. Although buyers initially may order only a small quantity of pieces to test how well your work will sell at their location, over a period of years, these small orders can be significant. Buyers will take orders for future delivery so you usually only need to bring samples to a wholesale fair. Selling your work wholesale allows you to plan your production schedule and spread the orders throughout the year. Wholesale fairs can be a cost-efficient way to get new accounts and make customers for life.

Buyers want a craftsperson with a businesslike approach and look for someone who can answer questions and explain unusual techniques. They appreciate a greeting, pieces with the prices marked on them, wholesale price lists, and catalogs that can be taken with them. Most importantly, buyers look for a business that will deliver the order when it says it will.

According to a study done by Dr. Pamela Brown, called "Inside the Buyer's Mind" in the October 1996 issue of the *Crafts Report,* buyers look for vendors who have an established history of delivering quality craft on time and according to the buyer's requirements. Buyers want to receive the same quality and look in a craft as they saw displayed at a fair. They also look for vendors or artisans with whom they can establish a good working relationship, almost to the extent of friendship. This relationship enables the buyer to work with the artisan to ensure timely delivery, solve problems, and develop the store's reputation for dependable crafts.

Jurying Process

In an effort to ensure consistent quality and fairness, many fairs are juried by outside jurors to ensure impartiality. The juror's job is to review slides and recommend admission to the fair.

Picture this: You have selected the fair to which you want to apply and have sent off your application and slides. The fair sponsor's office has received hundreds of applications for this fair. Volunteers begin sorting slides into carousels by medium. A viewing room is set up with slide projectors and the jurors sit down. The jurors are not told your name, so unless they recognize your work, they do not know who has done it. As your pieces are projected simultaneously, each juror assigns a score to your work. At the end of the review, the scores are added up and the applicants with the best scores get in the fair. The rest are either put on a waiting list or rejected.

What does this process tell you? Send the highest quality slides possible, the number of slides requested, and label each slide so they won't get lost. Even if you do everything right and were in the fair last year, you are not guaranteed re-admission. If you didn't get in the fair this year, it doesn't necessarily mean you won't get in next year. Jurors and the competition constantly changes. The fair promoters strive for a balance of mediums. For example, if one hundred jewelers and ten weavers apply to a fair, each weaver has a better chance of getting into the fair than the jewelers, assuming the promoters are trying to balance the fair by medium.

The application and jury process make it hard for craftspeople to plan their schedules. As a result, many craftspeople apply to more fairs than they could possibly handle just to make sure they get into some. In an effort to help craftspeople, some promoters have instituted a tenure process so that once a craftsperson has been accepted into a fair, they can plan on doing it again the next year if they want to. While this is good for the craftspeople who have already been in the fair, it can leave less booth spaces available and make it more competitive for new exhibitors. However, juried fairs are still the best way to keep the process open to everyone and to maintain a high level of quality.

Booth Design

You have a very short time to get the customers or buyers walking by your booth to stop, take a look, and decide whether or not they might want to buy something. At a craft fair, the design of your booth and the display of your work are almost as important as the quality of your work. Strive to create a booth that enhances what you sell.

When designing your booth, you should consider lighting, signage, and the visual look of the display itself, but also the ease of setup and takedown. There should be adequate space to make sales and a place to store extra inventory. Finally, consider safety issues such as fire, wind (if the booth is outdoors), and theft.

Before you invest in a booth, visit craft fairs to see how other craftspeople have designed their booths. If you see one you like, figure out what it is that you like and ask the exhibitor where it was purchased. Look through craft magazines and order several catalogs from companies that make booths to compare features and prices.

Have your booth made out of lightweight materials, preferably in a style that comes apart easily and can be shipped and stored in manageable pieces. Think about how you will display your work within the space. Do you need pedestals? If you make jewelry, do you have display cases to protect it from theft? If you make clothing, do you have a space for people to try the garments on and a mirror to see themselves? Is there a place for you to sit down when you need to take a break? What do you need?

Once you have purchased or made your booth, set it up at home and try different arrangements until you feel satisfied with the presentation. Think about how to display your pieces to show off their beauty and function. Consider how your pieces will be used and, whenever possible, duplicate that setting. If you sell jewelry, wear it and have a mirror available so your customers can see how the pieces look on them. If you sell tote bags, display them filled with groceries or items to take to the beach. Make it easy for people to see how to use your crafts if they are functional.

Make a packing list of everything you need to bring when you do a fair, and keep all these items stored with your booth display. For example, you may need a few cleaning products such as glass cleaner for your cases or an extension cord to connect your lights. Buy whatever you need and remember to replace things when you run out of them, before the next fair.

The way you dress and present yourself is another important part of your presentation. Not only do you need to look the part of a successful craftsperson, but you need to make sure you are comfortable. Can you stand in your shoes all day long? Are your clothes comfortable? Do you have water to drink? Something easy to snack on between customers? Taking care of yourself is very important. This is supposed to be fun, right?

Making a Sale

You have been accepted into a fair, your booth is set up, and a customer is walking your way looking with interest at the pieces in your booth. Now what? Selling your work is telling people about your work, finding out if it is something they want or need to buy, and helping them to make the decision to purchase. Some craftspeople love the opportunity to mingle with customers, while others dread meeting customers and making a sale. If you feel good about your work, the prices you are charging, and your booth display, you may find that you enjoy talking with customers and selling your work.

Bill Pearson, in his article "Recover the Lost Art of Selling" in the June 1997 issue of the *Crafts Report*, says: "I don't know about you but I like to be sold. It happens so seldom that it's actually a shock. I don't feel ripped off—I feel served. Help is what I want. To spend money is what I want. Why else would I be in the store? Selling gets a bad name because the process gets abused; it always has, always will." Salesmanship is not usually self-taught, nor is it rocket science. People shop to satisfy needs and wants, and effective salespeople assist favorably in that process. Sometimes customers know what they want to buy, but more often they do not.

Consider this scenario: It's mid-December and Bill and Jane have done none of their holiday shopping. They have agreed to spend $50 each for ten people on their gift list. They enter their local gift store and proceed to look around. An hour later, bags in hand, they head home. Ten gifts were purchased and $500 spent.

Now consider a second scenario: It's late in December and Bill has yet to buy a gift for Jane. He has no list and about $100 to spend. Bill enters a local craft store and proceeds to look around. When approached, it's obvious Bill needs help. An hour later, gift box in hand, Bill heads home. One gift was purchased and $200 spent.

The first scenario was pretty routine. Ten gifts were purchased and right on budget. No fuss, no muss, and not much selling. Bill and Jane got "clerked." The second scenario is all about selling. Bill knew he needed a gift, but little else. He thought he'd spend $100, but happily spent $200. Bill encountered a *salesperson.*

To help you make sales, consider the following tips:

Think about what you can do before the fair to help you make sales.

For example, do a direct mailing to let current customers, buyers, and the media know that you will be exhibiting in this fair and note your booth number. Send the mailing out as least three weeks before the fair. Although sometimes the promoters will give you preprinted invitations to send to your mailing list, gallery owners and buyers often receive large numbers of these so they have lost their effectiveness as a personalized promotion tool. Have your own invitations made up and use the free invitations as a handout at other fairs or in your showroom.

Your work will not sell by itself no matter how good it is.

If you are uncomfortable selling your work, maybe you need to practice. Try switching the emphasis from trying to sell your work to thinking of the situation from the customer's point of view. For example, use questions as sales tools to engage potential customers in conversation so you can find out some important information about their needs. Are they buying for themselves, their companies, or gifts?

Make a list of questions to start a conversation, such as Are you enjoying the show? What are you shopping for today? What other work at the show are you interested in? and What is your price range?

Think about how you are phrasing your questions. For example, saying "You wouldn't want to buy that, would you?" suggests a negative response. "Can I help you?" allows the customer to give a yes or no answer, while asking "Why are you shopping today?" requires the customer to respond with more than one word. You want to have a response so you have something to go on to ask the next question.

Outline the features and benefits of your product and why it might meet their needs.

Make a list of your product's features and benefits ahead of time so you can incorporate them into your sales pitch. Features are what makes your product good; for example, the quality of the piece, how it is made, or the use of special materials. Benefits might be what customers will gain by owning one of your pieces. Are they collectors who see your work as an investment? Do they want to be thought of as people who buy unusual gifts, or who are knowledgeable about the crafts? Will owning the piece bring beauty or pleasure to their life?

Closing a sale is getting a decision from the customer.

Don't be afraid to ask if the customer would like to buy the piece or how he or she would like to pay for it. Start out by saying something like, "I can see you really like my work and especially this piece. Are you interested in buying it?" Wait for the customer to answer. The worst thing that he or she can say is "No" or "I need to think about it."

You may also start to get buying signals from the customer, such as "Do you have this in stock?" or "Do you take a personal check?" or "Can you make me one like this in purple?" Try to respond in a way that gets the person to make a commitment, such as "Would you like me to make you one in purple?"

Have at least one assistant to help you answer questions and make sales at the fair.

Spend time to train your assistants about your products and policies so that they can speak intelligently with customers and buyers. Empower them to make sales and decisions without needing your input, except in special circumstances, in case you are really busy.

Successful selling requires a willingness to help people, a positive attitude, knowledge about the products, an ability to offer solutions to the needs of the customer, and being able to work quickly in today's fast-paced environment—people do not like to wait. People will make a purchase for any number of reasons. Consider which of the following describes your customers:

- They buy what they want regardless of the price
- They purchase only because the price is high
- They purchase what they don't need because the price is right
- They won't purchase what they want because the price is too high

Typical customer comments have many meanings. If a customer says, "It's too expensive," this might mean:

- I can't afford it
- I can buy the same thing for less money from someone else
- It's not well made for the price
- I will buy it, but let's see if I can get a lower price

When a customer tells you, "I'll think about it," he or she could be saying:
- I don't understand what you told me
- I'm not sure I should buy it
- I need someone else's approval
- I want to get away from this salesperson

Here are some sample steps for making a sale:
1. Greet all potential customers, make eye contact, and smile
2. Ask them questions and listen to their responses
3. If they seem interested, give them an overview of your work, telling them about its features and benefits
4. Encourage them to buy with incentives such as a special
5. Ask for the sale
6. Say thank-you when you make a sale
7. Find a way to keep in touch with the customer

Even though your work is good, worth the money, and you do everything "right," only a fraction of your interactions with customers will result in a sale. The reality of selling is that you don't get a yes from every customer. Treat each person as if he or she is interested in your work and will buy. Keep trying to improve by learning from your successes and failures. Review what did and did not work. Compare your sales goals with actual sales. With practice, a selling style you feel comfortable with, and belief in your product and your price, you can be a great salesperson. You may even find you start to enjoy making sales rather than dreading them!

CHAPTER 23

GALLERIES

Many craftspeople think that if they could only get their work in a gallery, all their problems would be solved. The fact is, even if your work is accepted by a gallery, you will probably still need to find other ways to sell your work. Some galleries may only sell a few of your pieces from each show or be able to give you a show every other year. Although there are some craftspeople who sell almost everything they put in a show, this is the exception rather than the rule.

What are your expectations regarding gallery sales? What percentage of your income can you realistically expect from gallery sales? If a gallery can sell your work and you have built all your expenses plus some profit into your wholesale prices, the commission the gallery receives is well spent. If a gallery keeps your work for a long time on consignment and doesn't sell any, you probably need to try another gallery or a different market.

Work for a gallery show is usually unique and one-of-a-kind, as opposed to work that is produced in multiples for sales in shops or at fairs. There are solo shows, group shows, and shows on specific themes. Shows may be juried, open to anyone who applies, or hand-picked by the gallery owners.

How do you know which type of gallery is right for your work? There are different types of galleries: those that specialize in a particular medium, showcase different types of work, or they may be a combination of a shop or framing business with a gallery space. There are also alternative spaces available including cooperatives, local restaurants, bookstores and cafés, as well as your own studio showroom. Galleries actively promote work through client lists, invitations and exhibitions rather than relying on walk-in customers or sale specials, as shops do. Keep in mind that many galleries are started by other craftspeople or collectors who may or may not have any formal business training in how to run a gallery.

Although there are galleries that show emerging talent, most of them are interested in showing work that has a track record because, after all, this is their business, they need to make money, and will be spending a lot of time and resources to promote their shows. Even when you find a gallery that is interested in exhibiting your work, you may have to get in line. Many galleries plan ahead and may have shows lined up for the next couple of years.

Finding the Right Gallery for Your Work

Locating the right gallery for your work is a perfect goal for a simple marketing plan (see chapter 17). The following sources will help you find out about craft galleries that are appropriate for your work:

- *Craft magazines* Available on newsstands or by subscription, look at the *Crafts Report, American Craft,* as well as those that are devoted to one medium, such as *Fiberarts* or *Fine Woodworking.*
- *Guidebooks* Examples include the *Art Now Gallery Guide,* which is published by region as well as internationally (to order call (908) 638-5255), and cultural guides produced in each state, such as the *Maine Cultural Guide* (published by the Maine Crafts Association; (207) 780-1807), or the *Vermont Crafts Guide* (published by the Vermont Crafts Council; (802) 223-3380).
- *Books with Resource Sections* Examples include *Crafting as a Business* by Wendy Rosen or *The Business of Crafts: A Complete Directory of Resources for Artisans* by the Craft Center, both available in bookstores.
- *Newsletters* Look for organizational newsletters published by your local or state crafts organization.
- *Mailing Lists* ArtNetwork rents mailing lists of galleries, museums, and store buyers for a fee. Contact ArtNetwork at P.O. Box 1360, Nevada City, CA 95959; (800) 383-0677; *www.artmarketing.com.*
- *Other Craftspeople* Many craftspeople are happy to give you suggestions of galleries that have worked for them and might even offer to set up an introduction for you.

When trying to find galleries suitable for showing your work, consider the following:

Is your work appropriate for the galleries in which you would like to show?

Before you send anything to a gallery or try to set up an appointment to have your work reviewed, research the kind of work it shows. As a gallery owner, would you want to receive a phone call or request for an appointment from someone who obviously has never visited your gallery and is not familiar with the type of work you show? Getting your work shown in a gallery is usually a long-term goal and requires preparation on your part.

Plan to visit galleries in which you are interested to see if your style of work is appropriate and to gather further information about the gallery.

This type of market research is a business expense that is tax deductible, so keep records of each trip (e.g., mileage, food, lodging, and tolls). If you aren't able to visit the gallery because it is too far away, use the sample questionnaire in this chapter as a guide when you call for information and ask to be put on its mailing list so you can receive show announcements.

When you call or visit a gallery, tell the gallery owner or staff person that you are a craftsperson right away.

Gallery owners are busy and need to know who is calling or visiting. Try to think of this from the gallery owner's perspective. Ask if the gallery represents emerging talent and find out what the policy is for reviewing work. Don't plan or insist on showing your work on the spot unless the owner suggests it. Remember, each gallery owner is approached by numerous craftspeople (more than one hundred craftspeople per week in one SoHo gallery), so there are reasons why some gallery owners have rules and specific timetables for reviewing work—whether it's monthly, every Friday, or even annually—in order to have time to sell. After all, selling crafts is their business, and having procedures for reviewing work makes sense.

Once you have chosen a gallery and submitted your materials, call a week or so after to make sure the work was received and whether it has been reviewed yet. If not, when will it be reviewed? Mark your calendar to check with the gallery again then.

If you are rejected, ask the gallery owner if it would be appropriate to resubmit work at another time. Can the owner tell you why you are being rejected? Does he or she have any suggestions for you? Thank the person for his or her time and feedback.

If your work is accepted, ask for a contract. It should include the dates of the show, delivery dates, list the pieces and prices, commission rate, handling of work, display requirements, shipping, insurance, publicity, and the responsibilities of both the artist and gallery. Keep a copy. Before you sign anything, ask someone else to review it. If the gallery doesn't have a contract, put your agreement in writing in a follow-up letter or supply your own contract. I have seen gallery owners shake someone's hand instead of using a contract or give a simple receipt from a sales receipt book. What if something goes wrong and you don't have anything in writing? Avoid problems that may take place later on by using a contract whenever possible.

Sometimes a gallery wants an exclusive arrangement with you asking you not to sell your work within a certain radius of the gallery. Are the sales you are likely to get at this gallery worth agreeing to an exclusive arrangement? Do you have any previous commitments that this will violate with other galleries or sales reps? What about doing fairs in this area? It's okay to agree to an exclusive arrangement, just approach it thoughtfully. A gallery that wants an exclusive arrangement just wants to be sure that the gallery down the street isn't selling your work as well.

The following descriptions of galleries have been selected from the 1997/ 98 issue of the *Maine Cultural Guide* (published annually by the Maine Crafts Association). Which ones do you think would be appropriate for your work? Can you tell from the descriptions?

Leighton Gallery, Blue Hill, Maine

Leighton Gallery, now in its seventeenth year, has been voted the best gallery in Maine. Featuring both strong and playful works by forty leading artists in shows that change monthly. Not to be missed is the superb outdoor sculpture garden.

This description doesn't tell you much about the kind of work shown at Leighton Gallery except that it is strong and playful, but maybe that's on purpose. After reading it, you know that the gallery has been around for a long time, was voted the best in Maine, changes shows monthly, and has a sculpture garden. This description, although not detailed, would spur me to pick up the phone to find out more.

Eastern Bay Gallery, Brooklin, Maine

Kate FairChild's Eastern Bay Gallery has a new home! Now housed in a wonderful renovated barn right in the heart of Brooklin Village. Eastern Bay still offers its exciting collection of contemporary Maine crafts, a series of rotating shows, and carefully selected new work.

The description lets you know that the gallery has moved and is open to reviewing new work. Does it only carry the work of Maine craftspeople? If you are not from Maine, it might be worth a quick call to find out.

The Turtle Gallery, Deer Isle, Maine

The Turtle Gallery just before Deer Isle Village. Specializes in fine art and contemporary crafts. Now newly relocated in the Old Centennial House Barn with two floors of paintings, prints, sculpture, and craft.

This gallery has also moved and sounds larger than the former space. You might want to call to find out what kind of craft sells the best here and about the upcoming show schedule.

Maine Coast Artists, Rockport, Maine

Since 1952, Maine Coast Artists has presented exhibitions of work by many of the best artists living and working in Maine. MCA has an extensive educational program with gallery talks, lecture series, and classes of instruction. The Gallery Shop specializes in handcrafted, Maine-made objects.

You need to live in Maine to show here. If you do, I would call for information about the gallery shop and education program.

Fibula, Portland, Maine

Fibula. A gallery with a breathtaking collection of oneofakind jewelry by Maine artists. Custom-designed pieces in high-karat gold and silver a specialty, with a selection of loose gemstones on display. Also jewelry repair.

Not only do you need to be from Maine to show in this gallery, but you must be a jeweler who makes one-of-a-kind pieces.

Questionnaire for Galleries (and Shops)

Date _____

Contact Name _____

Gallery _____

Address _____

_____

Telephone _____

Type of Gallery _____

"Hello, my name is _____. I'm calling as a craftsperson interested in finding out more about your gallery to see if it might be an appropriate place to exhibit and sell my work. I heard about your gallery through _____.

"Do you have a few minutes to talk with me? If not, is there a better time I can call?"

Call the gallery back at the time suggested by noting it on your calendar. It may take several calls to get the owner at the right time. And, yes, he or she really may be in a meeting! Call at least three times if you have to. Do not expect the person to call you back and do not feel rushed because it may be a long-distance call. This is important. If you can't get through to the owner, perhaps the person answering the phone can answer the questions or send you some information.

Briefly describe the type of work you make and your customer profile. Then ask the following questions:

Maine Potters Market, Portland, Maine

Celebrating our eighteenth year, Maine's largest pottery cooperative offers a tremendous selection of functional pottery and one-of-a-kind pieces. The gallery features stoneware, porcelain, earthenware, raku, majolica, ceramic jewelry, Judaica, and more!

You need to work in clay and live in Maine for this gallery. You may also have to be a member of the cooperative as well. If you are a potter who lives in Maine, it would be worth a call or visit.

Many places that call themselves a gallery are really shops featuring fine crafts or a combination shop and gallery. If you are interested in getting your work into a craft shop, follow the same procedures outlined here to approach a gallery.

How long have you been in business? _____

How many craftspeople do you exhibit? _____

Who are your customers? _____
_____

How often do you select work to be in your gallery? _____

Do you prefer to look at slides, photographs, the original work? _____

Do you buy work outright? _____

Do you sell by consignment? What is the percentage? _____

How soon would I get paid after a piece sells? _____

Do you use a contract? ☐ Yes ☐ No   Can I see a copy?_____

What price range sells the best? _____

Who pays for shipping?_____

How long do you keep work?_____

Where do you advertise your gallery? _____

Do you provide insurance for exhibitors? _____

Do you require an exclusive agreement? _____

Do you have any suggestions of other places I might contact about my work?

1. _____

2. _____

3. _____

Thank you for your time.

If a gallery wants to show your work but requires you to leave it on consignment to test the market, I would consider taking advantage of the offer when you are just starting out. If it sells well, chances are good that the gallery will want more and may pay you up front the next time. The following is a sample consignment contract for you to use:

What the Gallery Can Do for You

A gallery can give you an opportunity to exhibit your work, pay you for sales, give you a public vote of confidence by showing interest in your work, and help you get valuable publicity through media contacts. A gallery can also host events such as openings, gallery talks, and opportunities for collectors to meet with the craftsperson.

Consignment Contract

Date _____

Contact Name _____

Gallery _____

Address _____

_____

Telephone _____

I, _____ owner of _____

gallery, agree to:

1. Pay the craftsperson _____% of each item sold using a retail price supplied by the craftsperson (usually a 60/40 or 50/50 split—the craftsperson gets 60%).

2. Assume full responsibility for the work while it is in my gallery. In the case of damage, my insurance policy will cover the cost and I will pay the craftsperson _____%.

3. Attractively display and promote the work. If I no longer have room for the work, I will contact the craftsperson to discuss returning the work.

4. Keep accurate records and pay for work sold within _____ days after the sale.

5. Return all work in good condition at my expense if not sold after _____.

6. Pay the craftsperson the same rate if I have a sale or show special.

You, _____ , the craftsperson, agree to:

1. Get your work to the gallery on time by _____.

2. Provide the gallery with promotional materials such as _____.

3. Ship or deliver the work to the gallery at your expense.

4. Give the gallery adequate notice or _____ days/weeks if you need to remove the work for any reason.

5. Return this contract.

The following pieces have been delivered to the gallery on _____ :

QUANTITY	TITLE	DESCRIPTION	WHOLESALE $	SUGGESTED RETAIL $

_____   _____

SIGNATURE OF CRAFTSPERSON   SIGNATURE OF GALLERY REPRESENTATIVE

What You Must Do for the Gallery

You are building a relationship with a gallery that you hope will provide income, be ongoing, and lead to future shows. You both have a common goal—to get work in front of an audience.

Delivering your work on time, calling when there is a problem to work jointly on a solution, keeping the gallery owner informed of your current activities, and appreciating the efforts of the gallery by saying thank-you are important aspects of developing your relationship.

You can also assist the gallery by having promotional materials available such as photographs and slides, a résumé or biographical statement, to help them get reviews or create a dynamite announcement of the show. Give them a press kit as well as the number of photographs they need.

Invite the gallery owner to visit your studio, alone or with a collector. A lot of collectors like to get to know the craftspeople whose work they buy, and a studio visit is an informal way for them to meet you, see more of your work, and feel special.

Keep in mind that if someone becomes aware of your work through a particular gallery and buys it from you directly, you should give the gallery the same percentage of the sale as a referral fee. Discuss with the gallery owner what seems appropriate before it happens, if possible, to make sure there are no misunderstandings. Your prices should be the same whether someone purchases your work in the gallery or out of your studio because you do not want to give the gallery owner the impression that you are undermining their efforts to sell and promote your work.

Cooperatives

A cooperative gallery is run by members, rather than by one owner, to share costs, responsibilities, and get valuable exposure for their work. Some cooperatives provide other benefits such as group discounts for supplies, workshops, and group insurance plans. A co-op can help you get exposure for your work without having to wait until you get accepted into a juried fair or show, provide an opportunity to learn about putting together and promoting an exhibit, and allow you to gain sales experience. Cooperatives can be very valuable training ground for any craftsperson interested in selling their work and running a business.

A cooperative is not organized for profit, and if there is a profit at the end of the year, it is usually distributed among members. Unlike a normal corporation in which stockholders vote according to the number of shares they own, most cooperatives operate on the basis of one vote per member. The members of the co-op elect a board of directors and may employ outside people to conduct the business affairs of the cooperative.

Some cooperatives have initiation fees and dues as well as charge a commission on sales while other co-ops don't believe in commissions, feeling that the members whose work sells the best are in effect supporting the gallery and subsidizing those who don't sell as well. Dues are usually calculated by estimating the annual expenses of the cooperative and dividing them by the number of members.

Alternative Spaces

In addition to cooperatives, there are many other alternative spaces to exhibit your work including university galleries, banks, restaurants, cafés, bookstores, frame shops, and anywhere else that makes sense. Will your customers see your work at an alternative space?

It's important to keep in mind that if you are exhibiting your work in an alternative space, you may be working with a well-intentioned business owner who hasn't got a clue about how to put together a show, promote it, or even make sales. However, if you go into the arrangement with a clear sense of what you want and how much you are willing to do, it can be a good way to get exposure and make sales.

Some alternative places already show work so all you have to do is find out who their customers are, how they select people for shows, and when the next available time slot is to exhibit. Ask if the work is insured or if you need to provide your own coverage. Do they take a percentage of any sales? Modify the gallery questionnaire form and make sure you have terms that are agreeable to both parties in writing.

Selling from Your Studio

There can be a lot of benefits to selling directly from your studio. People love to meet craftspeople and have a chance to see where you make your work. Is it worth the effort and expense to have a showroom in your studio? Are you in an area that your customers can travel to easily? How will they find out about your business? Is this the best way to spend your time?

A couple of potters I know did craft fairs for years until they built up a following of retail customers and buyers before they decided to market their work solely through their studio showroom. Now they make their entire living from their showroom, filling orders from established accounts and selling to customers who visit their showroom. They are located in a small town near a ski area so it has been just a matter of getting the word out about their business through local tourist venues.

If you decide you want to have a showroom and sell out of your studio on a regular basis, you are basically opening a small retail operation. You need to dedicate a space, put up a sign, figure out where people will park, make displays for your work, have cash on hand to make change, and advertise your studio. A lot of craftspeople have their studios open by appointment or chance so they are not tied down to specific hours or only have regular hours seasonally. Make sure your insurance covers you for liability before you have customers come to your studio.

If you are selling from your studio on an annual basis, rather than opening a regular retail operation, pick a date, send out information to the media, figure out the guest list, make up an invitation including directions, check your inventory, create displays, plan refreshments, designate parking, and find assistants to help you during the event. You may want to hold a training session a week ahead of the event so that your assistants can answer questions and process sales on their own. Selling out of your studio is a lot of work, but is a good way to learn what people buy and test your prices.

Whether you market your work through galleries or shops, cooperatives, or alternative spaces, make sure you have a contract or letter of understanding. When looking for places to sell your work, determine what your expectations are regarding getting into a show or being represented by a gallery. Is your work more appropriate for a gallery or a shop? Always deliver your work on time and offer to provide promotional materials to the gallery. Set sales goals for your shows and evaluate the results. Combined with other methods of selling your crafts, galleries can be a significant portion of your income.

CHAPTER 24

COMMISSIONS

A lot of the commissioned work you see is the result of craftspeople actively promoting their work to both public and private sources. There's a lot of opportunity for craftspeople to do pieces for public spaces as well as for private individuals. If you are interested in pursuing commission, do research and learn the necessary procedures.

One nationally known quiltmaker I know makes approximately 80 percent of her income creating sculptures for public spaces, whether through the Percent for Art program or through private commissions. Although she is known as a quilt artist, the truth is that the current market doesn't have enough collectors to support her work through sales of her quilts. As a result of doing commissions to earn her living, she can design her quilts with aesthetic rather than financial concerns.

How will interested parties, private and public, find out about your work in order to commission a piece? Will they see your work exhibited in a gallery or at a fair, view your slides at a slide registry, read a review of your work in a magazine, see your advertisement in a sourcebook such as *The Guild*, receive a referral from a customer, arts consultant, or interior designer, or receive a proposal from you looking for a commission? If you are interested in doing this kind of work, you need to start getting your work to the appropriate places.

Writing Proposals

If you have an idea for a piece, you may want to generate a commission by writing a proposal and approaching possible funding sources. You may be asked to put together a proposal in response to a request. Writing a proposal is often difficult for craftspeople because it's not something they are trained to do. Use the worksheet in this chapter to help you get started.

Here are the basic steps to writing a proposal:

1. Contact the customer or organization for the name of the person who handles commissions and see if you can run your idea by him or her for feedback before you submit a proposal. The person may be able to help you write the proposal in such a way that it fits the organization's guidelines or the client's needs and increases your chances for success. Ask if he or she would like to see slides of your work or a mock-up of your idea.

2. Write the proposal and send it. Keep a copy for your records.

3. Call in a week to check whether the proposal has been received. The person may say he or she never received your request or that he or she isn't the person who should have received it. The person may say he or she remembers seeing it but can't locate it now. Resend it, if necessary, and still keep a copy.

If your proposal is accepted, you should receive a contract. (Refer to the section in this chapter on what should be in a contract.) Have your lawyer review the contract before you sign it so it can be amended if necessary. If you are rejected, ask why so you can learn from the experience and increase your chances for success the next time you submit a proposal. Can you resubmit the proposal with changes? What does the person recommend? Keep in touch to let the person know what you are currently working on because there may be another opportunity that will be more appropriate. Say thank-you.

Produce your commissioned piece adhering to established deadlines and budget. If there are any unforeseen problems or changes, keep the customer or organization informed and work out solutions together. Document your work with photographs and slides for your portfolio. Use them with a press release to garner publicity. Make sure that you thank the customer or organization for the opportunity.

If you are given the opportunity to make a commissioned piece for a client, first determine what the client needs or wants, how much the person is

Writing a Proposal Worksheet

What are you proposing to do? _____

_____

_____

Who will work on the project? (Attach résumés)

1. _____

2. _____

3. _____

When will the project take place or when will the piece be done? _____

Where will it take place or be installed? _____

How will it be publicized? Or distributed? _____

_____

Why is your project important? Who will it benefit and why? _____

_____

_____

willing to pay, and when the piece needs to be completed. You should also find out how to protect yourself in case the finished piece is not well received by the client, and what reserved rights you should specify. Show the client your portfolio and see what type of work they think is appropriate. Then, if you are both in agreement, draft a simple contract and set up a payment schedule—before you start the piece—to avoid problems or misunderstandings later on. You want the client to feel confident that you not only know what you are making, but that you can handle the details of installing a commissioned piece within a specified deadline. Indicate any relevant experience or references you may have.

A contract for a commission should include the following:

- *A description of the piece specifying size and materials* Include a photograph or drawing in addition to the written description of the piece. Feel free to visit the site and take measurements or ask for an architect's blueprint, if applicable.

- *A preliminary model or drawing and the fee* Before making the final piece, it's a good idea to present a model or drawing for approval by the client for a fee of $100–$250. A model allows you to find out if the piece looks the way the client envisions it. If it doesn't, you can de-

·

sign something else, again for a fee, or if the client doesn't think the work is suitable, neither one of you has wasted a lot of time or money.

- *Your copyright statement* Not everyone is familiar with copyright law, so specify that although the client owns the actual commissioned piece, the copyright of the piece belongs to you. This means that the piece cannot be reproduced without your permission.
- *The overall fee and payment plan* You should request payment in four installments: one as a deposit, two while you make the piece, and the final payment upon delivery.
- *An indication that you will acquire building permits, if necessary* Depending on what kind of piece you are making, you may need a building permit.
- *A statement that you will insure the piece until delivery* You should cover the piece with your insurance policy until it is delivered, then it is the responsibility of the client.
- *Who will pay for shipping or delivery as well as installation* Usually, you will pay for delivery and installation, which should be included in your budget.
- *The start date as well as the date the piece is due* After establishing a start date, choose a date that you will deliver the finished piece, giving yourself a reasonable amount of time to complete the work.
- *Cancellation information and fee* If the client cancels the commission, you should be entitled to any money paid or agreed upon by that date. You should specify a percentage of the fee that will be owed if the client cancels. You can also terminate the agreement if the client doesn't pay in a timely manner.
- *A clause about what will happen if you are unable to finish the piece* Will you refund the client's money? All or part of it? What if you are ill, disabled, or die?
- *Any reserved rights you would like to specify* Examples of reserved rights include borrowing the piece (if that's possible) for exhibition, expectations regarding ongoing maintenance of the work, as well as proper credit for the piece in any publicity.
- *The signatures of both parties*

Percent for Art Program

What is the Percent for Art program? The Percent for Art handout distributed by the Maine Art Commission asks: What town is without its monument to native sons slain in defense of their country? What country academy is without ornamental stained-glass windows to brighten the days of its students? What town hall or public library is without its symbols of civic pride—works of art created to be enjoyed by the people who use those facilities? The Percent for Art program exists to extend this tradition, to allow people of today to commission new artworks that will convey our ideas about ourselves and our world to one another, and to those who will follow us. One school district may commission a mural depicting the area's history, while another may commission an abstract multimedia piece; a state agency may purchase paintings on an intimate scale depicting the agency's purpose, while a university campus may commission a large-scale outdoor sculpture. All of these speak to both the specific public using those facilities as well as the casual observer, and to future generations.

Percent for Art commissions, required by law in almost every state, specify that new construction or renovation of stateowned buildings (such as schools, universities, and state buildings) set aside 1 percent of the budget (up to a maximum of $40,000) to acquire art for the buildings.

Work is selected by a panel that usually consists of one or two representatives of the site, one or two art professionals, and the project architect. The representatives of the site might be a school principal or administrator, while the art professional may be a curator, collector, or craftsperson. The panel makes a recommendation that needs to be approved by the governing board of the site and by the art council. Community involvement is encouraged, and meetings are open to the public.

Work may be selected (1) directly from slides and purchased, (2) through a limited competition where several artists and craftspeople are asked to submit proposals, or (3) by open competition where any number of artists and craftspeople may submit proposals for consideration.

To be kept informed of opportunities and have your work available for review, submit your work to be included in the slide registries at your local and state art council. You may also submit work to other states. Many interior designers, architects, and art consultants turn to slide registries when looking for a specific type of work as well as when working with the Percent for Art program.

Slide Registries

If you are interested in getting your work into slide registries, here are some
suggestions:

- To locate your state art council, contact the National Assembly of
  State Arts Agencies at 1029 Vermont Avenue NW, 2nd floor, Washington, D.C.: 20005; (202) 347-6352; *www.nasaa-arts.org.*
- The American Craft Council (ACC) also keeps a database of craft artists as a resource. Contact ACC at 72 Spring Street, New York, NY
  10012; (212) 274-0630; *www.craftcouncil.org.*
- ArtNetwork rents mailing lists of art consultants, art councils, and
  more. Contact ArtNetwork at P.O. Box 1360, Nevada City, CA 95959;
  (800) 383-0677; *www.artmarketing.com.*
- Call the Visual Artists Hotline at (800) 232-2789.

Designing a Budget

Once you have developed an idea for a commissioned piece, you need to allocate costs to making the piece. If you are designing a piece for a Percent for
Art commission, for example, you know how much money is available and
can plan accordingly. If you are working with an individual client, you may
need to negotiate. Does the client want to pay you one fee? Does it include
materials, framing, installation, and labor for you and an assistant? Make a
list of everything you will need and assign a dollar value to it to facilitate a
discussion for a budget.

Not all craftspeople want to, or are suited to, do commissioned work. It
requires working with a client or committee and may have a long lead time
from start to finish. If you do choose to pursue commissioned work, take the
time to research opportunities and send your slides to places that have slide
registries. Prepare a proposal, draft a contract, have a model or mock-up of
your idea approved, establish a payment schedule, and design a budget. Don't
forget to document the finished project for your portfolio and future commission opportunities. It can be a lucrative venture.

Commission Budget Form

Model Fee	$ _____
Supplies and Materials	$ _____
	$ _____
Equipment (over $500)	$ _____
Labor	$ _____
Travel	$ _____
Shipping	$ _____
Installation	$ _____
Insurance	$ _____
Other	$ _____

*Total Estimated Cost** $ _____

*Note: If revisions are requested by the client, the client will be billed at $_____ per hour plus materials, with an estimate provided by the craftsperson.

CHAPTER 25

INTERIOR DESIGNERS AND ARCHITECTS

Many interior designers and architects have a need for unusual pieces for their projects whether it is a large sculpture for a lobby of a bank, furniture for a conference room, or light fixtures for a hallway. Although working with an interior designer or architect requires flexibility and additional paperwork, it can be both satisfying and lucrative.

Finding Firms That Specify Craftwork

Craftspeople are a valuable resource for interior designers and architects looking for unusual pieces to put into their designed space. Designers are essentially acting as collectors who instead of displaying the work in their homes or offices are specifying it for one of their clients.

How can you find interior design and architectural firms that specify crafts? A good place to start is to associate yourself with organizations that put you in contact with these professions. Most interior designers belong to the American Society of Interior Designers (ASID), which has over 30,000 members with eight different specialities: residential, office, facilities management, hospitality, healthcare, retail store planning, government, and institutional. The headquarters are located at 608 Massachusetts Avenue NE, Washington, D.C. 20002. Call ASID at (202) 546-3480 to find a local chapter near you or check out its Web page at *www.asid.org.*

Plan to attend meetings and workshops to meet interior designers, and request a listing of members near you so that you can send them information about your work. Affiliate members receive mailings and a membership card, which provides access to trade shows and design centers that are not open to the public. Design Centers are located around the country, primarily in large cities like Boston, New York, Los Angeles, Seattle, and Chicago. They are comprised of showrooms open to the trade only. Ask your local ASID chapter where a design center is located nearest you. Some cities have more than one.

Most architects belong to the American Institute of Architects (AIA), which has 59,000 members nationwide with state and local chapters. The headquarters are located at 1735 New York Avenue NW, Washington, DC. 20006. Call AIA at (800) AIA-3837 or visit its Web site at *www.aia.org.* If you decide to join AIA as an affiliate member, you will receive a subscription to *Architectural Records* magazine, a newsletter, and announcements of conferences and meetings. You will be able to select a professional interest area and be apprised of other opportunities to advertise your business. Ask for a list of affiliated architects in your area so you can contact them.

You may want to contact the galleries you work with, or those in your area, and ask if they can recommend interior designers or architects. Also try contacting colleges and universities in your state that offer degrees in interior design or architecture, and speak to the professors. Finally, look up interior design companies and architects in the yellow pages and call to find out who should receive information.

How do interior designers or architects find a craftsperson to design special pieces for some of their projects? They might have attended a craft fair, seen the artist's work in a gallery or shop, or asked someone for a referral. Interior designers and architects also look at slides in slide registries and listings in sourcebooks. Make it easy for them to know about you and your work by approaching them, giving them the materials they need to have on file, and keeping them apprised of your activities.

When working with interior designers and architects keep the following tips in mind:

- *Understand that you are being hired to satisfy the needs of the client.* You would not have gotten the job in the first place if the designer or architect didn't already like your work. However, the client may want something in a different color, size, or texture than you normally make. Tell them what you can and cannot do. Do they prefer slides or photographs, copies of your brochure or a résumé? If possible, include images that show your work displayed in a lobby, conference room, or restaurant. Depending on which market you are approaching, this will take away some of the guesswork for them of trying to visualize your work in a real space.

- *As a craftsperson, you may be hired as a subcontractor by the interior designer or architect.* In some cases, the designer or architect will take complete control of a project, subcontracting craftspeople, writing proposals, and handling the invoicing. Others will recommend that a craftsperson must handle their own proposal writing and billing. Be prepared to write simple proposals and contracts, set up an invoicing system, and work with clients, if necessary.

- *Describe in detail the materials and processes to be used.* Commercial interior design can make special demands on craft. For example, fabric must meet fire codes for flame resistance. Craftspeople must be willing to give the client a warranty on the work and to do repairs, if necessary. You may also be asked to use alternative materials or processes to bring down a price.

- *When designing your budget, keep the following in mind:*
  — How will changes requested by the client be billed? Will you charge an hourly fee plus materials?
  — Set up your billing so that you receive a nonrefundable deposit as well as installment payments. When you deliver the finished piece, there will be only a small portion of the payment remaining.
  — On your price page, consider listing the price per running or square foot in addition to unit price so that the interior designer or architect can estimate the cost based on the size of the space, if necessary.
  — Make sure that the price you quote allows you to make a profit after the interior designer or architect gets his or her commission and you have paid for all the materials and labor.

- *Your ability to meet a deadline is crucial.* Allow yourself plenty of time to finish your work. If you can't meet your deadline, call and work out a solution together.

- *Interior designers and architects appreciate the extra effort made by craftspeople to keep in touch.* Send them postcards, pick up the phone to ask what they are working on and if they need any help, and send them your latest designs. Put them on your mailing list so they receive information from you periodically. Then, when an opportunity presents itself, chances are good your work will come to mind.

The Guild Sourcebooks

If you are interested in marketing your work to architects and interior designers, a good place to start is *The Guild: A Sourcebook of American Craft Artists*, published by Kraus-Sikes, Inc. *The Guild* is published in three annual volumes: *Architectural Arts and Sculpture: The Architect's Sourcebook; Art for the Wall, Furniture and Accessories: The Designer's Sourcebook;* and *The Handbook: The Wholesale Buyer's Guide to Craft Artists*.

When the first edition was published in 1986, *The Guild* broke new ground in the marketing of crafts by becoming a bridge between craftspeople and the people who commission crafts. According to the 1997 rate card, an advertisement in *The Guild* will be seen by 7,000 architects, interior designers, art consultants, public art administrators, and other specialists who work in the architectural field who receive the book free. Another 3,000 books are sold through fine bookstores and direct mail in North America and abroad.

A full-page, full-color display ad with two photos and 80–120 words of copy, including layout, typesetting, and a black-and-white laser proof, will vary in cost depending on which of the three sourcebooks you choose. Additional photographs cost extra, and one thousand reprints are available for a fee. Half-page ads are available in *The Handbook* only.

Before you choose to advertise through *The Guild,* call to ask what type of response other craftspeople in your medium have received through their ads. It may take awhile for your ad to generate a profit, but in the long run, the results should be worthwhile. As an advertiser, you will receive added benefits such as mailing lists of design professionals, discounted rates on additional space in future editions and repeat pages, free listings, password-protected access to project announcements through the online Commissions Clearinghouse, application schedules and procedures, and the ability to be linked to its home page at no cost.

For an informational packet including a rate sheet, sample pages, and a complete listing and description of sourcebooks, contact Kraus-Sikes Inc. at 931 East Main Street, Suite 9, Madison, WI 53703; (800) 969-1556 or (608) 257-2590, or visit its Web site at *www.guild.com.*

You should realize that working with interior designers and architects is a long-term project, so you should be applying for new projects while you are still working on current ones. Although the process can require additional paperwork and flexibility to meet their specific needs, many craftspeople are successfully selling their work to this market.

CHAPTER 26

MAIL ORDER

According to Kathy Borrus in *The Business of Crafts,* a book by the Crafts Center, the mail-order business is a $60 billion-a-year business. Many department stores, specialty shops, and museum stores send out mail-order catalogs as a separate additional business, or as an advertisement to enhance their product offerings and bring customers into their stores. Other catalogs are a retail mail-order business only, with no store outlets. Catalogs often target a special market segment, such as gardening, home furnishings, ready-to-wear, and kitchen accessories. Many magazines also put out special issues devoted primarily to crafts.

Whether you sell your work through catalogs that already exist or decide to produce your own catalog, the same issues apply. How will the catalog be distributed? Will your customers buy your work through the mail? What percentage of your income do you think catalog sales can generate? Can you handle a large volume of orders?

Going into the mail-order business generally requires a willingness to produce your work in multiples and being able to easily fill orders of high-quality work in a timely fashion. Before you decide to sell your work through a catalog, find out if the catalog is mailed to people who fit your customer profile and include any costs of selling through the catalog in your pricing. You need to have an item that sells well and should maintain realistic expectations regarding sales.

Approaching Existing Companies

What is the best way to approach a catalog company to see if it is interested in carrying your work? Request catalogs to learn as much as you can about the catalog before approaching the buyers, to see if your work will complement the current work, the price range sold, and the type of work that fits the catalog's image. Then, call to find out to whom you should send information and what they need to see to make a decision. For example, catalog buyers generally prefer photographs rather than slides of your work.

Buyers are looking for consistent quality, your ability to supply your work in the necessary quantities, and the dollar amount an item can earn. Catalog companies do a lot of testing of their products and tend to find new items at craft or trade shows. Rather than order current designs, some buyers will want to work with you to design a special piece that will be exclusively marketed through their catalog.

When working with catalog companies, you will discover that different companies have different ways of working with craftspeople and may do any of the following:

- Ask the craftsperson to pay for the space his or her photograph and copy takes up in the catalog as well as the cost of the photography itself
- Pay for the photography and space that the copy requires but won't stock your product, sending you orders as received to be filled by you
- Buy the work outright from you at your wholesale prices
- Allow customers to order directly from you, charging you an insertion fee plus a commission on sales.

Noelle Backer relates in the article "Catalogs: Keeping Up with the Demand," published in the November 1997 issue of the *Crafts Report,* that craftsperson Tom Torrens sells his functional home and garden sculpture through catalogs like the Nature Company, Wind and Weather, and Gump's by Mail. All the catalogs Torrens deals with buy his work outright at wholesale prices, warehouse the inventory, and then fill orders directly. They also pay for shipping. For Torrens, this arrangement provides many benefits without the costs other types of catalogs may incur, such as insertion fees or commissions. "The best thing about it," says Torrens, "is that it's basically free advertising. It allows more people the opportunity to see your work; it's exposure."

Some mail-order retail firms buy only enough inventory to do the photography and require you to do the shipping. Even though the company believes your work will sell in its catalog, it is impossible to predetermine which items will and which won't. As a result, for every order the catalog company receives, it sends you a packing slip and mailing label for you to ship the work. This is a costly way for you to ship because you are giving the catalog company a volume discount, yet shipping to fill individual orders. Some companies will pay a small fee to offset this cost. You need to decide if the exposure and amount of orders you receive from a particular catalog company make it worth your while.

Just like anything else, it is important to develop a good relationship with the buyers at the catalog companies you work with. If you are having problems filling orders, let them know when you can have it done by and see if they still want the pieces.

Starting Your Own Mail-Order Business

If you are thinking of starting your own mail-order business, write a simple marketing plan, look at other catalogs for ideas, and call up companies whose catalogs you like for suggestions. You are designing this catalog to attract your customers, so write the copy as if you are speaking directly to them. Be sure to include whatever they need to place an order, such as your telephone number, an order form, and your policies. After you have done research, consider the following:

Having high-quality and attractive photographs taken of your work.

This is not the time to hire your friend who photographs weddings to take the photographs for your catalog. You want to work with someone who has done product shots or catalog work before, because photographs for a catalog are different than the slides of your work that you use to apply to craft fairs. Instead of highlighting one piece per frame as you would for a craft fair application, think about settings that show how your product is used. For example, if you make clothing, you may want to have a model, or if you make furniture, you may want to have a vase of flowers or a few books on a table, in a room setting to show how your work functions.

Hiring someone to write the copy.

Consider hiring the services of a professional writer if you are not good at writing or just don't have the time. If you do decide to do this yourself, review your product descriptions and write the copy as if you are speaking to your customers. Leave plenty of time to rewrite if necessary.

Working with a graphic designer and printer.

The same issues of putting together a brochure apply here. Figure out the way you want the catalog to look in terms of layout, design, typeface, the kind of paper, and ink colors.

How you will distribute it and how many copies do you need?

Will you mail it to your current customers, buy a mailing list, hand it out at fairs, or mail it in response to inquiries from an advertisement? Look over your marketing plans and estimate the number you will need.

How much time and money can you spend to have the catalog produced, printed, and mailed?

Will it be black and white or four color? The costs of putting together the catalog will be the same no matter how many copies you have printed. What about the costs of handling the orders, packing, shipping, postage, returns, complaints, and keeping your mailing list updated?

What about having your catalog online?

If you decide to offer your products online, your customers will be able to find out if the pieces are available or will have to be back-ordered, may be given expert advice on how to care for and use your products, and will be able to access your schedule of fairs or places where your work is sold.

Is there any way to follow up your catalog mailing?

Should you send a catalog more than once? What about sending some other direct-mail pieces as well, such as a postcard or sale special? Should you call on the phone?

When you get an order, can you ship it right away or do you need a few weeks to produce enough pieces?

How much inventory do you need to have on hand? A general rule of thumb is that all mail orders should be shipped within thirty days unless you specify another time period. If you need to delay the shipping of an item, it's a good idea to furnish customers with postcards to let them know when they can expect the item and allow them a chance to cancel or change the order if they can't wait.

Selling your work through a catalog can complement other methods of selling. Keep track of the results so you can evaluate the effectiveness of this way to market your work. How many catalogs were sent and how many orders were generated? Does this percentage match your goals? Although you may make less per sale by marketing your work through an existing catalog, having your work in an established catalog is a lot less work than starting your own catalog. Craftspeople with an established business may find that producing a simple catalog, as a printed piece or online, can be an easy way for buyers to reorder and be kept up-to-date on new products.

CHAPTER 27

SALES REPS

Are you comfortable with someone else selling your work? Do you make items that can be produced in volume to easily fill orders generated by a sales rep? Can your pricing handle the extra 10–30 percent commission for the sales rep in the wholesale price, while still keeping the retail price affordable? Can you handle the extra paperwork having a sales rep requires?

Most of the craftspeople I meet think if they just had a sales rep, all their problems would be solved. They would never have to promote themselves or make sales again, and they could spend all their time in the studio just making their pieces. Even if you locate a great sales rep who is able to sell your work, chances are you will still have to promote yourself and make sales in other ways. You may even have to make sure the sales rep is doing his or her job by checking in with them periodically.

Craftsperson Patti Dowse, in an article entitled "How Many Toads Do We Have to Kiss to Find Our Prince?" in the November 1994 issue of the *Crafts Report,* asserts that many people think hiring a sales rep is a risk-free way to increase sales. Since a sales rep's fees are based on sales, no sales would mean no fees. But there are other costs to consider before starting a search for a rep. The most obvious cost of doing business with a sales rep is the cost of samples. For Dowse's line of leather products, rep samples can cost $3,000. These are vulnerable to wear and tear, obsolescence, and outright thievery, which often happens when a rep is not reputable. She counts these items as a cost of sale, then adds fees for support services including phone calls to the rep, travel to meet with the rep, sending updated sales literature and color sheets, and book-keeping to keep track of commissions.

What materials would you need to provide to sell your work through the services of a sales rep? To help ensure a successful relationship, sales reps need the following:

- Excellent promotional material in sufficient quantities to give to buyers, such as catalogs, brochures with complete descriptions and photographs, wholesale and retail price sheets, samples of your work, and starter assortments of your best selling items.
- To be paid their commissions in a timely manner and sent a listing of accounts. Sales reps need to know that current customers have received their shipments before visiting them.
- Communication from you concerning production schedules and availability of work, new items introduced in time for seasonal buying (such as in the summer for the holiday buying season), and any problems or changes.
- Orders to be filled promptly. Reps prefer that you fill orders within two to four weeks, so that buyers receive their orders when they expect to.
- An exclusive territory. Note any exceptions, such as preexisting accounts.
- Reasonable prices that can be marked up to retail and still sell easily.

In exchange, a good sales rep can give the craftsperson:
- Valuable marketing and pricing feedback from the buyers and their customers.
- Information on current trends.
- Suggestions for improvement to current pieces or for new pieces based on customer feedback.
- Exposure at trade shows and permanent showrooms as well as road sales.
- Enough sales to justify the expense of paying them.
- More time in the studio producing work.

Finding the Right Sales Rep for Your Work

You can always find a sale rep, but how do you find a good one? Before you start your search, decide why you want a sales rep so you will know what is important. Do you want to increase your sales, sell to a new market, or sell in a different part of the country? Once you know what you want a sales rep to accomplish, it will be easier to find prospective reps who can help you meet your goals. Look for someone with whom you enjoy working that can garner results and give you constructive feedback as well.

I want a sales rep because:

1. _____
2. _____
3. _____

You can find a sales rep for your work through a referral from another craftsperson or gallery, a directory or registry service, advertising in trade magazines, looking at show directories, or by referring to the following sources:

- *Jill Ford's Rep Registry* is a service that will match sales reps and producers. For a fee, she will search her database and give you appropriate names. If you hire one, you owe her another fee. She has also written a book called *Working with Wholesale Giftware Reps: A Beginner's Handbook.* Contact Jill Poulsen Ford at Box 2306, Capistrano Beach, CA 92624; (949) 240-3333; *www.giftbusiness.com.*
- *The Directory of Wholesale Reps for Crafts Professionals* lists over one hundred reps giving information about territories, showrooms and shows, types and numbers of accounts, commission rate, crafts wanted, and material required from craftspeople interested in their services. For more information, contact Northwoods Trading Company at 13451 Essex Court, Eden Prairie, MN 55347-1708; (800) 715-9594; *www.craftassoc.com/olson.*
- ArtNetwork rents mailing lists of reps, consultants, and dealers for a fee. Contact ArtNetwork at P.O. Box 1360, Nevada City, CA 95959; (800) 383-0677; *www.artmarketing.com.*

When contacting sales reps, send your brochure, high-quality color photos, and a wholesale price list, along with a cover letter on your stationery. Include an SASE or a response card to help guarantee a response. Send samples only if they are requested.

A week or two later, make a follow-up call to make sure your information has been received. Ask the sales rep for estimates of how much work he or she can sell, if any other information is needed, or if the person would like to see a sample piece. If the rep is interested in representing your work, ask for references of other craftspeople he or she represents.

Contracts

You have done your research and have found a sales rep. Congratulations! The next step is to draw up a contract outlining your arrangement. Ask your lawyer to review the contract, and you and the rep should each sign and keep a copy. A contract with a sales representative should address the following issues:

- The sales territory. Note any exceptions, such as sharing it with another rep or gallery, or the right to change the territory from exclusive to nonexclusive.
- How the commission rate is determined for original orders and reorders and the dates when commissions will no longer be given on reorders.
- The time frame in which commissions are paid.
- Clarification of who owns the product samples.
- Terms that spell out whether the rep is an independent contractor or employee.
- Acknowledgement that the agreement is with this particular rep and cannot be transferred to another rep without your permission.
- A clause requiring the rep to keep certain information about your business confidential such as customer lists.
- A clause restricting your rep from using confidential information about your business to compete with you after your relationship ends.
- Just cause for termination of the contract for you and the sales rep.
- A period of time to allow for termination without cause based on reasonable notice, such as two months.

If you do give a rep an exclusive territory, only do so for a specific period of time. This way you can evaluate the level of sales that he or she is making, and if things are going well, you can renew the exclusive territory clause. If the rep is not selling your work well, then you have a valid reason to hire the services of another rep without losing a lot of valuable time.

If you are able to fill orders of your work in a timely manner and feel that you can work with a sales rep, this can be a lucrative way to make sales. Using a sales rep is not for every craftsperson so you need to decide if having a rep is valuable and profitable. Start out slowly and keep good records so you can easily evaluate your progress.

CHAPTER 28

THE INTERNET

Imagine having a low-cost way to reach potential customers all over the world, 365 days a year, seven days a week, twenty-four hours a day, at the very instant that they decide they want to purchase a handmade art or craft object. According to Ilise Benun (*www.selfpromotiononline.com*), "You must spread the word. You must speak up if you want to be heard; your work will not speak for itself. You must listen and respond to your prospects. You must offer something of substance and of value. You must participate. So get ready to add a very powerful medium to your message, because if you make a commitment to promoting yourself and your services, both online and offline, your business will grow."

Visualize your Web site from your potential customers' point of view regarding not only what they would need to know to make a purchase but also what will set you apart from your competitors and make the selling process over the Internet more personalized. For example, say you need to buy a wedding present and decide to look for some pottery using the Internet. Your search locates two potters who have Web sites to market and sell the type of work you want. The first potter's site has all the basic tools she needs to sell her work online: samples of the work, prices, and ordering information. The second potter's site has all of the above, and also includes features like a schedule of upcoming craft fairs where you can meet the potter and watch him make his work; links to other sites that you will find useful, such as sites with information on collecting and caring for handmade pottery; sample glaze recipes and tips sharing how the potter gets the beautiful effect you love on his pieces; and an e-mail link or real-time database that you can use to send him an inquiry, so that you can see what he currently has in stock. Who would you buy from? Customers at a crafts fair like to buy from the craftsperson who is fun to talk to, who provides a story to bring home along with the work, and who teaches them a little something about the craft. Customers surfing the net want to have a personal experience, too.

What does a Web site offer a craftsperson interested in selling her work online? Although the Internet is just another communications tool, it has several important qualities that make it different from other selling venues:

- Speed and round-the-clock access
- Low cost
- Deeper and deeper levels of detailed content
- Easy updates
- The option to personalize a sale with the aid of e-mail and digital photography
- A variety of ways to have an online presence, whether you choose to have your own Web site or are included on an online listing
- The opportunity to share information and give back to the crafts community

The Internet offers the ability to reach potential and current customers with timely information, anytime, at a low cost. At the touch of a button, the consumer can learn about you and your work and, even better, make a purchase. Increasingly, as time goes on, craftspeople who do not have a presence on the Internet may be bypassed by buyers, shop owners, and galleries, because it is much more convenient to communicate with craftspeople who are online.

What are your expectations for your site? Do you just want to have an easy way for people to see your work, or do you want to sell your work directly from the site? Take a few minutes to jot down some of your reasons for having a Web site, then read the following ways other artists and craftspeople have decided to use a Web site.

Your Reasons for Having a Web Site:

_____

_____

_____

_____

_____

How to Use the Web as Part of Your Business Plan

How do craftspeople use Web sites to help promote their businesses? While some craftspeople see the Internet as a way to easily sell potential customers their work, others use it to find new markets, keep information current, or as a follow-up tool for commission requests.

According to a study done by the *Crafts Report* magazine (*www.craftsreport.com*) called "Are Craftspeople Making Money on the Internet?," nearly half the respondents said they make less than $500 in a year, a quarter are making between $500 and $5,000 a year, and a very small percentage are making more than $15,000 on Internet sales. A third of the respondents who were making $8,000 to $15,000 a year had had a presence on the Internet for more than five years, compared to less than 4 percent who had had a presence for only one or two years. For many artists, these online retail sales make up a large percentage of their total annual income, with nearly a third of them having online retail sales constituting 75 to 100 percent of their total income!

Although the *Crafts Report* readership may include more established and marketing-savvy craftspeople, Peace Fleece (*www.peacefleece.com*), a Russian-American and Middle East—American wool, knitting, and felting products company, found that after only one year on the Internet, 90 percent of its orders were coming in online rather than over the phone or through the mail. "Before using the Web, we had about eight thousand retail customers and our products where sold through four hundred stores," says Peter Hagerty, owner of Peace Fleece. "After designing our Web page, we decided not to put out a paper catalog. The printing and mailing costs were getting so expensive, and many of the catalogs were not getting delivered. Now we probably have over ten thousand retail customers and enjoy the flexibility the Internet offers to respond quickly to customer inquiries."

Although the Internet may seem to some like an impersonal way to shop, there is the potential to personalize the medium that will help you successfully sell your work. Glass artist Josh Simpson (*www.megaplanet.com*) has had a Web site since 1995 and has been amazed at the growth of sales through his site. "The Internet can be a personal way of shopping," says Josh. "For example, when we get an e-mail request, we send back a personalized response and include digital photographs of the glass work currently in our inventory. With this kind of information, a customer can pick a vase directly off our shelves and have it shipped immediately. Although I never thought I would sell my work online when I first got my site, annual sales currently equal to one craft fair." For many professional craftspeople, even one crafts fair can be a significant source of income.

If you make different types of work, how can you design your Web site to attract different types of customers? Tile-maker, potter, and sculptor Chris Gustin (*www.gustinceramics.com*), says, "My Web site was designed to serve two functions. The first is to advertise and promote my tile work, with the primary audience being architects and designers. The second is to promote myself as an artist, highlighting my pottery and sculpture work, and promote events held at my studio (such as firings done in my wood kiln), which target ceramic collectors, galleries, artists, and students. Both functions have been very successful and have offered me a way to give vast amounts of information to a large group of people. For example, the tile studio section of the site offers an online catalog that allows me, for a very small price, to publish an extensive amount of information on the tile company, while the sculptural ceramics section is a resource on my work, listing galleries that show my current work, as well as archives of my past work. My Web site is where I can put my professional life on view, so anyone who is interested in my work can find information on me. This has been invaluable to me in many ways and has proved to be a tremendous asset to my studio."

What if you are looking for a way to not only find new markets but also keep in touch with customers with whom you have already had contact? Artist Elizabeth Busch (*www.elizabethbusch.com*), an artist who makes her living from a combination of public art commissions, teaching, and art quilts, says, "I see it as a connection with the people taking my workshops, as well as another way to connect with art consultants, interior designers, and architects to expand my commission work."

Some craftspeople use a Web site as a follow-up tool. Candace Jackman (*www.jackmansglass.com*), who designs and makes custom-designed stained glass, says, "My site is set up as a gallery of my work for potential customers not only to see samples of my work, but also to show the pieces to someone else who is a part of the decision-making process. I rarely make a sale at a fair, and the Web site functions as an important follow up tool for me."

If you use a Web site to sell your work, will your Web address be the same name as your business? How will a prospective customer find your page? Will you be linked to another company or organization for additional exposure? How will you successfully advertise or get publicity for your site? And what can you do to keep a customer at your site long enough to generate an inquiry or sale?

Domain Names

To make your Web site easy to find by anyone who knows the name of your business, use a service that can provide a Web address (also called a Universal Resource Locator or URL) in the form "*www.yourbusiness.com.*" If your business has high name recognition, this could be a valuable feature for you. For example, when I decided to get a Web site, I registered my business as *www.artbiz.info,* utilizing not only my business name but also the implied sense of service with the ".info" domain, instead of ".com." For more information about registering your domain name, check out *www.register.com* or *www.networksolutions.com.* If you already have a Web site and don't want to change hosts, you may want to upgrade to a more marketable address by using a domain forwarding service to direct traffic from the new name to your existing site.

Search Engines

What if someone is looking for your product and has never heard of your business? The Internet has a form of the yellow pages, called a search engine. For example, if a gallery owner is interested in finding new fiber artists who work specifically in cotton and make blankets, she might type into a search engine "*artists* and *fiber* and *cotton* and *blankets.*" If any sites are found that meet the search criteria, a list appears on her screen. She could look at any or all of the sites at any time, day or night. The only cost would be her time and her Internet connection fee. As a craftsperson interested in marketing your work through the Internet, you would want to identify as many characteristics (also known as keywords or Metatags) about your business as possible, to aid someone using a search engine in locating your type of products. If you are interested in submitting your Web address to search engines, check out the following sites: *www.submit.com,* *www.123add-it.com, www.selfpromotion.com,* or *www.websitegarage.com.*

Linking Your Site

Many visitors will find your site by a circuitous route, rather than typing your Web address directly into the address bar on their browser. For example, a visitor to your site may have started out at the site of a state craft organization and found a link to your page by reviewing the membership list. Links are an important Internet marketing tool and can increase traffic, boost your credibility, and add value to your site. But how can you get your site linked to other sites? Try bartering links with your competition as a way to increase traffic and add value to both sites, by not only educating but also giving visitors more choices. Many craft or business organizations offer members the ability to link their Web site to the organization's Web site. For example, the Maine Crafts Association (*www.mainecrafts.org*) allows those with a professional-level membership to be linked to its page, with both an image and a small amount of text listed on the membership list page. The National Craft Organization (*www.craftassoc.com*) offers links to your Web site for a small fee and also offers affordable Web-page design. Even if you have to pay to join an organization, or join at a higher level than you had planned, to be eligible for the link, it may be worthwhile for all the extra "hits" your site will receive as a result. For more ideas on linking your site, check out *www.artmarketing.com* or *www.artisthelpnetwork.com*. And don't forget, if there are places you think would be good links for your page, contact them and find out if they offer that service. All they can say is no, right?

Advertising and Publicity

Your Web page or online presence should be part of your overall advertising and publicity efforts. One of the easiest ways to advertise your site is to add your Web site and e-mail address to all of your printed materials (including your business card, brochure, price pages, newsletter, stationery, and invoices) as a way to direct people to your site. For example, consider sending out a postcard mailing announcing your site (once it's ready), not only to your current mailing list but to places you want to know about your business. Write informational articles for on- and offline publications that show you as an expert in your field, as a way of directing people to your Web site. Participate in online chat rooms and note your Web site address with your comments. The possibilities for promoting your Web site are endless!

Designing a Web Site

When designing your site, start by translating the information and images from your brochure or catalog into a format suitable for a Web site presentation. Think about what you want the customers to do after they see your site. Should they call you and leave their address and telephone number so you can send them something and follow up with a call, or will they place an order immediately online? Which method would be easiest not only for you but for your customers?

One of the advantages of using a Web site over print media is that you can change the information quickly. For example, if your prices change or something is out of stock, you can either change the price or delete the product from your Web site, even temporarily. With a brochure or catalog the item would still remain in your brochure until you have the piece reprinted. "I can continually update and change the site according to my needs," says Chris Gustin of *www.gustinceramics.com,* "and because it's online, there is little cost incurred. The site also allows me to advertise the tile to a much larger client base than a paper catalog would, due to cost issues, and a significant amount of business has come in because of this."

Some people design their own Web sites, while others pay a fee to have someone else design the site. If you are interested in designing your own site, there are templates you can buy that you can download and modify, or you can learn how to design your own by taking a class. If you do choose to hire a designer, be sure to inquire about how your site will be updated. Some designers allow you to make the necessary updates to your site right from your own computer through the use of a password, while others require you to pay a small fee to have their staff make the changes. In addition to paying a fee to design a Web site, you may have a monthly service fee. The monthly fee should be reasonable, and you can get a package that usually includes: (1) an e-mail account, (2) connection to the Internet, and (3) a dedicated amount of space on the designer's server. There are also packages available that will allow more than one e-mail address, and more space on the server. Comparison shop by contacting at least three companies. Try to evaluate the companies' reputation and viability, as well as cost. Interruptions of service or having to replace a defunct host can be very disruptive to your marketing efforts.

Although designing a Web site is similar to putting together a brochure or catalog, there are some fundamental differences. Here are a few things to keep in mind when designing your Web site:

- The Internet is a medium that encourages skimming and scanning until you find something of interest; then you should be able to delve into more detail.
- The Web site must offer an easy way for a customer to inquire or place an order.
- The easier a Web site is to navigate and the more content your site offers, the longer a visitor may stay.
- Remember—you don't have to show everything. It's better to offer samples of your best or most recent work.

Other aspects of Web page design to keep in mind are the things you shouldn't do:

- Don't let your site be "under construction" for a sustained period of time.
- Avoid posting information that lacks real content.
- Never keep information on your site that is out of date—it will compromise the credibility of your Web presence.
- A site that is too slow to load will frustrate potential customers. Make sure the technical aspects of your site function well.

Maintaining Your Site

Your Web site is finally done and now you can forget about it and go back to the studio (you think). Just as you need to update your printed materials on a regular basis, your Web site will need regular review, as well. The fast-moving nature of the Internet makes it inappropriate to display outdated information. Nothing is worse than a "What's New" page that is full of old news or that never changes. Have you designed a new piece or product line? Did you recently receive an award at a show? Have you changed your prices, or are some of your items on sale? Where will you be showing your work in the near future? Give visitors a reason to bookmark your site and return on a regular basis by sharing not only new work but your achievements and stories, as well. It is also quick and easy to rotate photographs and graphics to give your site a fresh look.

E-mail

Communication via e-mail can be a timesaver, provides an unobtrusive way to approach and court a new customer, and is a quick way to follow up a conversation or meeting. E-mail allows you to send a message that is received immediately, and it can help to eliminate phone tag. Like other forms of communication, e-mail can be used as an introduction, a follow up, or as a means to network, ask questions, get feedback, or simply send a thank you. Again, the Internet is all about speed and responsiveness, so set a goal of replying to all valid e-mail messages daily. For some people, even the lag time in e-mail can be frustrating. As a result, instant message programs are beginning to be used for business communication.

How can you use e-mail to your advantage in terms of your overall marketing efforts? Believe it or not, your customers and potential customers really do want to hear from you and to see your latest work. Compile a mailing list for an online marketing plan, come up with a targeted list of e-mail addresses, and start sending out information on a periodic basis. You may be surprised at the results.

Web Site Promotion and Marketing Plans

What can you do to market and promote your Web site? According to the *Crafts Report* survey mentioned above, here are the methods of the artists who made more than $8,000 in annual online sales:

- Advertising in magazines, craft and noncraft
- Direct marketing
- Submitting the sites to search engines regularly
- Writing articles for publication on other craft-related Web sites
- Displaying work on free, online galleries
- Linking exchanges with related sites
- Advertising on craft mall sites
- Classified advertising

Those that want their sites to be part of their crafts business need to make sure that the sites are visited regularly by potential customers, as well as figure out how and where Web sites fit into their business plans.

Not all artists and craftspeople make sales directly from their sites. Artist Amanda Barrow (*www.amandabarrow.com*) has had a Web site since 1996 and, to date, has never made a direct sale from it. When asked why she continues to maintain her site, she said, "When I first got my Web page, I think people paid more attention to it. Now everyone has one, and it isn't as special or unusual as it once was. I got it because I felt that in order to reach more people quickly, the Internet was, and still is, the most efficient and inexpensive tool I could use to get my visual message across. Although I haven't sold one thing directly from it, I refer people to it, especially gallery people, so they can get a taste of my work before they receive my slides. Basically, it's just one more tool an artist can use to get her message out into the world. That's the bottom line. At this point, I ask my artist friends, 'Why wouldn't you have a Web site?' It's so easy and cheap to maintain."

CHAPTER 29

CUSTOMERS

Your potential customers are everywhere. They are young and old, male and female, friends, neighbors, and relatives, other craftspeople, people who like to go to craft fairs, shop through mail-order catalogs, or use the Internet, wholesale buyers from craft shops and galleries, as well as interior designers and architects.

As a craftsperson interested in selling your work, your job is to figure out who your potential customers are and let them know about your work so they can buy it. Sounds simple. Knowing who your customers are makes all the other tasks you need to do to run your business easier, because you will know you are spending your marketing time and dollars wisely to attract the people who will actually buy your work.

After you have determined who your customers are, using the customer profile worksheet included in this chapter, develop customer service policies that will enable you to treat customers fairly and retain them. It is a well-known fact that it is much more cost effective to retain current customers than to find new ones.

Profiles

To figure out who your customers are, look at a piece of your work and think about who would buy it and where they shop? Most craftspeople have more than one customer type, so you many want to do the customer profile worksheet several times in order to come up with all the possibilities for your work. If you have already made some sales, remember who bought your work and translate that into a customer profile.

Devise a set of questions tailored to your business to ask customers so you can keep detailed notes to see if your profiles are on target or if there are more types than you imagined. Use the questions on the worksheet on the next page to help you get started and add a couple of your own.

For example, let's say there is a company called Wearable Weavings for Women and we are looking at a beautiful brown and black handwoven jacket with a dark brown silk lining and very unusual buttons that retails for $500. Who do you think would like this jacket, could afford it, and would actually buy it? Where would they find it? You might guess that the customers for this garment are interested in unusual clothing, shop at craft fairs and boutiques, are primarily women over the age of twenty-five, with an annual income of $40,000, who would spend between $200 and $500 on a special garment they really want to own. Other customers might buy these garments as a gift. Does the customer profile in this example sound right?

Now try to figure out who your customers are by filling out the Customer Profile Worksheet.

Customer Service Policies

All customer services policies should be based on the golden rule: Treat other people the way you would like to be treated. What should you do if someone wants to return one of your pieces for a refund; orders a piece to be shipped and when it arrives, it's broken; or pays with a check and it bounces? You need to have customer service policies in place to manage situations like these.

How will your customers know about your policies? You should have them posted in your showroom, listed on your order form, or in your brochure or catalog. Customer service policies give you and your staff guidelines to handle customer questions, problems, and complaints in a consistent way. Although policies are usually the result of your wish to avoid problems, you need to stay flexible and decide when it's appropriate to make an exception to a policy. Empower your employees to be able to make decisions without your okay so that when a situation warrants an adjustment to the policy, the employee can resolve the problem without having to keep the customer waiting while trying to find you.

Welcome the opportunity to fix a problem or listen to a complaint. Although the customer standing in front of you may seem difficult, the person

Customer Profile Worksheet

Who is most likely to buy my work? _____

Are my customers most likely men or women or both? _____

Is there any age group that is most likely to buy my work? _____

Do my current customers have anything in common? _____

Where do they like to shop? (Check all that apply)

☐ Craft Fairs ☐ Craft Shop ☐ Gallery ☐ Mail-Order Catalog

☐ Studio Sales ☐ Malls ☐ Internet ☐ Other

How would they find out about my business? (Check all that apply.)

☐ Sign ☐ Advertisement ☐ Directory ☐ Fair

☐ Gallery ☐ Shop ☐ Internet ☐ Other

Do they live in the city or the country? _____

How far will they travel to shop? _____

Do they make purchases on vacations? _____

How much money do they earn annually? _____

What price range for a piece could they afford? _____

Are they buying for themselves or shopping for gifts? _____

Who makes the buying decision? _____

Do they have to check with someone before purchasing? _____

What magazines and newspapers do they read? _____

_____

Where could I advertise to reach them? _____

How many times do I have to contact customers before they will buy? _____

Will they buy from me more than once? _____

Description of a typical customer: _____

_____

_____

is in fact giving you a chance to make things right by complaining. If you can come up with a good solution, the customer will not only be pleased but will tell everyone he or she knows about how well you handled the situation. If you can't rectify the situation, the person will *not* be pleased and will, unfortunately, tell everyone he or she knows. It's not a question of *if* something will go wrong; it's a question of how you will handle things that *do* go wrong that's important.

If a customer doesn't seem pleased when quoted a policy, ask the customer what he or she feels would be fair given the situation. The person may come up with a viable solution that makes him or her happy and may not ask you for as much as you think. By asking customers for their input, they become an active part of the solution. Err on the side of doing the right thing whenever possible.

Consider the following questions when determining the policies you want to have in place:

- *Return policies* Under what circumstances will you accept your work back, if at all? For example, will you only accept returns of your work with a receipt? Is there a time limit on returns (e.g., within 30 days of purchase)? Will you give a cash refund or a credit toward another purchase? What if the work is damaged? Will your insurance policy cover this?

- *Methods of payment* Will you offer a discount for cash? Will you accept bills larger than twenties? Will you accept checks? Will you require a telephone number or another form of ID in case the check is returned? Will you charge a fee for a returned check? Which credit cards will you accept? What if the card is maxed out? Will you charge customers who use a credit card an extra fee or build it into your overall pricing?

Have a place where you and your staff can keep track of things you aren't sure how to handle so you can incorporate them into your customer policies.

Retaining Customers

In addition to the bottom line, some indicators of how well your business is doing may be if you are retaining your customers, if your customers give you repeat business, or if your customers refer your product or services to other people. Do your customers compliment you on what a good job you are doing? How will you measure your ability to retain customers?

What can you do to retain your customers? Having quality products, at an affordable price, with fast, friendly, and knowledgeable service is a good start. But more than that, you should consider other incentives to give your customers a reason to keep coming back. Can you offer incentives for current customers such as gift wrapping, shipping, free local delivery, a newsletter, special previews, or demonstrations? Put your creativity to work to find ways of treating your current clientele well and you will retain your customers with ease.

Whether you are beating the bushes looking for customers or trying to withstand the constant flood of customers, determining who they are, designing policies to treat them fairly, and offering incentives to retain them are very important aspects of your business. Without your customers, you wouldn't be in business.

RESOURCES

CHAPTER 30

NETWORKING

If you feel uncomfortable talking about yourself and your work, and the idea of networking is the last thing you would choose to do, you're not alone. Many people feel as if they're not supposed to talk about themselves because that would be bragging, or having a big ego, or seem pushy. But how will anyone know about your work if you don't talk about it? If you don't tell them, who will?

Networking is simply going to places that attract the kind of people who are your customers to have a chance to meet them, talk about your business, and find a way to keep in touch with them. How do you know which organizations your customers belong to? For example, if you are interested in breaking into the interior design market, you may want to join the local ASID chapter. If your products are garden sculptures, you might want to join the local garden club.

Networking also gives you the opportunity to meet other people in business to share valuable tips and information, take workshops, and gain access to much needed business services such as group health insurance. For example, you might try joining the chamber of commerce or your local crafts organization.

Just joining an organization or attending a couple of events isn't enough. You have to get out there, mingle, and figure out ways to let people know about your business—or it doesn't count. Here are a couple ideas to help get you started:

Attend events and talk with people.

Ask people questions to start a conversation such as if they have been to these meetings before, how long they have been a member, or what their business is. Many of the other people there will feel just as awkward as you do at first and will be happy to have a conversation with someone. Think of a few questions that you would feel comfortable asking so you are prepared when you meet someone new, and write them below.

Questions

1. _____

2. _____

3. _____

Join a committee and help organize some of the events.

Although this requires a time commitment on your part, you will get to know several people very well by working on a committee and, more importantly, they will get to know you. Perhaps you could host one of the meetings at your studio or donate one of your pieces to be used as a door prize to increase your visibility in the organization.

Exchange business cards.

You are not trying to give away as many of your business cards as you can but to get cards from the people you think should know more about your business. For example, with one of their business cards, you can follow up with a mailing or a telephone call. People expect to exchange business cards so feel free to suggest it if you think someone may be a potential customer or can refer you to someone else.

Keep in touch with the people you meet.

Put them on your mailing list and invite them to see your studio or visit your booth at a fair. Although they may not have a need to purchase one of your pieces now, something may come up later and they will remember you. People like to work with people they know.

There is no right or wrong way to network. You may even already be doing it but didn't realize that by attending a workshop, you were actually promoting your business.

Craft Organizations

Joining a crafts organization may be one of the best business decisions you can make. A craft organization will usually give you information and announcements of upcoming events; access to having your work sold in a shop, fair, or show; slide registries; group health and studio insurance; workshops; and the chance to meet other craftspeople in your area. Call your local crafts organization for membership information and benefits. If you aren't aware of one, call the American Craft Council listed in this chapter for suggestions.

Many state craft centers also publish a guide to craft galleries, shops, and individual showrooms, which are usually distributed free in information booths, shops and galleries. In addition, there are numerous organizations dedicated to specific mediums. Ask your reference librarian to show you the guide to nonprofit organizations or contact the American Craft Council at (212) 274-0630; *www.craftcouncil.com*. Some craft organizations are listed below.

- Arizona Designer Craftsmen, 218 West Knox Drive, Tucson, AZ 85705; (520) 791-4063; *www.intrec.com/adc*.
- Arkansas Craft Guild, P.O. Box 800, Mountain View, AR 72560; (870) 269-3897; *www.arkansascraftguild.org*.
- Craft Alliance of Missouri, 6640 Delmar Boulevard, St. Louis, MO 63130; (314) 725-1177; *www.craftalliance.org*.
- Florida Craftsmen, 501 Central Ave., St. Petersburg, FL 33701; (727) 821-7391.
- Kentucky Art and Craft Foundation, 609 West Main Street, Louisville, KY 40202; (502) 589-0102; *www.kentuckycrafts.org*.
- League of New Hampshire Craftsmen, 205 North Main Street, Concord, NH 03301; (603) 224-3375; *www.nhcrafts.org*.
- Maine Crafts Association, 15 Walton Street, Portland, ME 04103; (207) 780-1807; *www.mainecrafts.org*.
- Michigan Guild Artists and Artisans, 118 North Fourth Avenue, Ann Arbor, MI 48104; (734) 662-3382; *www.michiganguild.org*.
- Ohio Designer Craftsmen, 1665 West Fifth Avenue, Columbus, OH 43212; (614) 486-4402; *www.saso-oh.org/odc*.

- Pennsylvania Guild of Craftsmen, P.O. Box 820, Richboro, PA 18954; (215) 579-5997; *www.Pennsylvaniacrafts.com.*
- Southern Highland Craft Guild, P.O. Box 9545, Asheville, NC 28815; (828) 298-7928; *www.southernhighlandguild.org.*
- Vermont State Craft Center, Frog Hollow, 1 Mill Street, Middlebury, VT 05753; (802) 388-3177; *www.froghollow.org.*

If you are interested in joining a national crafts organization, contact the American Craft Council (ACC) at 72 Spring Street, New York, NY 10013; (212) 274-0630, (800) 724-0859; *www.craftcouncil.org.* Membership includes a subscription to *American Craft* magazine, access to group health insurance, library privileges, free admission to its museum, and information about the ACC juried craft fairs.

Business Associations

Don't overlook the opportunities that may be available to you through local business associations such as your local chamber of commerce, Rotary, and Kiwanis Clubs, as well as other small-business management organizations like the SBA or SCORE. Although the membership will be made up of a wide variety of types of businesses and professions, there are valuable contacts to be made here and services to use.

For example, many chamber of commerce offices have information booths where you can put your brochures so visitors can find your showroom. They also offer workshops on various business topics and provide access to group health insurance. Chambers of commerce host a variety of functions to help promote different businesses as well as the area where they are located, such as early-bird breakfast meetings, annual dinner meetings, and business after-hours receptions. Call your local chamber of commerce for details.

The most important thing is to find an organization you like where you can increase your skills, meet other people, and get the word out about your business. Networking is just talking about your business.

CHAPTER 31

WORKSHOPS

Whether you take a continuing education course or a workshop offered through a guild, association, or small business center, there are a lot of people and services available to help you run your business better. Sign up for the next available workshop, because the longer you wait, the more time you will waste until you get the assistance you need. Business help can translate directly into time and money.

Continuing Education Programs

Art and craft schools are beginning to offer formal business courses to their students as well as workshops to the public through their continuing education programs. Not only are these geared specifically to artists and craftspeople, but they offer an opportunity to meet other craftspeople in your area that may be running their own businesses too. Some workshops may be offered for college credit as well.

Many of the business seminars I have taught through ArtBiz have been at places that had not previously offered a business seminar for artists and craftspeople. These places include continuing education programs at colleges and universities, local art associations, galleries and craft shops, craft supply stores, and high school adult education programs. Call your local art school or craft organization to see if there is a course or workshop offered near you. If there are places that you think should offer a class, ask them to arrange either a one-day workshop or a series of speakers on various topics. They may be surprised at the large response.

Here are a few business courses and resources available to the general public:

- **Oregon College of Art & Craft**, 8245 Southwest Barnes Road, Portland, OR 97225; (503) 297-5544; *www.ocac.edu*. Offering a three-quarter-long sequence course called Business Practices, as well as short-term topic-specific workshops in which practicing artists and craftspeople seeking a stronger career focus can gain skills in handling the business side of their work through presentations by business professionals and hands-on classroom practice. The sequence covers gallery representation, legal issues, marketing, grants-manship, finances and accounting, forms of doing business, developing a portfolio, and professional presentations. The course is available for college credit.

- **School of the Museum of Fine Arts**, 230 The Fenway, Boston, MA 02115-5596; (617) 369-3638; *www.smfa.edu*. The Artists Resource Center at the School of the Museum of Fine Arts is dedicated to helping artists with career development. Paid subscribers receive the biweekly *Artist's Resource Letter,* access to Jobline, a resource library, and can schedule individual appointments with trained staff.

    The center also offers a two-semester-long credit course called Survival and Business Skills for the Visual Artist, offered through the continuing education office, which addresses the special questions that artists face in their careers. What does marketing mean? Is public art a real opportunity? How do I get grants? How do juries work? What are my legal rights? What about insurance? What about health hazards? How do I find a studio and keep it? Coordinated by a professional artist, each session has a guest speaker that is a well-seasoned professional.

- **Worcester Center for Crafts**, 25 Sagamore Road, Worcester, MA 01605; (508) 753-8183; *www.worcestercraftcenter.org*. Offering a one-semester course called Business Practices Seminar, this course covers portfolio requirements, artist's statements, résumés, slide photography, taxes, business cards and letterhead design, grant writing, trade shows, retail and consignment options, and gallery visits. Coordinated by a member of the faculty, the center has several visiting instructors.

Guilds and Associations

Many craft organizations offer business workshops for their members at their annual conferences. If you aren't aware of any, look in the nonprofit directories at your public library for topic-specific associations that may offer business and marketing workshops at their annual meetings. For example, under Crafts, there are about seventy-five organizations listed, such as the American Association of Woodturners, the Handweavers Guild of America, the Knifemakers Guild, the Knitting Guild of America, the Marquetry Society of America, the National Council on Education for the Ceramic Arts (NCECA), and the Society of North American Goldsmiths (SNAG), to name a few. Or call the Visual Artists Information Hotline at (800) 232-2789 for information.

The following two places periodically offer business assistance for artists and craftspeople:

- **The Center for Design and Business**, 20 Washington Place, Providence, RI 02903; (401) 454-6558. Started in 1996, the Center for Design and Business—a joint venture between Bryant College and Rhode Island School of Design—organizes business workshops for artists, craftspeople, and other visual and performing artists, and also works with businesses to increase creativity and problem-solving skills in the business world. Contact the center for a schedule of events.
- **Arts Business Institute**, 2229 Paseo de los Chamisos, Santa Fe, NM 87505; (505) 424-1261; *www.artbusinessinstitute.org*. Held annually, this three-day conference covers more than two dozen business topics and offers excellent networking opportunities. Scholarships are available.

Small Business Centers

Small business centers can be found all over the country. Although their services are not primarily geared to the concerns of craftspeople, they can offer valuable advice and services to new businesses of any type and size.

- **Small Business Administration (SBA)**, (800) 8-ASK-SBA, *www. sba.gov.* The SBA offers assistance for starting a business, writing business plans, finding shareware computer programs, workshops, information files, and more. Contact the association for the office nearest you.
- **Service Corps of Retired Executives Association (SCORE)**, (800) 634-0245, *www.score.org.* SCORE offers free management assistance and

low-cost workshops for starting or expanding a business by retired executives who volunteer their time and expertise. SCORE offers pre-business workshops for people just getting started as well as special-ized seminars for those further along in the process. SCORE's volunteer leadership is divided into ten regions in order to foster the development of community-oriented chapters. For example, in 1996, SCORE offered over more than 4,000 workshops in the United States.

- **Volunteer Lawyers for the Arts (VLA)**, 1 East 53rd Street, Sixth Floor, New York, NY 10022; (800) 864-0476; *www.vlany.org*. Volunteer lawyers offer advice and workshops on topics such as copyright law and leases in various locations around the United States to artists and craftspeople who qualify financially. Call for the VLA office nearest you.

You should plan to continue your business education by taking work-shops periodically through continuing education programs, guilds, and asso-ciations, as well as taking advantage of the services offered through small business centers. Workshops can be important ongoing sources of business information to craftspeople running their own businesses.

CHAPTER 32

BUSINESS MAGAZINES

Subscriptions to magazines, periodicals, and newsletters will help keep you informed, give you tips and ideas to sell your work, and encouragement to run your business more successfully.

Even though magazine subscriptions are a legitimate business expense, the cost can add up, especially if you get more than one. Consider subscribing with a friend, asking your public library to subscribe, or visiting the library at your local crafts organization. Suggest a subscription to a magazine as a gift idea to your friends and family.

Although there are many magazines from which to choose, I suggest that you subscribe to at least one magazine created solely for your medium as well as a general business magazine for craftspeople. If you are not familiar with magazines designed for craftspeople, go to several large bookstores and look at what they sell. Ask other craftspeople what they read or call your local crafts organization for suggestions.

Here are ten sample magazines to consider:

- *American Craft* magazine, P.O. Box 3000, Denville, NJ 07834; (888) 313-5527; *www.craftcouncil.org*. Founded in 1943, this magazine is published bimonthly by the American Craft Council for its members and is also available on newsstands. *American Craft* features interviews and profiles of craftspeople, articles on craft history, and profiles emerging crafts-people in the portfolio section. Informative listings of opportunities in the back include exhibits, events, and workshops.

- *American Style,* 3000 Chestnut Avenue, Suite 304, Baltimore, MD 21211; (800) 272-3893; *www.americanstyle.com.* Published by the Rosen Group, this magazine is primarily geared to craft collectors.
- *Ceramics Monthly.* P.O. Box 6102, Westerville, OH 43081; (614) 523-1661; *www.ceramicsmonthly.org.* Published monthly, this magazine is geared to the ceramics field and includes profiles, how-to articles, and listings and suppliers.
- *The Crafts Report,* P.O. Box 1992, Wilmington, DE 19899; (800) 777-7098; *www.craftsreport.com.* This business journal for the crafts industry is published monthly to inspire the professional craftsperson and crafts retailer with how-to articles on business management, industry news, current trends and issues, a forum for exchanging ideas, encouragement, and recognition. The Craft Showcase is an advertising section specifically for craftspeople.
- *Fiberarts,* 67 Broadway, Asheville, NC 28801; (828) 253-0467; *www.fiberartsmagazine.com.* For craftspeople working in the fiber arts—spinning, weaving, surface design, and wearables—this magazine offers profiles, how-to articles, and listings of opportunities and suppliers.
- *Fine Woodworking,* The Taunton Press, P.O. Box 5506, Newtown, CT 06470; (203) 426-8171; *www.finewoodworking.com.* Published monthly for woodworkers, this magazine includes profiles, how-to articles, and listings of opportunities and suppliers.
- *Hand Papermaking,* P.O. Box 77027, Washington, D.C. 20013; (800) 821-6604; *www.handpapermaking.org.* Published for craftspeople working with handmade paper, this magazine includes profiles, how-to articles, and listings of opportunities and suppliers.
- *Metalsmith,* 710 East Ogden Avenue, Suite 600, Napeville, IL 60563; (630) 579-3272; *www.snagmetalsmith.org.* Published by the Society of North American Goldsmiths (SNAG) for metalsmiths, this magazine contains profiles, how-to articles, and listings of opportunities and suppliers.
- *NICHE,* 3000 Chestnut Avenue, Suite 304, Baltimore, MD 21211; (410) 889-3093; *www.nichemag.com.* Published by the Rosen Group, this publication for craft retailers and galleries contains profiles and advertising opportunities for craftspeople.
- *Sunshine Artists,* 3210 Dade Avenue, Orlando, FL 32804; (407) 228-9772; *www.sunshineartist.com.* This monthly publication, calls itself "America's premier show and festival publication," and features show reviews, extensive listings, and business articles.

These magazines are only a sampling of what is available. Magazines are a good way to keep up with what's going on in your specific field and the craft world in general. You should incorporate information gleaned from magazines into your business and take advantage of the opportunities listed such as exhibits, competitions, and workshops.

A WORD FROM THE AUTHOR

Now that you have read this book, you have the basic information you need to help sell your crafts—whether you are about to start a craft business or want to run an existing one more successfully. Perhaps you may have decided that running a craft business is not for you at this time. Whatever you decide, find ways to keep motivated and producing your pieces. Rent a studio in a building with other craftspeople, join a crafts organization, take classes, or read magazines to stay involved and informed.

Don't get discouraged if you are not able to work in your studio consistently. There are different phases in each of our lives. Sometimes we will find it easy to create, while other times there will be obstacles to doing our work. If you feel discouraged, remember that it took several of the craftspeople profiled in chapter 2 a few years before they were self-supporting. Nurture your creativity—it's a gift.

If you decide you want to sell your crafts and make your living as a craftsperson, feel good about your work and your prices. Keep working, trying new things, and your work will continue to improve and change. It may be only a matter of time before you will be either supplementing or completely supporting yourself with your crafts business.

Take the time to do the necessary planning. Set up the support system you need to keep yourself on track. Other craftspeople are selling their crafts right now. You can do it too!

Please contact me and let me know your questions and concerns, successes and failures, so that I may continue to help others sell their crafts. Best of luck to you!

Susan Joy Sager, *ArtBiz*

P.O. Box 222, South Berwick, ME 03908

ssager@artbiz.info

www.artbiz.info

BIBLIOGRAPHY

Aude, Karen. "Copyrighting Your Designs: Is It Worth It?" *Crafts Report,* October 1995.

Backer, Noelle. "Are Craftspeople Making Money on the Internet?" *Crafts Report* Web page, *www.craftsreport.com,* Industry News section.

Backer, Noelle. "Catalogs: Keeping Up with the Demand." *Crafts Report,* November 1997.

Benun, Ilise. "The Do-Able Marketing Plan." *Art of Self-Promotion,* Winter 1995.

Benun, Ilise. "Does Advertising Work?" *Art of Self-Promotion,* Winter 1996.

Benun, Ilise. *Self Promotion Online.* Cincinnati, OH: North Light Books, 2001.

Biow, Lisa. *How to Use Your Computer.* Emeryville, CA: Ziff Davis Press, 1996.

Borden, Kay. *Bulletproof News Releases.* Marietta, GA: Franklin Sarrat Publishers, 1994.

Brill, Jack and Alan Reder. *Investing from the Heart.* New York: Crown Trade Paperbacks, 1993.

Brown, Pamela. "Inside the Buyer's Mind." *Crafts Report,* October 1996.

The Craft Center. *The Business of Crafts.* New York: Watson-Guptill Publications, 1996.*

Dowse, Patti. "How Many Toads Do We Have to Kiss to Find Our Prince?" *Crafts Report,* November 1994.

---

*Books highly recommended by the author.

DuBoff, Leonard. *The Law (in Plain English)® for Crafts.* New York: Allworth Press, 1999.*

Edwards, Sarah and Paul. *Making It on Your Own.* New York: Jeremy P. Tarchers, Inc., 1991.

Grant, Daniel. "You've Got a College Degree in Your Craft, What Now?" *Crafts Report,* March 1996.

Hoover, Deborah. *Supporting Yourself as an Artist.* New York: Oxford University Press, 1989.

Janecek, Lenore. *Health Insurance: A Guide for Artists, Consultants, Entrepreneurs, and Other Self-Employed.* American Council for the Arts, 1993.*

Kraus-Sikes, Inc. Rate Card, *The Guild,* Madison, WI: 1997.

Louis, Robert. "Estate Planning for Artists." *Crafts Report,* August 1997.

Maine Art Commission. *Percent for Art Handbook.* Augusta, ME.

Maine Crafts Association. *Maine Cultural Guide 1997/98.* Deer Isle, ME.

Meltzer, Steve. *Photographing Your Craftwork.* Loveland, CO: Interweave Press, 1986.*

Ortalda, Robert Jr. *How to Live within Your Means and Still Finance Your Dreams.* New York: Simon and Schuster, 1989.

Pearson, Bill. "Compensation for Today's Employees." *Crafts Report,* October 1997.

Pearson, Bill. "Recover the Lost Art of Selling." *Crafts Report,* June 1997.

Rosen, Wendy. *Crafting as a Business.* New York: The Rosen Group Inc., 1994.*

Scott, Michael. Edited by Leonard DuBoff. *The Crafts Business Encyclopedia.* San Diego, CA: Harcourt, Brace & Co., 1993.*

Snell, Tricia. *Artists' Communities.* New York: Allworth Press, 1996.*

Williams, Gerry. *Apprenticeship in Craft.* Goffstown, NH: Daniel Webster Books, 1981.*

ABOUT THE AUTHOR

Susan Joy Sager founded ArtBiz in 1992 to facilitate the professional development of artists and craftspeople through business seminars and counseling services. In the first five years, ArtBiz provided individual guidance to over fifty artists and craftspeople through career counseling sessions as well as business information to over one thousand artists and craftspeople through business seminars taught throughout New England.

In 1996, Susan self-published *The ArtBiz Workbook,* a fifty-page handbook designed to supplement the business seminars with simple how-to information and worksheets. In addition, Susan published articles in several craft magazines and newsletters such as "Assessing Your Own Success" in the October 1996 issue of the *Crafts Report,* "Pricing Your Work Based on Cost" in the August 1996 issue of *WOODSHOP News,* and "Approaching Galleries" in the November/December issue of the *Maine Crafts Association Newsletter.*

Susan is a graduate of the Lake Placid School of Art in Lake Placid, New York, with a diploma in painting and photography, and Hampshire College in Amherst, Massachusetts, with a B.A. degree in photography and history.

Susan's work as an arts administrator includes institutions such as the Program in Artisanry at Boston University; Swain School of Design in New Bedford, Massachusetts; Portland School of Art in Maine; and the Haystack Mountain School of Crafts and Maine Crafts Association, both in Deer Isle, Maine. In addition, Susan was a member of the board of directors of the Watershed Center for the Ceramic Arts in Edgecomb, Maine, serving on the executive committee as secretary, and was a regional representative for the Maine Crafts Association.

Susan now makes her home in South Berwick, Maine.

INDEX

Books from Allworth Press

Crafts and Craft Shows: How to Make Money
by Philip Kadubec (paperback, 6 × 9, 208 pages, $16.95)

Business and Legal Forms for Crafts
by Tad Crawford (paperback, 8¹/₂ × 11, 176 pages, $19.95)

The Law (in Plain English)® for Crafts
by Leonard DuBoff (paperback, 6 × 9, 224 pages, $18.95)

The Artist-Gallery Partnership: A Practical Guide to Consigning Art,
Revised Edition *by Tad Crawford and Susan Mellon* (paperback, 6 × 9, 216 pages, $16.95)

**The Artist's Guide to New Markets: Opportunities to Sell Art Beyond
Galleries** *by Peggy Hadden* (paperback, 5¹/₂ × 8¹/₂ , 248 pages, $18.95)

How to Grow as an Artist
by Daniel Grant (paperback, 6 × 9, 240 pages, $16.95)

The Quotable Artist
by Peggy Hadden (hardcover, 7¹/₂ × 7¹/₂, 224 pages, $19.95)

The Fine Artist's Career Guide *by Daniel Grant* (paperback, 6 × 9, 304 pages, $18.95)

The Business of Being an Artist, Third Edition
by Daniel Grant (paperback, 6 × 9, 352 pages, $19.95)

The Artist's Complete Health and Safety Guide, Third Edition
by Monona Rossol (paperback, 6 × 9, 416 pages, $19.95)

Licensing Art & Design, Revised Edition
by Caryn R. Leland (paperback, 6 × 9, 128 pages, $16.95)

The Artist's Resource Handbook, Revised Edition
by Daniel Grant (paperback, 6 × 9, 248 pages, $18.95)

**Caring For Your Art: A Guide for Artists, Collectors, Galleries, and Art
Institutions,** Third Edition *by Jill Snyder* (paperback, 6 × 9, 256 pages, $19.95)

Legal Guide for the Visual Artist, Fourth Edition
by Tad Crawford (paperback, 8¹/₂ × 11, 272 pages, $19.95)

The Fine Artist's Guide to Marketing and Self-Promotion
by Julius Vitali (paperback, 6 × 9, 224 pages, $18.95)

Please write to request our free catalog. To order by credit card, call 1-800-491-2808
or send a check or money order to Allworth Press, 10 East 23rd Street, Suite 510,
New York, NY 10010. Include $5 for shipping and handling for the first book ordered
and $1 for each additional book. Ten dollars plus $1 for each additional book if
ordering from Canada. New York State residents must add sales tax.

If you would like to see our complete catalog on the World Wide Web, you can find
us at ***www.allworth.com.***